Microsoft® PowerPoint® 2013

Step by Step

Joyce Cox
Joan Lambert

PUBLISHED BY
Microsoft Press
A Division of Microsoft Corporation
One Microsoft Way
Redmond, Washington 98052-6399

Library of Congress Control Number: 2012956092
ISBN: 978-0-7356-6910-9

Printed and bound in the United States of America.

First Printing

Microsoft Press books are available through booksellers and distributors worldwide. If you need support related to this book, email Microsoft Press Book Support at mspinput@microsoft.com. Please tell us what you think of this book at http://www.microsoft.com/learning/booksurvey.

Microsoft and the trademarks listed at http://www.microsoft.com/about/legal/en/us/IntellectualProperty/Trademarks/EN-US.aspx are trademarks of the Microsoft group of companies. All other marks are property of their respective owners.

Native plant photographs courtesy of Rugged Country Plants, which is no longer open to the public.

The example companies, organizations, products, domain names, email addresses, logos, people, places, and events depicted herein are fictitious. No association with any real company, organization, product, domain name, email address, logo, person, place, or event is intended or should be inferred.

This book expresses the author's views and opinions. The information contained in this book is provided without any express, statutory, or implied warranties. Neither the authors, Microsoft Corporation, nor its resellers, or distributors will be held liable for any damages caused or alleged to be caused either directly or indirectly by this book.

Acquisitions Editor: Rosemary Caperton
Editorial Production: Online Training Solutions, Inc.
Technical Reviewer: Rob Carr
Copyeditor: Jaime Odell
Indexer: Joyce Cox
Cover: Microsoft Press Brand Team

Contents

PART 1

Basic presentations

1   Explore Microsoft PowerPoint 2013   3

2   Create presentations   45

3   Work with slides   75

4   Work with slide text   103

PART 2

Presentation enhancements

8   Fine-tune visual elements   229

9   Add other enhancements   263

10   Add animations, audio, and videos   287

PART 3

Additional techniques

14 Work in PowerPoint more efficiently 391

Introduction

Part of the Microsoft Office 2013 suite of programs, Microsoft PowerPoint 2013 is a full-featured presentation program that helps you quickly and efficiently develop dynamic, professional-looking presentations and then deliver them to an audience. *Microsoft PowerPoint 2013 Step by Step* offers a comprehensive look at the features of PowerPoint that most people will use most frequently.

Who this book is for

Microsoft PowerPoint 2013 Step by Step and other books in the *Step by Step* series are designed for beginning-level to intermediate-level computer users. Examples shown in the book generally pertain to small and medium businesses but teach skills that can be used in organizations of any size. Whether you are already comfortable working in PowerPoint and want to learn about new features in PowerPoint 2013 or are new to PowerPoint, this book provides invaluable hands-on experience so that you can create, modify, and deliver professional presentations with ease.

How this book is organized

This book is divided into three parts. Part 1 explores the everyday experience of working in PowerPoint 2013. Part 2 discusses ways of enhancing presentation content. Part 3 covers more advanced PowerPoint techniques, in addition to customizing program functionality to fit the way you work. This three-part structure allows readers who are new to the program to acquire basic skills and then build on them, whereas readers who are comfortable with PowerPoint 2013 basics can focus on material that is of the most interest to them.

Chapter 1 contains introductory information that will primarily be of interest to readers who are new to PowerPoint or are upgrading from PowerPoint 2003 or an earlier version. If you have worked with a more recent version of PowerPoint, you might want to skip directly to Chapter 2.

This book has been designed to lead you step by step through all the tasks you're most likely to want to perform with PowerPoint 2013. If you start at the beginning and work your way through all the exercises, you will gain enough proficiency to be able to create and work with most types of PowerPoint presentations. However, with the exception of the topics in Chapter 1, which build on each other, the topics are self-contained, so you can jump in anywhere to acquire exactly the skills you need.

Download the practice files

Before you can complete the exercises in this book, you need to download the book's practice files to your computer. These practice files can be downloaded from the following page:

http://aka.ms/PowerPoint2013sbs/files

IMPORTANT The PowerPoint 2013 program is not available from this website. You should purchase and install that program before using this book.

The following table lists the practice files for this book.

Chapter	File
Chapter 1: Explore Microsoft PowerPoint 2013	BuyingTrips.pptx
	DesigningColor.pptx
	SalesMeetingA.pptx
	SalesMeetingB.pptx
Chapter 2: Create presentations	BuyingTravelB.pptx
	ProjectProcess.pptx
	ServiceA.pptx
	ServiceB.pptx
	ServiceOutline.docx
Chapter 3: Work with slides	CommunityA.pptx
	CommunityB.pptx
	CommunityC.pptx
	CompanyMeeting.pptx
	DesignWithColor.pptx
	LandscapingA.pptx
	LandscapingB.pptx

Chapter	File
Chapter 4: Work with slide text	CommunityServiceA.pptx
	CommunityServiceB.pptx
	CommunityServiceC.pptx
	TripsA.pptx
	TripsB.pptx
Chapter 5: Add simple visual enhancements	Agastache.jpg
	JournalingA.pptx
	JournalingB.pptx
	Penstemon.jpg
	WaterConsumption.xlsx
	WaterLandscapingA.pptx
	WaterLandscapingB.pptx
	WaterLandscapingC.pptx
Chapter 6: Review and deliver presentations	Harmony.pptx
	MeetingA.pptx
	MeetingB.pptx
	ServiceProjectsA.pptx
	ServiceProjectsB.pptx
	YinYang.png
Chapter 7: Present content in tables	MayMeeting.pptx
	NewEquipment.xlsx
	WaterSavingA.pptx
	WaterSavingB.pptx
Chapter 8: Fine-tune visual elements	JuneMeeting.pptx
	NativePlant1.jpg through NativePlant8.jpg
	NativePlants.pptx
	NaturalGardening.pptx
	SavingWater.pptx
Chapter 9: Add other enhancements	JulyMeeting.pptx
	NewWaterSaving.pptx
	OrganizationA.pptx
	OrganizationB.pptx
	OrganizationC.pptx
	Procedures.docx

Chapter	File
Chapter 10: Add animations, audio, and videos	AGKCottage.pptx
	Amanda.wma
	Bird.jpg
	Butterfly.wmv
	HealthyEcosystemsA.pptx
	HealthyEcosystemsB.pptx
	NaturalGardenA.pptx
	NaturalGardenB.pptx
	Wildlife.wmv
Chapter 11: Share and review presentations	CottageShowA.pptx
	CottageShowB.pptx
	HomeHarmony.pptx
	MeetingSH.pptx
	MeetingTA.pptx
	MeetingThemeA.pptx
	MeetingThemeB.pptx
	MeetingThemeC.pptx
	Projects.pptx
	WaterUse.pptx
Chapter 12: Create custom presentation elements	AnnualMeeting.pptx
	NativePlant1.jpg through NativePlant3.jpg
	NaturalA.pptx
	NaturalB.pptx
	NaturalC.pptx
	PhotoAlbum.pptx
Chapter 13: Prepare for delivery	CommunityProjects.pptx
	GettingOrganized.pptx
	Jounal.pptx
	Procedures.docx
Chapter 14: Work in PowerPoint more efficiently	BuyersSeminar.pptx
	ColorDesign.pptx

If you would like to be able to refer to the completed versions of practice files at a later time, save the modified practice files at the end of each exercise. If you might want to repeat the exercises, either save the modified practice files with a different name or in a different folder.

Your companion ebook

With the ebook edition of this book, you can do the following:

- Search the full text
- Print
- Copy and paste

To download your ebook, please see the instruction page at the back of the book.

Get support and give feedback

The following sections provide information about getting help with this book and contacting us to provide feedback or report errors.

Errata

We've made every effort to ensure the accuracy of this book and its companion content. Any errors that have been reported since this book was published are listed on our Microsoft Press site at oreilly.com, which you can find at:

http://aka.ms/PowerPoint2013sbs/errata

If you find an error that is not already listed, you can report it to us through the same page.

If you need additional support, email Microsoft Press Book Support at *mspinput@microsoft.com*.

Please note that product support for Microsoft software is not offered through the addresses above.

We want to hear from you

At Microsoft Press, your satisfaction is our top priority, and your feedback our most valuable asset. Please tell us what you think of this book at:

http://www.microsoft.com/learning/booksurvey

The survey is short, and we read every one of your comments and ideas. Thanks in advance for your input!

Stay in touch

Let's keep the conversation going! We're on Twitter at: *http://twitter.com/MicrosoftPress*.

Basic presentations

Chapter at a glance

Work

Work in the PowerPoint 2013 user interface, page 10

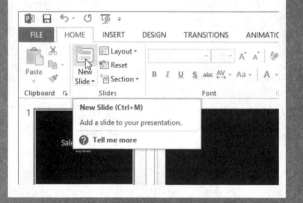

Navigate

Open, navigate, and close presentations, page 28

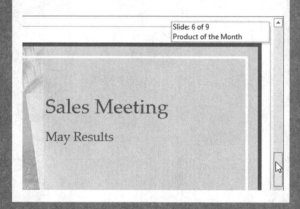

View

View presentations in different ways, page 33

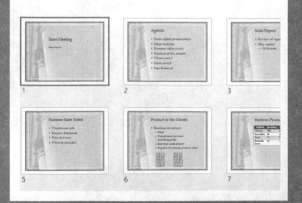

Search

Search for help with PowerPoint 2013, page 40

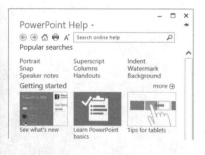

Explore Microsoft PowerPoint 2013

1

IN THIS CHAPTER, YOU WILL LEARN HOW TO

- Identify new features of PowerPoint 2013.

- Work in the PowerPoint 2013 user interface.

- Open, navigate, and close presentations.

- View presentations in different ways.

- Search for help with PowerPoint 2013.

Microsoft PowerPoint 2013 and a little creativity are all you need to develop professional presentations ready for delivery to any audience. You can use PowerPoint to:

- Introduce an idea, proposal, organization, product, or process with professionally designed, high-impact slides.

- Add visual appeal by using themes, styles, and formatting options to achieve the right combination of colors, fonts, and effects.

- Reinforce bullet points by adding pictures, shapes, and fancy display text.

- Convey numeric data in easy-to-grasp ways by using attractive charts and tables.

- Illustrate a concept by using the SmartArt Graphics tool to create sophisticated diagrams that reflect processes, hierarchies, and other relationships.

- Maintain branding consistency by creating custom themes, designs, and layouts.

- Collaborate with colleagues, giving and receiving feedback to ensure the best possible presentation.

In this chapter, you'll learn about the different PowerPoint programs that are available so that you can identify the one you are using. Then you'll get an overview of the new features in recent versions of PowerPoint to help you identify changes if you're upgrading from a previous version. You'll explore the program's user interface, and open, navigate, view, and close presentations in various ways. Finally, you'll explore how to get help with the program.

PowerPoint 2013 is part of Microsoft Office 2013, which encompasses a wide variety of programs, including Microsoft Access 2013, Excel 2013, InfoPath 2013, Lync 2013, OneNote 2013, Outlook 2013, Publisher 2013, and Word 2013. Office is available in various editions that include different combinations of programs; you can also purchase most of the programs individually.

The programs in the Office suite are designed to work together to provide highly efficient methods of getting things done. You can install one or more Office programs on your computer. Some programs have multiple versions designed for different platforms. Although the core purpose of a program remains the same regardless of the platform on which it runs, the available functionality and the way you interact with the program might be different. We provide a brief description of the various PowerPoint 2013 programs here so that you can identify any differences between what is displayed on your screen and what is described in this book.

- **PowerPoint 2013 standard desktop installation** The program we work with and depict in images throughout this book is a desktop installation of PowerPoint 2013, meaning that we installed the program directly on our computers. The desktop installation has all the available PowerPoint functionality. It is available as part of the Office 2013 suite of programs, as a freestanding program, or as part of an Office 365 subscription that allows users to install the desktop programs from the Internet.

  TIP Office 365 is a cloud-based solution that provides a variety of products and services through a subscription licensing program. Depending on the subscription plan purchased, users will have access either to the full PowerPoint 2013 desktop installation and PowerPoint Web App or only to PowerPoint Web App.

- **PowerPoint 2013 RT** Tablet-style computers that run Windows RT (an installation of Windows 8 that runs only on devices that use a type of processor called an *ARM processor*) come preloaded with Office Home and Student 2013 RT, which includes Word, Excel, PowerPoint, and OneNote.

  The Office Home and Student 2013 RT programs have the functionality of the full programs and also include a Touch Mode feature to help you work with the program and enter content by tapping the screen with your finger or by using a tool such as a stylus. When Touch Mode is turned on, the user interface is slightly modified to simplify on-screen interactions, and an on-screen keyboard is readily available for text input. (You can simplify your interactions even further by attaching a keyboard and mouse to your Windows RT computer and interacting with Office in the usual manner.)

- **PowerPoint Web App** When you want to work with a presentation that is stored on a Microsoft SkyDrive or Microsoft SharePoint site, you might be able to review and edit the presentation in your web browser by using PowerPoint Web App. Office Web Apps are installed in the online environment in which you're working and are not part of the desktop installation on your computer. PowerPoint Web App is available as part of Office 365 and SharePoint Online subscriptions, and is free on SkyDrive storage sites.

SEE ALSO For more information about saving presentations to SkyDrive folders and SharePoint sites, see "Starting and saving presentations" in Chapter 2, "Create presentations."

PowerPoint Web App displays the contents of a presentation very much like the desktop application does. Although the Web App offers only a subset of the commands available in the full desktop application, it does provide the tools you need to create and edit most elements of a presentation. Commands that are not available in PowerPoint Web App control higher-level functionality such as that for managing slide layout, text box layout, and advanced font and paragraph formats; inserting tables, screen captures, charts, actions, specialized text or symbols, and media clips; changing the size or background of a slide; managing special features of animations and transitions; and working with slide masters, multiple windows, and window elements. Slide show management and presentation reviewing tools, other than simple comments, are also not available in the Web App.

Both PowerPoint Web App and the desktop version of the program might be available to you in the online environment. When viewing a presentation in the Web App, you can click the Edit Presentation menu and then choose the version you want to use by clicking Edit In PowerPoint or Edit In PowerPoint Web App. If you're editing a presentation in the Web App and find that you need more functionality than is available, and you have the full PowerPoint program installed on your computer, you can click Open In PowerPoint to open the presentation and use the full program.

TIP At the time of this writing, Office Web Apps are compatible with recent versions of Windows Internet Explorer, Firefox, Google Chrome, and Safari.

Identifying new features of PowerPoint 2013

PowerPoint 2013 builds on previous versions to provide powerful tools for all your presentation needs. If you're upgrading to PowerPoint 2013 from a previous version, you're probably most interested in the differences between the old and new versions and how they will affect you, and you probably want to find out about them in the quickest possible way. The following sections list new features you will want to be aware of, depending on the version of PowerPoint you are upgrading from. Start with the first section and work down to your previous version to get the complete picture.

If you are upgrading from PowerPoint 2010

If you have been using PowerPoint 2010, you might be wondering how Microsoft could have improved on what seemed like a pretty comprehensive set of features and tools. The new features introduced between PowerPoint 2010 and PowerPoint 2013 include the following:

- **Windows 8 functionality** PowerPoint 2013, like all Office 2013 programs, is a full-featured Windows 8 application. When it is running on the Windows 8 operating system, it not only has the sleek new Windows 8 look but it also incorporates the latest touch technologies designed for tablet and mobile devices.

- **Starting screen** PowerPoint opens to a screen that provides easy access to presentation templates, the presentations you recently worked on, and locations where existing presentations might be stored.

- **Cloud access** When you connect Office or PowerPoint to a Microsoft account (formerly known as a Windows Live account) or Office 365 account, you have the option of saving presentations "in the cloud" to a SharePoint document library or SkyDrive. After saving a presentation in a shared location, you and your colleagues can simultaneously work on one version of the presentation, using either the full version of PowerPoint or PowerPoint Web App.

- **Previous location bookmark** When you close a presentation, PowerPoint marks the location where you were working. The next time you open the presentation, a resume reading flag enables you to quickly jump back to that location.

- **Smart guides** Dynamic on-screen alignment guides help you intuitively align graphics for a clean, professional look.

- **Outline view** The old Outline tab has been replaced with a full-fledged Outline view that makes it easier than ever to enter and edit the text of a presentation.

- **Improved charting** Linked Excel data now appears in a window, and filters enable you to select which of the data series in the linked data you want to appear in the chart.

- **Improved comments** The Comments button on the status bar and the Comments pane make it easier to enter and respond to comments.

- **Enhanced Presenter View** New tools make Presenter View setup easier and give you more control during the presentation. For example, thumbnails of all the slides give you an overview and help you pinpoint your current location, and new zoom functionality enables you to focus your discussion.

- **Web-based presentation delivery** The Present Online feature makes it simpler than ever to deliver a presentation via the web. After you send a link to the presentation, audience members who don't have PowerPoint can follow along in their web browser as you move from slide to slide.

If you are upgrading from PowerPoint 2007

In addition to the features discussed in the previous section, if you're upgrading from PowerPoint 2007, you'll want to take note of the following features that were introduced in PowerPoint 2010:

- **The Backstage view** All the tools you need to work with your files, as opposed to their content, are accessible from one location. You display the Backstage view by clicking the File tab, which replaces the Microsoft Office Button at the left end of the ribbon.

- **Customizable ribbon** The logical next step in the evolution of the command center: create your own tabs and groups to suit the way you work.

- **A window for each presentation** You no longer display all presentations in the same window, so you can arrange open presentations for easy comparison or work on different presentations at the same time.

- **Reading view** This way of previewing presentations makes it easy to quickly check the effect of one or two changes.

- **Presentation videos** Turning a presentation into a Windows Media Video is a simple matter of saving in that format.

- **Paste preview** No more trial and error when moving items to new locations. Preview the appearance of an item in each of the available formats, and then choose the one you want.

- **Animation Painter** If you spend time developing a complex animation for one object, you can copy the animation settings to another object with a few mouse clicks.

- **New themes and transitions** Adding pizzazz to your presentations is just a matter of applying a professional-looking theme or a snazzy dynamic-content transition.

- **Graphics editing** Found the perfect picture, but its colors or style aren't quite right for your presentation? After inserting a picture, you can edit it in new ways. In addition to changing color, brightness, and contrast, you can remove the background and, most exciting of all, apply artistic effects that make it appear like a watercolor, pencil drawing, or pastel sketch.

- **Improved cropping** Not only can you drag crop handles to manually crop a picture but you can also apply a built-in cropping ratio and then move a cropping window around the picture until you get precisely the part you want.

- **Text effects** WordArt has had a makeover. You can still use WordArt to create distinctive headlines, but now you can use its effects on any selected text.

- **Screen shots** You don't need to leave PowerPoint when you want to capture a graphic and insert it on a slide.

- **Improved SmartArt Graphics tool** Include pictures in addition to text in your SmartArt diagrams.

- **Video tools** Found a perfect video, but it is too long to include in a presentation? You can insert the video and then use the video editing tools built into PowerPoint to trim and format it. You can also insert a link to a video on a website into a slide.

- **Version merging** You can merge two versions of the same presentation and accept or reject changes.

- **Team collaboration** Team members can work simultaneously on a presentation stored on a SharePoint site or a SkyDrive.

- **Broadcasting** You can review a presentation with colleagues over the Internet by working through a free broadcasting service. Your colleagues can view the presentation in their web browsers and give feedback via a conference call.

- **Language support** If you need to conduct business internationally across language lines, you can easily tailor the language of your working environment. You can also use translation tools to collaborate with team members in other countries.

- **Unsaved file recovery** PowerPoint preserves your unsaved files for a period of time, allowing you to recover them if you need them.

If you are upgrading from PowerPoint 2003

In addition to the features discussed in the previous section, if you're upgrading from PowerPoint 2003, you'll also want to take note of the new features that were introduced in PowerPoint 2007. The PowerPoint 2007 upgrade provided a more efficient working environment and included a long list of new and improved features, including the following:

- **The ribbon** No more hunting through menus, submenus, and dialog boxes. This interface organizes all the commands most people use most often, making them quickly accessible from tabs at the top of the program window.

- **Live Preview** You can display the effect of a style, theme, or other option before you apply it.

- **Custom layouts** It's easy to create your own layouts with placeholders for specific objects, and then save them for use in other presentations.

- **SmartArt Graphics tool** Use this awesome diagramming tool to create sophisticated diagrams with three-dimensional shapes, transparency, drop shadows, and other effects.

- **Improved charting** Enter data in a linked Excel worksheet and watch as your data is instantly plotted in the chart type of your choosing.

- **Presentation cleanup** Have PowerPoint check for and remove comments, hidden text, and personal information stored as properties before you declare a presentation final.

- **New file format** The Microsoft Office Open XML Formats reduce file size and help avoid loss of data.

Working in the PowerPoint 2013 user interface

As with all Office 2013 programs, the most common way to start PowerPoint is from the Start screen (Windows 8) or the Start menu (Windows 7) displayed when you click at the left end of the Windows Taskbar. When you start PowerPoint without opening a specific presentation, a program starting screen appears. From this screen, you can create a new presentation or open an existing one. Either way, the presentation is displayed in a program window that contains all the tools you need to add content and format slides to meet your needs.

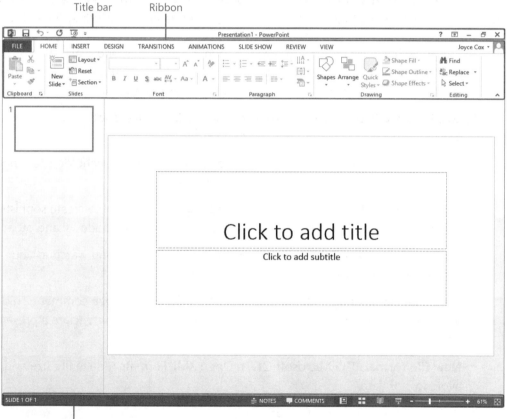

The PowerPoint 2013 program window, showing a new blank presentation.

Identifying program window elements

The program window contains the following elements:

- **Title bar** This bar across the top of the program window displays the name of the active presentation and provides tools for managing the program and the program window.

The title bar for a new, unsaved presentation.

At the left end of the title bar is the program icon, which you click to display commands to restore, move, size, minimize, maximize, and close the program window.

To the right of the PowerPoint icon is the Quick Access Toolbar. By default, the Quick Access Toolbar displays the Save, Undo, Redo/Repeat, and Start From Beginning buttons, but you can customize it to display any command you want.

TIP You might find that you work more efficiently if you organize the commands you use frequently on the Quick Access Toolbar and then display it below the ribbon, directly above the workspace. For information, see "Manipulating the Quick Access Toolbar" in Chapter 14, "Work in PowerPoint more efficiently."

On the far-right side of the title bar are five buttons: the Microsoft PowerPoint Help button that opens the PowerPoint Help window, in which you can use standard techniques to find information; the Ribbon Display Options button that controls how much screen space the ribbon occupies; and the familiar Minimize, Maximize/Restore Down, and Close buttons.

- **Ribbon** Below the title bar, all the commands for working with a PowerPoint presentation are gathered together in this central location so that you can work efficiently with the program.

TIP If your ribbon appears as a row of tabs across the top of the workspace, click the Home tab to temporarily display that tab's buttons. For information about how to control the display of the ribbon, see "Viewing presentations in different ways," later in this chapter.

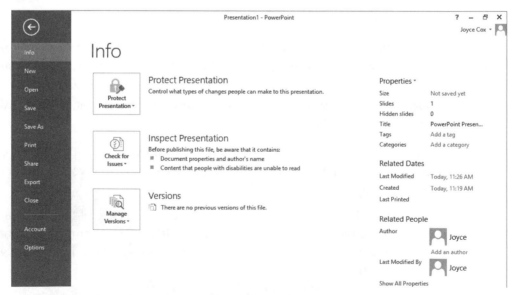

The ribbon, with the Home tab active.

TIP Don't be alarmed if your ribbon looks different from those shown in our screens. You might have installed programs that add their own tabs to the ribbon, or your screen settings might be different. For more information, see "Working with the ribbon" later in this topic.

Across the top of the ribbon is a set of tabs. Clicking a tab displays an associated set of commands.

Commands related to managing PowerPoint and PowerPoint presentations (rather than slide content) are gathered together in the Backstage view, which you display by clicking the colored File tab located at the left end of the ribbon. Commands available in the Backstage view are organized on pages, which you display by clicking the page tabs in the colored left pane. You redisplay the presentation and the ribbon by clicking the Back arrow located above the page tabs.

The Backstage view, where you can manage files and customize the program.

Commands related to working with slide content are represented as buttons on the remaining tabs of the ribbon. The Home tab, which is active by default, contains the commands most PowerPoint users will use most often. When an object is selected on a slide, one or more tool tabs might appear at the right end of the ribbon to make commands related to that specific object easily accessible. Tool tabs disappear again when their associated object is no longer selected.

TIP Some older commands no longer appear as buttons on the ribbon but are still available in the program. You can make these commands available by adding them to the Quick Access Toolbar. For more information, see "Manipulating the Quick Access Toolbar" in Chapter 14, "Work in PowerPoint more efficiently."

On each tab, buttons representing commands are organized into named groups. You can point to any button to display a ScreenTip with the command name, a description of its function, and its keyboard shortcut (if it has one).

SEE ALSO For information about controlling the display and content of ScreenTips, see "Changing default program options" in Chapter 14, "Work in PowerPoint more efficiently." For more information about keyboard shortcuts, see "Keyboard shortcuts" at the end of this book.

Related but less common commands are not represented as buttons in a group. Instead, they're available in a dialog box or pane, which you display by clicking the dialog box launcher located in the lower-right corner of the group.

About buttons and arrows

Some buttons include an integrated or separate arrow. To determine whether a button and its arrow are integrated, point to the button to activate it. If both the button and its arrow are shaded, clicking the button will display options for refining the action of the button. If the button is shaded but the arrow isn't, clicking the button will carry out its current default action. You can change the default action of the button by clicking the arrow and then clicking the action you want.

The Arrange button, which has an integrated arrow,
and the New Slide button, which has a separate arrow.

- **Status bar** cross the bottom of the program window, this bar displays information about the current presentation and provides access to certain program functions.

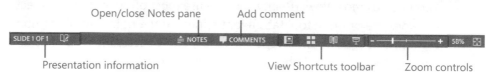

The status bar.

At the left end of the status bar is the number of the active slide and the total number of slides in the presentation. To the right of the number is a button representing the spell checker, which checks the spelling of the text you enter and displays a check mark if there are no errors or an X if there are.

In the middle of the status bar are buttons for displaying and hiding notes or working with comments.

SEE ALSO For information about entering notes, see "Preparing speaker notes and handouts" in Chapter 6, "Review and deliver presentations." For information about entering comments, see "Adding and reviewing comments" in Chapter 11, "Share and review presentations."

To the right of the Comments button is a set of buttons called the *View Shortcuts toolbar*, which provides convenient methods for switching the view of the presentation.

SEE ALSO For information about the various ways you can view a presentation, see "Viewing presentations in different ways" later in this chapter.

At the right end of the status bar are the Zoom Slider, the Zoom Level button, and the Fit Slide To Current Window button. These tools enable you to adjust the magnification of the active slide.

The goal of all these user interface features is to make working on a presentation as intuitive as possible. Commands for tasks you perform often are readily available, and even those you might use infrequently are easy to find. The user interface also makes it easier to decide which formatting options you want by displaying the possibilities in a gallery of images, called *thumbnails*, that provide a visual representation of each choice.

When you point to a thumbnail in a gallery, the Live Preview feature displays what the current presentation, slide, or selection will look like if you click the thumbnail to apply its associated formatting.

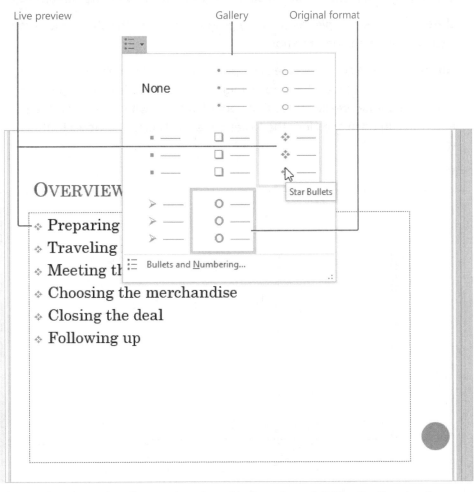

Live Preview shows the effect on the selected bullet points of clicking the thumbnail you are pointing to in the Bullets gallery.

You can display the content of the active presentation in five primary views: Normal view, Outline view, Slide Sorter view, Reading view, and Slide Show view. You carry out most of the development work on a presentation in Normal view, which is the default.

Normal view consists of the following panes:

- **Thumbnails** This pane appears by default on the left side of the program window and displays small thumbnails of all the slides in the active presentation.

- **Slide** This pane occupies most of the program window and shows the current slide as it will appear in the presentation.

- **Notes** This pane sits below the Slide pane and provides a place for entering notes about the current slide. These notes might be related to the development of the slide, or they might be speaker notes that you will refer to when delivering the presentation. You can open and close the Notes pane by clicking the Notes button on the status bar.

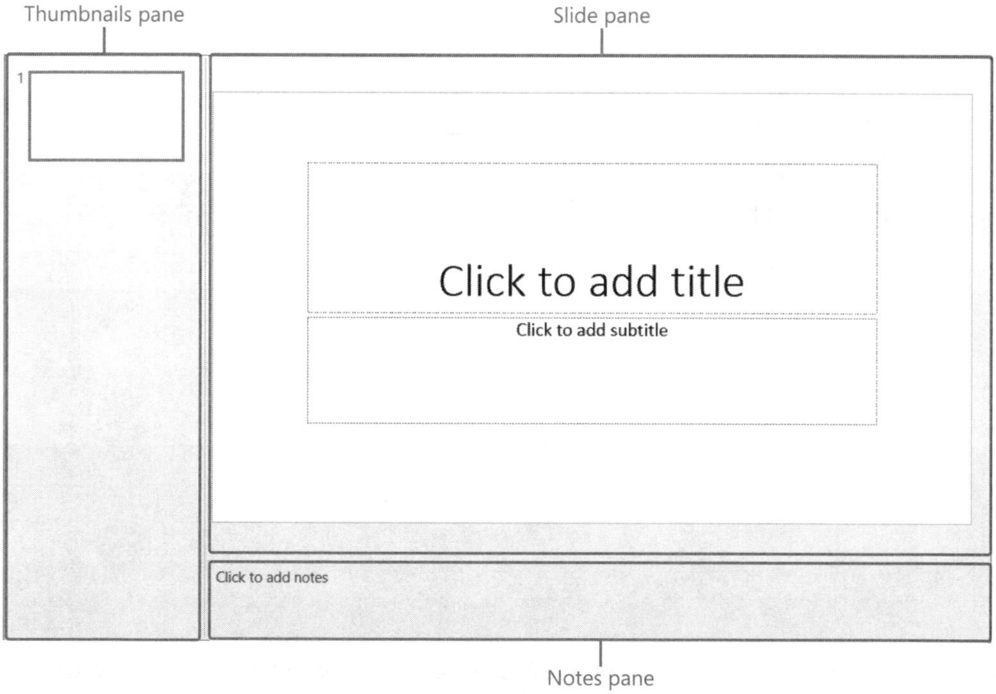

Thumbnails pane   Slide pane

Click to add title

Click to add subtitle

Click to add notes

Notes pane

The three panes of Normal view.

Working with the ribbon

As with all Office 2013 programs, the PowerPoint ribbon is dynamic, meaning that as its width changes, its buttons adapt to the available space. As a result, a button might be large or small, it might or might not have a label, or it might even be an entry in a list.

For example, when sufficient horizontal space is available, the buttons on the Home tab are spread out, and the available commands in each group are visible.

Large button   Small, labeled button

Drop-down list   Small, unlabeled button

The Home tab at 1024 pixels wide.

If you decrease the horizontal space available to the ribbon, small button labels disappear and entire groups of buttons might hide under one button that represents the entire group. Clicking the group button displays a list of the commands available in that group.

Small, unlabeled buttons   Group buttons

The Home tab at 712 pixels wide.

When the ribbon becomes too narrow to display all the groups, a scroll arrow appears at its right end. Clicking the scroll arrow displays the hidden groups.

Scroll arrows

The Home tab at 323 pixels wide.

The width of the ribbon depends on three factors:

- **Program window width** Maximizing the program window provides the most space for the ribbon. To maximize the window, click the **Maximize** button, drag the borders of a nonmaximized window, or drag the window to the top of the screen.

- **Screen resolution** Screen resolution is the size of your screen display expressed as pixels wide × pixels high. Your screen resolution options are dependent on the display adapter installed in your computer, and on your monitor. Common screen resolutions range from 800 × 600 to 2560 × 1600. The greater the number of pixels wide (the first number), the greater the number of buttons that can be shown on the ribbon.

To change your screen resolution:

1   Display the **Screen Resolution** control panel item in one of the following ways:

- Right-click the Windows desktop, and then click **Screen Resolution**.

- Enter screen resolution in Windows 8 Search, and then click **Adjust screen resolution** in the **Settings** results.

- Open the **Display** control panel item, and then click **Adjust resolution**.

2   On the **Screen Resolution** page, click the **Resolution** arrow, click or drag to select the screen resolution you want, and then click **Apply** or **OK**.

You can set the resolution by clicking or dragging the pointer on the slider.

- **The magnification of your screen display** If you change the screen magnification setting in Windows, text and user interface elements are larger and therefore more legible, but fewer elements fit on the screen. You can set the magnification from 100 to 500 percent.

You can change the screen magnification from the **Display** page of the **Appearance and Personalization** control panel item. You can display the **Display** page directly from **Control Panel** or by using one of the following methods:

- Right-click the Windows desktop, click **Personalize**, and then in the lower-left corner of the **Personalization** window, click **Display**.

- Enter display in Windows 8 Search, and then click **Display** in the **Settings** results.

On the Display page, you can choose one of the standard magnification options or change the text size of specific elements.

To change the screen magnification to 125 or 150 percent, click that option on the **Display** page. To select another magnification, click the **Custom sizing options** link and then, in the **Custom sizing options** dialog box, click the magnification you want in the drop-down list or drag the ruler to change the magnification even more.

After you click **OK** in the **Custom sizing options** dialog box, the custom magnification is shown on the **Display** page along with any warnings about possible problems with selecting that magnification. Click **Apply** on the **Display** page to apply the selected magnification.

Adapting exercise steps

The screen shots shown in this book were captured at a screen resolution of 1024 x 768, at 100-percent magnification. If your settings are different, the ribbon on your screen might not look the same as the one shown in this book. As a result, exercise instructions that involve the ribbon might require a little adaptation. Our instructions use this format:

- On the **Insert** tab, in the **Illustrations** group, click the **Chart** button.

If the command is in a list, our instructions use this format:

- On the **Home** tab, in the **Slides** group, click the **Section** button and then, in the list, click **Add Section**.

If differences between your display settings and ours cause a button to appear differently on your screen, first click the specified tab, and then locate the specified group. If a group has been collapsed into a group list or under a group button, click the list or button to display the group's commands. If you can't immediately identify the button you want, point to likely candidates to display their names in ScreenTips.

If you prefer not to have to adapt the steps, temporarily set up your screen to match ours while you read and work through the exercises in this book.

In this book, we provide instructions based on traditional keyboard and mouse input methods. If you're using PowerPoint on a touch-enabled device, you might be giving commands by tapping with your finger or with a stylus. If so, please substitute a tapping action any time we instruct you to click a user interface element. Also note that when we instruct you to enter information in PowerPoint, you can do so by typing on a keyboard, tapping an on-screen keyboard, or even speaking aloud, depending on your computer setup and your personal preferences.

In this exercise, you'll start PowerPoint and explore the Backstage view and ribbon. Along the way, you'll experiment with galleries and Live Preview.

 SET UP **You need the SalesMeetingA presentation located in the Chapter01 practice file folder to complete this exercise. Start your computer, but don't start PowerPoint. Then follow the steps.**

1   Start **File Explorer**, and navigate to your **Chapter01** practice file folder. Then double-click the **SalesMeetingA** presentation to open it in PowerPoint.

TIP In Windows 8, File Explorer has replaced Windows Explorer. Throughout this book, we refer to this browsing utility by its Windows 8 name. If your computer is running Windows 7, use Windows Explorer instead.

TROUBLESHOOTING Don't worry if an Information bar below the ribbon tells you that the presentation has been opened in Protected view. By default, PowerPoint opens any presentation that originates from a potentially unsafe location, such as a website or email message, in Protected view. Your computer can then display but not interact with the presentation. If you trust the file and want to work with it, click the Enable Editing button in the Information bar.

2   If the program window is not maximized, click the **Maximize** button. Notice that on the **Home** tab, only the buttons representing commands that can be performed on the currently selected presentation element (the entire slide) are active.

On the Home tab, buttons related to creating slide content are organized in six groups: Clipboard, Slides, Font, Paragraph, Drawing, and Editing.

TROUBLESHOOTING If your ribbon shows the tab names but no buttons, click Home, and then click the Pin The Ribbon button (shaped like a pushpin) at the right end of the ribbon to permanently display it. Throughout this book, the exercise instructions assume that the ribbon is displayed unless we explicitly tell you to hide it.

3   Point to each button on the **Home** tab to display the ScreenTips that name them, describe their functions, and give their keyboard shortcuts (if any).

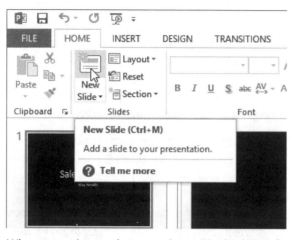

When you point to a button, a ScreenTip displays information about the button's function and keyboard shortcut.

Now let's explore the other tabs.

4   Click the **Insert** tab, and then explore its buttons.

On the Insert tab, buttons related to all the items you can insert into a presentation and its slides are organized in nine groups: Slides, Tables, Images, Illustrations, Links, Comments, Text, Symbols, and Media.

5   Click the **Design** tab, and then explore its buttons.

On the Design tab, buttons related to the appearance of a presentation are organized in three groups: Themes, Variants, and Customize.

6   In the **Themes** group, point to (but don't click) each of the visible thumbnails to display a live preview of what the slide will look like if you click the thumbnail you're pointing to.

7   On the scroll bar to the right of the thumbnails in the **Themes** group, click the scroll down arrow to display the next row of theme thumbnails.

8   At the bottom of the **Themes** scroll bar, click the **More** button to display a menu that includes the entire **Themes** gallery.

The menu includes a gallery of thumbnails of all the themes you can apply to this presentation and two commands related to themes.

9   Point to various thumbnails in the **Themes** gallery, observing the live preview on the slide.

10   Press the **Esc** key to close the gallery without applying a theme.

11   Click the **Transitions** tab, and then explore its buttons.

On the Transitions tab, buttons related to the movement from slide to slide in your presentation are organized in three groups: Preview, Transition To This Slide, and Timing.

12 Click the **Animations** tab. Note that all the buttons except Preview, Animation Pane, and Reorder Animation are gray and unavailable until an object on the slide is selected.

On the Animations tab, buttons related to the animation of objects on slides are organized in four groups: Preview, Animation, Advanced Animation, and Timing.

13 Click the **Slide Show** tab, and then explore its buttons.

On the Slide Show tab, buttons related to displaying your presentation are organized in three groups: Start Slide Show, Set Up, and Monitors.

14 Click the **Review** tab, and then explore its buttons.

On the Review tab, buttons related to editorial tasks are organized in four groups: Proofing, Language, Comments, and Compare.

15   Click the **View** tab, and then explore its buttons.

On the View tab, buttons related to changing the view or the display of the presentation are organized in seven groups: Presentation Views, Master Views, Show, Zoom, Color/Grayscale, Window, and Macros.

16   In the lower-right corner of the **Show** group, click the dialog box launcher to open the **Grid And Guides** dialog box.

In the Grid And Guides dialog box, you can set options to control tools that help you align objects on a slide.

17   At the bottom of the **Grid and Guides** dialog box, click **Cancel**.

18   On the slide, click anywhere in the **Sales Meeting** title, and then click the **Format** tool tab that appears on the ribbon.

On the Format tool tab, buttons related to formatting text placeholders are arranged in five groups: Insert Shapes, Shape Styles, WordArt Styles, Arrange, and Size.

Let's investigate the Backstage view, where commands related to managing presentations (such as creating, saving, and printing) are available.

19 Click the **File** tab to display the **Backstage** view with the **Info** page active.

20 In the left pane, click the **New** page tab.

You can start a presentation based on a template from the New page of the Backstage view.

SEE ALSO For information about creating presentations, see "Starting and saving presentations" in Chapter 2, "Create presentations."

21 In the left pane, click each of the next six page tabs to get an overview of the options available on these pages. Stop when the **Export** page is displayed.

22 Skipping the Close page tab, click the **Account** page tab to display information about your intallation of Office.

The Account page displays information and settings related to your version of Office 2013.

23   In the left pane, click **Options** to open the **PowerPoint Options** dialog box.

This dialog box provides access to settings that control the way the program looks and behaves.

SEE ALSO For information about the PowerPoint Options dialog box, see "Changing default program options" in Chapter 14, "Work in PowerPoint more efficiently."

24   At the bottom of the **PowerPoint Options** dialog box, click **Cancel**.

⊗ CLEAN UP Leave the SalesMeetingA presentation open for the next exercise.

Opening, navigating, and closing presentations

In the previous exercise, you double-clicked an existing presentation in File Explorer to start PowerPoint and open the presentation. If you start PowerPoint from the Windows 8 Start screen or the Windows 7 Start menu, a screen appears that enables you to create a new presentation, open a presentation you worked on recently, or open any existing presentation.

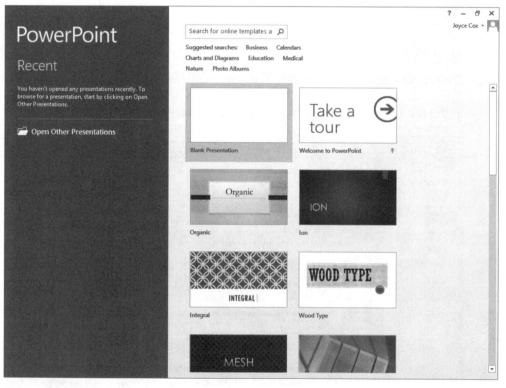

The screen displayed when you start PowerPoint.

If the name of the presentation you want to open appears in the Recent list on this starting screen, simply double-click the name to open the presentation. To open an existing presentation that is not in the Recent list, click Open Other Presentations in the left pane to display the Open page of the Backstage view. Then clicking a storage location displays options in the right pane for opening a presentation from that location.

To open a presentation that is stored on your computer, click Computer in the Open pane.

When Computer is selected, clicking Browse in the right pane opens the Open dialog box. The first time you use this command, the Open dialog box displays the contents of your Documents library. If you display the dialog box again in the same PowerPoint session, it displays the contents of whatever folder you last used. To open a presentation from a different folder, use standard Windows techniques to navigate to the folder and then double-click the name of the presentation you want to work with.

TIP In the Open dialog box, clicking a file name and then clicking the Open arrow displays a list of alternative ways to open the selected file. To look through a presentation without making any inadvertent changes, you can open the file as read-only, open an independent copy of the file, or open it in Protected view. You can also open the file in a web browser. In the event of a computer crash or other similar incident, you can tell PowerPoint to open the file and try to repair any damage.

When a presentation is open, you can use several techniques to move from slide to slide, including the following:

- Click the slide you want to move to in the **Thumbnails** pane.
- Use the scroll bar on the right side of the **Slide** pane.
- Click the **Previous Slide** or **Next Slide** button at the bottom of the **Slide** pane scroll bar.
- Press navigation keys on the keyboard.

TIP When you open a presentation you have worked on recently, PowerPoint displays a flag adjacent to the Slide pane's scroll bar. Clicking the flag displays a link to the slide you were working on when you closed the presentation, with the date and time of your last change. Simply click the link to jump to that slide.

Every time you open a presentation, a new instance of PowerPoint starts. If you have more than one presentation open, clicking the Close button at the right end of a presentation's title bar closes that presentation and exits that instance of PowerPoint. If you have only one presentation open and you want to close the presentation but leave PowerPoint running, display the Backstage view and then click Close.

In this exercise, you'll open an existing presentation and explore various ways of moving around in it. Then you'll close the presentation.

➡ SET UP You need all the presentations located in the Chapter01 practice file folder to complete this exercise. With the SalesMeetingA presentation from the previous exercise still open on your screen, follow the steps.

1   Click the **File** tab to display the **Backstage** view, click **Open** to display the **Open** page, and then click **Computer**.

2   At the bottom of the right pane, click **Browse** to open he **Open** dialog box. Then if the contents of the **Chapter01** practice file folder are not displayed, use the **Navigation** pane or the **Address** bar to display the contents of that folder.

In the Open dialog box, you display the contents of the folder you want by clicking locations in the Navigation pane on the left or the Address bar at the top.

3   Double-click **BuyingTrips** to open it in a new program window.

4   Display the **Open** page again, click **Computer** in the **Places** pane, and then in the **Current Folder** area, click **Chapter01** to display the contents of that folder in the **Open** dialog box.

5   Double-click **DesigningColor** to open it in a new program window.

6   Repeat steps 4 and 5 to open the **SalesMeetingB** presentation in a new program window.

Now let's practice moving around in this presentation.

7   In the **Thumbnails** pane, click the slide **3** thumbnail.

8   At the bottom of the scroll bar on the right side of the **Slide** pane, click the **Next Slide** button to move to slide **4**.

9   Click the **Previous Slide** button to move back to slide **3**.

10   Drag the scroll box slowly down to the bottom of the scroll bar.

As you drag the scroll box, a ScreenTip tells you the number and title of the slide that will be displayed if you release the scroll box at that point.

11   Press the **Page Up** key until slide **3** is displayed.

12   Press **Home** to move to slide **1**.

Now let's experiment with closing open presentations.

13   At the right end of the title bar, click the **Close** button to close the **SalesMeetingB** presentation.

14   On the **Windows Taskbar**, point to the **PowerPoint** button to display thumbnails of the three open presentations.

15   Point to the **SalesMeetingA** thumbnail, and then click the **Close** button that appears in its upper-right corner.

16   Repeat either step 13 or step 15 to close the **DesigningColor** presentation.

17   With the **BuyingTrips** presentation active, display the **Backstage** view, and then click **Close** to close the presentation without exiting the program.

> **TROUBLESHOOTING** If you click the Close button at the right end of the title bar instead of displaying the Backstage view and then clicking Close, you'll close the presentation and exit the PowerPoint program.

❌ CLEAN UP **Leave PowerPoint running for the next exercise.**

Viewing presentations in different ways

PowerPoint has four primary views to help you create, organize, and preview presentations. There are other views, but these are the ones you'll use most frequently for your development work:

- **Normal** As described earlier, this view includes the **Thumbnails** pane, which you use for navigation, and the **Slide** pane, where you work on the content of an individual slide. It also has a **Notes** pane where you can enter notes to help with presentation development and delivery.

  SEE ALSO For information about working with notes, see "Preparing speaker notes and handouts" in Chapter 6, "Review and deliver presentations."

- **Outline** In this view, the **Thumbnails** pane changes to the **Outline** pane, where a text outline of the presentation is displayed. You can enter text either directly on the slide or in the outline.

  SEE ALSO For information about working with outlines, see "Entering text in place-holders" in Chapter 2, "Create presentations."

- **Slide Sorter** In this view, the slides of the presentation are displayed as thumbnails so that you can easily reorganize them. You can also apply transitions from one slide to another, as well as specify how long each slide should remain on the screen.

  SEE ALSO For information about changing the order of slides, see "Rearranging slides and sections" in Chapter 3, "Work with slides." For information about applying transitions, see "Adding transitions" in Chapter 5, "Add simple visual enhancements."

- **Reading view** In this view, which is ideal for previewing the presentation, each slide fills the screen. You can click buttons on the navigation bar to move through or jump to specific slides.

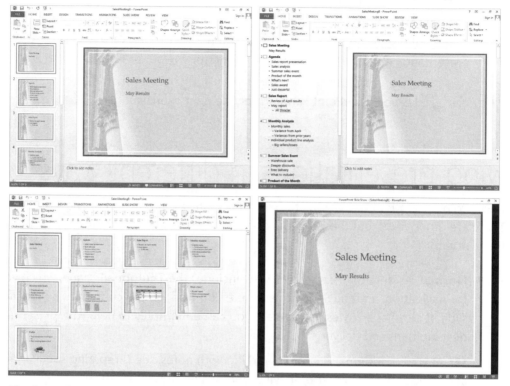

The four primary presentation-development views: Normal view, Outline view, Slide Sorter view, and Reading view.

While you are developing a presentation, you can switch among Normal, Outline, Slide Sorter, and Reading views in two ways:

- Click the buttons on the **View Shortcuts** toolbar at the right end of the status bar. (Clicking the **Normal** button while it is active toggles between **Normal** and **Outline** views.)

- Click the buttons in the **Presentation Views** group on the **View** tab.

The Presentation Views group also includes a button for Notes Page view. In this view, you can create speaker notes that contain elements other than text. Although you can add speaker notes in Normal view's Notes pane, you must be in Notes Page view if you want to add graphics, tables, diagrams, or charts to your notes.

SEE ALSO For information about creating more elaborate notes, see "Preparing speaker notes and handouts" in Chapter 6, "Review and deliver presentations."

TIP Are you wondering what the Master Views group on the View tab is all about? You can control the default look of a presentation by working with the masters displayed in Slide Master view, Handout Master view, or Notes Master view. For information about masters, see "Viewing and changing slide masters" in Chapter 12, "Create custom presentation elements."

The View tab includes other buttons that do the following:

- Display rulers, gridlines, and guides to help you position and align slide elements.

- Change the zoom percentage of the current slide.

- Show how a colored slide will look if rendered in grayscale or black and white (usually for printing).

- Arrange and manipulate windows.

TIP Clicking the Macros button displays the macros embedded in a presentation. The subject of macros is beyond the scope of this book. For information, refer to PowerPoint Help.

When you are working in Normal view, you can adjust the relative sizes of the panes to suit your needs by dragging the borders that separate them. When you point to a movable border, the pointer changes to a bar with opposing arrows, and you can drag in either direction. You can hide the Thumbnails or Notes pane by dragging the border to shrink the pane as far as it will go. (You cannot hide the Slide pane.) Click the Thumbnails or Notes button to display the pane again. If you adjust the width of the Thumbnails pane, the size of the slide thumbnails is adjusted accordingly—that is, there are more small thumbnails in a narrow pane and fewer large thumbnails in a wide pane.

TIP Any changes you make to a view, such as adjusting the sizes of panes, are saved with the presentation that is open at the time and do not affect other presentations.

When you are working in Normal, Outline, or Slide Sorter views, you can increase the amount of available screen space by clicking the Collapse The Ribbon button, which appears as an upward-pointing arrow in the group area at the right end of the ribbon. Clicking this button hides the groups and their buttons but leaves the tab names visible. When the groups are hidden, the Collapse The Ribbon button changes to the Pin The Ribbon button, which is shaped like a pushpin. You can click any tab name to temporarily display its groups.

Clicking anywhere other than the ribbon hides the groups again. When the groups are temporarily visible, you can click the Pin The Ribbon button to make their display permanent.

KEYBOARD SHORTCUT Press Ctrl+F1 to collapse or pin the ribbon. For a complete list of keyboard shortcuts, see "Keyboard shortcuts" at the end of this book.

In any of these three views, you can also hide the title bar, ribbon, and status bar by clicking the Ribbon Display Options button at the right end of the title bar and then clicking Auto-hide Ribbon. To temporarily display the hidden program window elements, click the three dots in the upper-right corner of the screen; to hide them again, click away from the ribbon. To permanently redisplay the title bar, ribbon, and status bar, click the Ribbon Display Options button, and then click Show Tabs or Show Tabs And Commands.

When you are ready to deliver a presentation to an audience, you display it in Slide Show view. In this view, each slide fills the screen, and PowerPoint implements transitions, animations, and media effects the way you have specified. How you switch to Slide Show view depends on which slide you want to start with.

- To start with slide **1**, click the **Start From Beginning** button on either the **Quick Access Toolbar** or in the **Start Slide Show** group on the **Slide Show** tab.

- To start with the current slide, click either the **Slide Show** button on the **View Shortcuts** toolbar or the **From Current Slide** button in the **Start Slide Show** group on the **Slide Show** tab.

SEE ALSO For information about delivering a presentation to an audience, see "Delivering presentations" in Chapter 6, "Review and deliver presentations."

In this exercise, you'll switch among different PowerPoint views and then return to Normal view, where you'll adjust the size of the panes. You'll display more than one presentation at the same time and experiment with adjusting the zoom percentage.

SET UP You need the BuyingTrips and DesigningColor presentations located in the Chapter01 practice file folder to complete this exercise. Open both presentations, and then with BuyingTrips displayed on your screen, follow the steps.

1   On the **View** tab, in the **Presentation Views** group, click the **Outline View** button to display the **Outline** pane instead of the Thumbnails pane on the left side of the window. Notice that PowerPoint automatically adjusts the sizes of the **Slide** pane and the **Outline** pane to accommodate the outline's text.

2   On the **View** tab, in the **Presentation Views** group, click the **Slide Sorter** button to display all the slides as thumbnails in one large pane, with slide 1 surrounded by an orange border to indicate that it is selected.

3   On the **View Shortcuts** toolbar, click the **Normal** button once to switch to the previous view (**Outline**) and again to switch to the view before that (**Normal**).

4   On the **View** tab, in the **Presentation Views** group, click the **Reading View** button to display a full-screen view of the first slide in the presentation.

5   Without moving your mouse, click its button to advance to the next slide.

> **TIP** You can also click the Previous or Next button on the status bar to move from one slide to another. To stop previewing a presentation, press the Esc key, or click the Normal or Slide Sorter button on the View Shortcuts toolbar.

6   Continue clicking the mouse button to advance through the presentation one slide at a time until PowerPoint displays a black slide, which signals the end of the presentation.

> **TIP** If you don't want a black slide to appear at the end of a presentation, display the Backstage view, and click Options. In the PowerPoint Options dialog box, click the Advanced page tab. Then in the Slide Show area, clear the End With Black Slide check box, and click OK.

7   Click again to return to **Normal** view.

Next let's adjust the size of the Normal view panes.

8   Point to the border between the **Slide** pane and the **Notes** pane, and when the pointer changes to a bar with opposing arrows, drag down until the **Notes** pane is completely closed.

9   On the status bar, click the **Notes** button to redisplay the **Notes** pane. Then drag the border between the **Slide** pane and the **Notes** pane upward as far as it will go to make it easier to enter notes about the slide.

10   Point to the right border of the **Thumbnails** pane, and drag it all the way to the left to hide the pane.

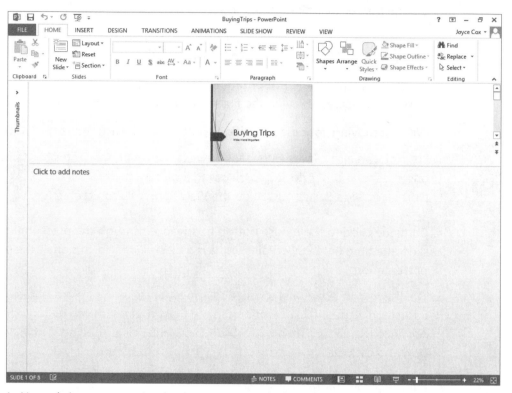

In Normal view, you can size the three panes to suit the task at hand.

11   On the **View** tab, in the **Window** group, click the **Switch Windows** button, and then click **DesigningColor**. Notice that customizing **Normal** view for the **BuyingTrips** presentation has not affected **Normal** view for this presentation.

Now let's view both open presentations at the same time.

12   On the **View** tab, in the **Window** group, click the **Arrange All** button.

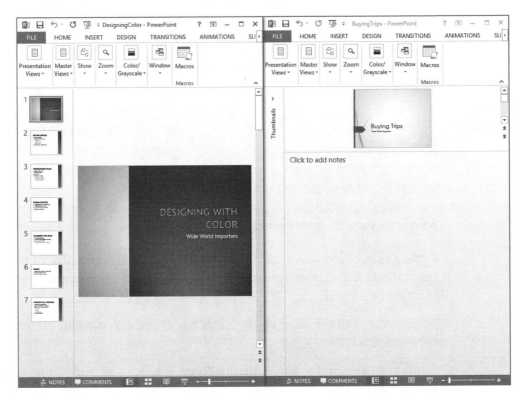

In this view, it is easy to compare two presentations or copy content from one to the other.

13 Experiment with the other commands in the **Window** group, and then close the **DesigningColor** presentation.

14 At the right end of the **BuyingTrips** title bar, click the **Maximize** button. Then click the arrow button at the top of the **Thumbnails** bar to display the hidden **Thumbnails** pane, and click the **Notes** button on the status bar to close the **Notes** pane.

Let's get a closer look at the open presentation.

15 On the **View** tab, in the **Zoom** group, click the **Zoom** button to open the **Zoom** dialog box.

You can select a zoom percentage or enter the percentage you want in the Percent box.

16   In the **Zoom** dialog box, click **100%**, and then click **OK**. Notice that at the right end of the status bar, the zoom percentage has changed and the indicator has moved to the middle of the slider.

17   At the left end of the slider on the status bar, click the **Zoom Out** button until the percentage is **50%**.

18   At the right end of the slider, click the **Zoom In** button once to increase the zoom percentage to **60%**.

Finally, let's expand the displayed slide to fit the available space in the Slide pane.

19   At the right end of the status bar, click the **Fit slide to current window** button.

❌ CLEAN UP Close the BuyingTrips presentation, but leave PowerPoint running for the next exercise.

Searching for help with PowerPoint 2013

Whenever you have a question about PowerPoint that is not answered by this book, your next recourse is the PowerPoint Help system. This system is a combination of articles, videos, and training available from the Office website for reference when you are online, and basic information stored on your computer for reference when you are offline. You can find Help resources in the following ways:

- To find out about an item on the screen, point to the item to display a ScreenTip. For example, pointing to a button without clicking it displays a ScreenTip giving the button's name, the associated keyboard shortcut if there is one, and a description of what the button does when you click it. Some ScreenTips also include enhanced information such as instructions and links to related Help topics.

- In the program window, click the **Microsoft PowerPoint Help** button (the question mark) near the right end of the title bar to display the **PowerPoint Help** window.

- In a dialog box, click the **Help** button (also a question mark) at the right end of the dialog box title bar to open the **PowerPoint Help** window and display any available topics related to the functions of that dialog box.

In this exercise, you'll explore the PowerPoint Help window and search for information about using SkyDrive.

➡️ SET UP You don't need any practice files to complete this exercise. If you want to follow the steps exactly, ensure that you have an Internet connection. Then follow the steps.

1   Near the right end of the title bar, click the **Microsoft PowerPoint Help** button to open the **PowerPoint Help** window.

KEYBOARD SHORTCUT Press F1 to display the PowerPoint Help window.

Your Help window might look different from this one because the material on the Office website is regularly updated.

TIP To switch between online and offline reference content, click the arrow to the right of PowerPoint Help and then click PowerPoint Help From Office.com or PowerPoint Help From Your Computer. You can print the information shown in the Help window by clicking the Print button on the toolbar. You can change the font size of the topic by clicking the Use Large Text button on the toolbar.

2   In the **Search** box, enter **activating,** and then click the **Search** button (the magnifying glass) to display a list of topics related to activating Office programs.

A typical list of Help topic search results.

3   Click the **Activate Office programs** topic to display the corresponding information.

4   At the top of the **PowerPoint Help** window, in the **Search online help** box, enter **SkyDrive**, and then press the **Enter** key.

5   In the results list, click **Save and share a PowerPoint presentation to Microsoft SkyDrive** to display that topic.

TIP When section links appear at the beginning of an article, you can click a link to move directly to that section of the article. You can click the Top Of Page link at the end of an article to return to the beginning.

Save and share a PowerPoint presentation to Microsoft SkyDrive

Touch Guide

You can save a PowerPoint 2013 presentation to Microsoft SkyDrive to make it easier to access, store, and share your files in the cloud.

IMPORTANT   This feature doesn't support synchronization between SkyDrive and your local drive in Office on a Windows RT PC. However, you can open and save your presentations to your SkyDrive by clicking the **File** tab, and then clicking the **Open** and **Save** tabs.

1. To set up a free SkyDrive account, you must have a Microsoft account. See Sign up for a Microsoft account.

The SkyDrive topic includes links to related topics, including a guide for using touch screens.

6 Jump to related information by clicking any hyperlink identified by blue text.

CLEAN UP When you finish exploring, close the PowerPoint Help window by clicking the Close button in the upper-right corner of the window.

Key points

- The core functionality of PowerPoint 2013 remains the same regardless of the version of the program you are using.

- The PowerPoint user interface provides intuitive access to all the tools you need to develop a sophisticated presentation tailored to the needs of your audience.

- You can move around a presentation by clicking thumbnails, scrolling, or pressing navigation keys.

- PowerPoint has four primary presentation-development views: Normal, Outline, Slide Sorter, and Reading. You can switch views by clicking buttons either on the View Shortcuts toolbar or in the Presentation Views group on the View tab.

- In Normal view, you can change the size of panes and the zoom percentage of slides to suit the way you work.

- The PowerPoint Help window gives you instant access via the web to information and training on most aspects of the program.

Chapter at a glance

Start

Start and save presentations,
page 46

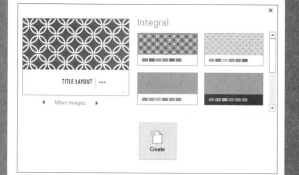

Enter

Enter text in placeholders,
page 56

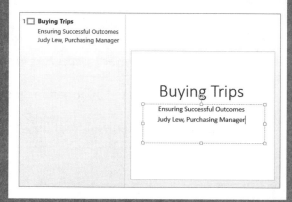

Add

Add and delete slides,
page 65

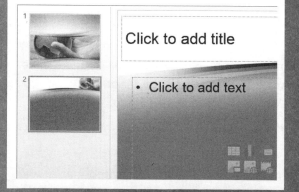

Import

Import slides from existing sources,
page 69

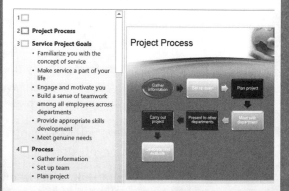

Create presentations 2

IN THIS CHAPTER, YOU WILL LEARN HOW TO

- Start and save presentations.

- Enter text in placeholders.

- Edit text.

- Add and delete slides.

- Import slides from existing sources.

Microsoft PowerPoint 2013 makes it easy to efficiently create effective presentations. Need to convince management to invest in a new piece of equipment? Need to present the new annual budget to the Board of Directors? Need to give a report about a recent research study? PowerPoint helps you get the job done in a professional, visually appealing way by making sophisticated presentation features easy to find and use, so even novice users can work productively with PowerPoint after only a brief introduction.

SEE ALSO If you are not familiar with features such as the Backstage view, tabs and groups, galleries, and Live Preview, be sure to read "Working in the PowerPoint 2013 user interface" in Chapter 1, "Explore Microsoft PowerPoint 2013."

In this chapter, you'll start by creating and saving several new presentations and entering and editing text. Then you'll add slides in various ways and delete slides you don't need.

PRACTICE FILES To complete the exercises in this chapter, you need the practice files contained in the Chapter02 practice file folder. For more information, see "Download the practice files" in this book's Introduction.

Starting and saving presentations

To work efficiently with PowerPoint 2013, you need to know the best way to start a presentation. The screen displayed when you start the program provides the following options for starting a new presentation:

- **Blank presentation** If you know what your content and design will be and you want to build the presentation from scratch, you can start with a presentation based on the Blank Presentation template. By the time you finish reading this book and working through its exercises, you'll be able to confidently create powerful presentations of your own. In the meantime, you'll probably want to use the other options available on the starting screen.

- **Design template** Creating attractive presentations from scratch is time-consuming and requires quite a bit of skill and knowledge about PowerPoint. You can save time by basing your presentation on one of the many design templates that come with PowerPoint. A design template is a blank presentation with a theme, and sometimes graphics, already applied to it. Some templates supply only a title slide and leave it to you to add the other slides you need; other templates supply an example of each of the available slide layouts.

    SEE ALSO For information about themes, see "Applying themes" in Chapter 3, "Work with slides."

- **Content template** From the PowerPoint starting screen, you can preview and download presentation templates that are available from the Office website. These templates provide not only the design but also suggestions for content that is appropriate for different types of presentations, such as reports or product launches. After downloading the template, you simply customize the content provided in the template to meet your needs.

TIP If you're already working in PowerPoint, you can start a new presentation by displaying the Backstage view, clicking New, and then choosing the presentation you want.

To start a new presentation with the design shown on a template thumbnail, double-click the thumbnail. Alternatively, you can click the thumbnail and then select a color variant of the design. Either way, you're not opening the template; instead you're creating a new file that has all the content and formatting of the template. And either way, the file exists only in your computer's memory until you save it.

You save a presentation the first time by clicking the Save button on the Quick Access Toolbar or by displaying the Backstage view and then clicking Save As. Both actions open the Save As page, where you can select a storage location.

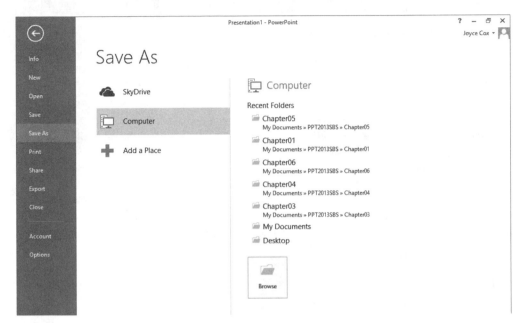

From the Save As page of the Backstage view, you can choose a storage location in which to save your presentation.

TIP Many countries have laws that require that certain types of digital content be accessible to people with various disabilities. If your presentation must be compatible with assistive technologies, you need to know the final file format(s) of your presentation before you create it and start adding content. Some types of content are visible in a PowerPoint file in Normal view but not in other accessible file formats such as tagged PDFs. Before basing a presentation on a template you have not used before, test it for accessibility.

You can save the presentation in a folder on your computer or, if you have an Internet connection, in a folder on your Microsoft SkyDrive. If your company is running Microsoft SharePoint, you can add your SharePoint SkyDrive or a different SharePoint location so that it is available from the Places pane of the Save As page, just like any other folder.

SEE ALSO For information about SkyDrive, see the sidebar "Saving files to SkyDrive" later in this chapter.

When Computer is selected as the save location, clicking Browse in the right pane displays the Save As dialog box, in which you assign a name to the file.

In the Save As dialog box, you can use standard Windows techniques either in the Address bar or in the Navigation pane to navigate to the folder you want.

TIP If you want to create a new folder in which to store the file, click the New Folder button on the dialog box's toolbar.

After you save a presentation for the first time, you can save changes simply by clicking the Save button on the Quick Access Toolbar. The new version of the presentation then overwrites the previous version.

KEYBOARD SHORTCUT Press Ctrl+S to save an existing presentation. If you have not yet saved the presentation, pressing Ctrl+S displays the Save As page of the Backstage view. For a complete list of keyboard shortcuts, see "Keyboard shortcuts" at the end of this book.

If you want to keep both the new version and the previous version, display the Save As page, and then save a new version with a different name in the same location or with the same name in a different location. (You cannot have two files with the same name in the same folder.)

TIP By default, PowerPoint periodically saves the presentation you are working on. To adjust the time interval between saves, display the Backstage view, and click Options. In the left pane of the PowerPoint Options dialog box, click Save, and then specify the period of time in the box to the right of the Save AutoRecover Information.

In this exercise, you'll start and save a couple of presentations based on templates.

→ SET UP **You don't need any practice files to complete this exercise. Start PowerPoint, and then from the starting screen, follow the steps.**

1   Press the **Esc** key to start a new presentation based on the Blank Presentation template.

   TIP By default, the slides in presentations you create based on the Blank Presentation template and the design templates that come with PowerPoint are set to Widescreen size. Before you begin adding content to a new presentation, you should consider how the presentation will be viewed. For example, all the practice files for this book have Standard size slides because we don't know what type of monitor our readers have. For information about slide sizes, see "Setting up presentations for delivery" in Chapter 6, "Review and deliver presentations."

   Now let's start a presentation based on a design template.

2   Display the **Backstage** view, and then click **New**.

3   On the **New** page, scroll the pane to view the ready-made presentation designs that are shipped with PowerPoint.

4   Click the **Integral** thumbnail to open a preview box that displays the title slide of the Integral design with four alternative color schemes and graphic backgrounds.

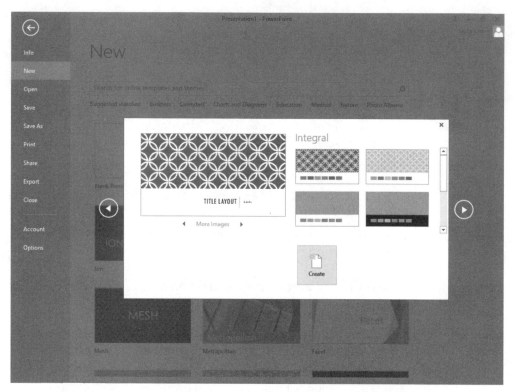

You can preview the slide layouts that are part of the template in each of the available variants.

5   In the preview box, click the right **More Images** arrow several times to display the
     other slide layouts for this template.

6   To the right of the preview box, click the arrow button several times to preview the
     other design templates that ship with PowerPoint. Then when you have finished
     exploring, click the **Close** button in the upper-right corner of the preview box.

7   On the **New** page, click the **Search** box at the top of the pane, enter world, and click
     the **Start searching** button. Then scroll the results, and double-click the thumbnail
     for the **World maps series, World presentation** template.

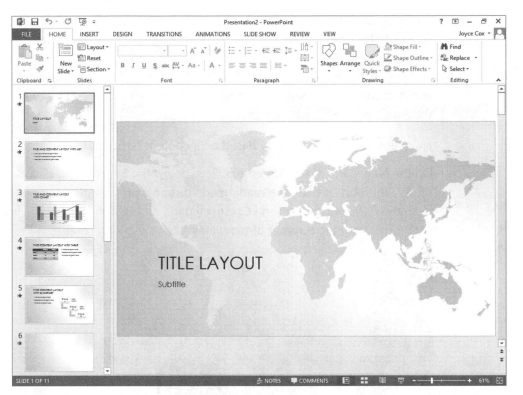

This design includes layouts for various types of slides, with graphics but no specific content.

8   On the **Quick Access Toolbar**, click the **Save** button to display the **Save As** page of the **Backstage** view.

9   Click **Compute**r, and then in the right pane, click **Browse** to open the **Save As** dialog box.

   TIP The dialog box displays the contents of the folder in which you last saved or opened a file from within the program. If the Navigation pane and toolbar are not displayed, click Browse Folders in the lower-left corner of the dialog box.

10 Use standard Windows techniques to navigate to the **Chapter02** practice file folder.

11 In the **File name** box, enter **My Presentation**, and then click **Save** to store the file in the **Chapter02** practice file folder.

TIP Programs that run on Windows use file name extensions to identify different types of files. For example, the extension .pptx identifies PowerPoint 2013, 2010, and 2007 presentations. Windows programs do not display these extensions by default, and you shouldn't enter them in the File Name box. When you save a file, PowerPoint automatically adds whatever extension is associated with the type of file selected in the Save As Type box.

Next let's start a presentation based on a content template.

12   On the **New** page of the **Backstage** view, below the **Search** box, click **Business** to display thumbnails of all the ready-made business presentation templates available from the Office website. In the **Category** pane on the right, notice the list of categories, with the number of templates available in each one.

From the New page, you can choose a template from a specific category. The selected template is indicated by a pink background.

TROUBLESHOOTING Don't be alarmed if your list of presentation templates is different from ours. New templates are continually being added. In fact, it is worth checking the Office website frequently, just to find out what's new.

13   Scroll down the center pane, noticing the wide variety of templates available.

14   Scroll down the **Category** pane, and click **Project** to display only the project-related templates. Then enter project status in the **Search** box, and click the **Start Searching** button.

15   In the center pane, click the **Project status report presentation** thumbnail. Then when the preview box appears, click the **More Images** right arrow a few times to preview each slide in the template.

16   Click **Create** to start a new presentation based on the selected template.

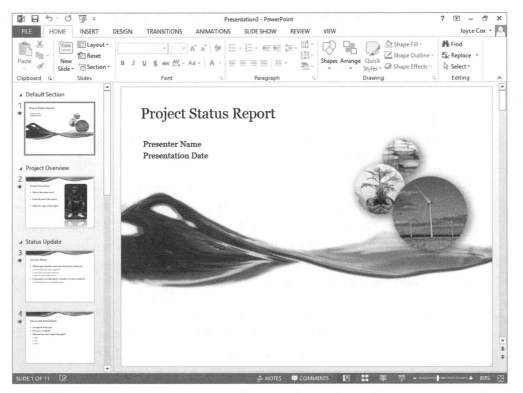

You can use the suggestions in the new status report presentation to develop the content of the presentation.

17   In the **Thumbnails** pane, click the slide **2** thumbnail. Then continue clicking thumbnails to display each slide of the presentation in turn.

The slides contain generic instructions about the sort of information you might want to include in a presentation for a project status report. You can replace these instructions with your own text. For now, let's simply save the new presentation.

18 Display the **Save As** page, and with **Computer** selected, click **Chapter02** in the **Recent Folders** list to open the **Save As** dialog box with that folder displayed.

19 On the dialog box's toolbar, click the **New folder** button to create a folder named **New Folder**, with the name selected for editing.

20 Enter **My Reports**, press **Enter**, and then double-click the new **My Reports** folder to make it the current folder.

21 In the **File name** box, click the existing entry, enter **My Presentation**, and then click **Save**.

You have now saved two presentations with the same name, but in different folders.

✖ CLEAN UP Close the My Presentation presentation.

Compatibility with earlier versions

The Microsoft Office 2013 programs use file formats based on XML. By default, PowerPoint 2013 files are saved in the .pptx format.

You can open a .ppt file created with an earlier version of PowerPoint in PowerPoint 2013, but the newer features of PowerPoint are not available. The presentation name appears in the title bar with [Compatibility Mode] to its right. You can work in this mode, or you can convert the presentation to the current format by clicking the Convert button on the Info page of the Backstage view, or by saving the presentation as a different file in the PowerPoint Presentation format.

If you work with people who are using a version of PowerPoint earlier than 2007, you can save your presentations in a format that they will be able to use by changing the Save As Type setting in the Save As dialog box to PowerPoint 97-2003 Presentation.

Saving files to SkyDrive

Whether you're working in a corporate environment or at home, you have the option of saving files to Microsoft SkyDrive. The SkyDrive location you save to might be part of your company's Microsoft SharePoint environment, or it might be a cloud-based storage location that is associated with your Microsoft account. Saving a file in either type of SkyDrive location provides the option of sharing the file with other people.

To save a presentation to SkyDrive, display the Save As page of the Backstage view, click your SkyDrive, and then specify the SkyDrive folder in which you want to save the file. If your SkyDrive doesn't already appear in the list of locations, click Add A Place, click SkyDrive, and then enter the credentials associated with the SkyDrive you want to access.

When you save a PowerPoint presentation to SkyDrive, you and other people with whom you share the presentation can work on it by using a local installation of PowerPoint or by using PowerPoint Web App, which is available in the SkyDrive environment.

SEE ALSO For information about PowerPoint Web App, see Chapter 1, "Explore Microsoft PowerPoint 2013."

Microsoft provides 7 gigabytes (GB) of free SkyDrive storage to Microsoft account holders. If you already have a Microsoft account, you can access your SkyDrive directly from any Office program, or from *skydrive.live.com*. If you don't yet have a Microsoft account, you can configure any existing email account as a Microsoft account at *signup.live.com*. (If you don't yet have an email account that you want to configure for this purpose, you can get a new account there too.)

SkyDrive Pro is available as part of a SharePoint 2013 environment, and your storage there will be managed by your company or SharePoint provider.

2

Entering text in placeholders

On each slide in a presentation, PowerPoint indicates with placeholders the type and position of the objects on the slide. For example, a slide might have placeholders for a title and for a bulleted list with bullet points and one or more levels of secondary subpoints. You can enter text directly into a placeholder on a slide in the Slide pane in Normal view; or you can switch to Outline view, where the entire presentation is displayed in outline form, and then enter text in the Outline pane.

When you point to a text placeholder or to an outline, the pointer changes to an I-beam. When you click, a blinking cursor appears to indicate where characters will appear when you enter them. As you enter text, it appears both on the slide and on the slide thumbnail (Normal view) or in the outline (Outline view).

In this exercise, you'll enter slide titles, bullet points, and subpoints, both directly in placeholders on a slide and in the presentation's outline.

 SET UP **You don't need any practice files to complete this exercise. Open a new, blank presentation, and save it as BuyingTravelA in the Chapter02 practice file folder. Close the Notes pane, and then follow the steps.**

1   On the slide, click the **Click to add title** placeholder. Notice that the cursor appears in the center of the box, indicating that the text you enter will be centered in the placeholder.

2   Enter **Buying Trips**. (Do not enter the period. By tradition, slide titles have no periods.)

   TIP If you make an error while working through this exercise, press Backspace to delete the mistake, and then enter the correct text. For information about more sophisticated ways of checking and correcting spelling, see "Correcting and sizing text while entering it" and "Checking spelling and choosing the best wording," both in Chapter 4, "Work with slide text."

3   On the **View** tab, in the **Presentation Views** group, click the **Outline View** button. Notice that the text you just entered in the title placeholder also appears in the **Outline** pane, adjacent to a slide icon.

4   On the slide, click the **Click to add subtitle** placeholder, and enter Ensuring Successful Outcomes, without the comma. (As you enter titles and bullet points throughout the exercises, don't enter any ending punctuation marks.)

5   Press **Enter** to move the cursor to a new line in the same placeholder, and enter Judy Lew, Purchasing Manager.

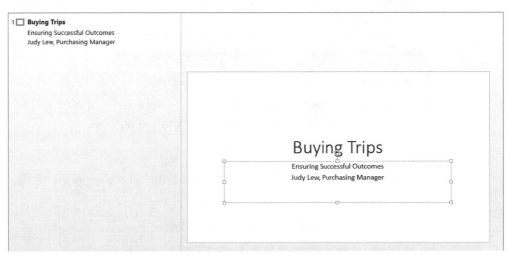

The Outline pane contains the text you entered on the adjacent title slide.

6   Save the presentation.

TIP We won't usually tell you to save your work; we assume you will save periodically.

Now let's enter text in the Outline pane.

7   Click a blank area of the **Outline** pane to position the cursor to the right of the word *Manager*.

8   Press **Enter**, which creates a new subtitle line.

9   Press **Shift+Tab**, which promotes the subtitle line to a second slide, as indicated in the **Outline** pane by the slide icon. Notice that a new slide, with placeholders for a title and either a bulleted list or a graphic, is displayed in the **Slide** pane, and the status bar displays **Slide 2 of 2**.

SEE ALSO For information about other ways to add slides, see "Adding and deleting slides" later in this chapter.

10 Without clicking the slide, enter Overview as the title of the slide, and press **Enter**, which creates another slide.

Instead of adding a third slide, let's add a bullet point to slide 2.

11 Press the **Tab** key to convert the new slide title to a bullet point with a gray bullet.

12 Enter Preparing for a buying trip, and then press **Enter** to add a new bullet point at the same level.

13 Enter Traveling internationally, and then press **Enter**.

14 Enter Meeting the client, and then press **Enter**.

If you know what text you want to appear on your slides, it is often quicker to work in the Outline pane. Let's add two more slides to the outline.

15 Press **Shift+Tab** to create the third slide.

16 Enter Preparing for a Buying Trip, press **Enter**, and then press **Tab** to add a bullet point.

17 Enter Know your needs, and then press **Enter**.

Instead of adding another bullet point, let's add a subpoint.

18 On the **Home** tab, in the **Paragraph** group, click the **Increase List Level** button to convert the new bullet point to a subpoint.

TIP You can click the Increase List Level button to change slide titles to bullet points and bullet points to subpoints in both the Slide and Outline panes. You can also click the Decrease List Level button to change subpoints to bullet points and bullet points to slide titles in both places. However, when you're entering text in the Outline pane, it's quicker to use keys—Tab and Shift+Tab—to perform these functions than it is to take your hands off the keyboard to click buttons.

19   Enter **Know your customers**, press **Enter**, and then enter **Know the current trends**.

Instead of creating another subpoint, let's add a new slide.

20   Press **Ctrl+Enter** to create a fourth slide.

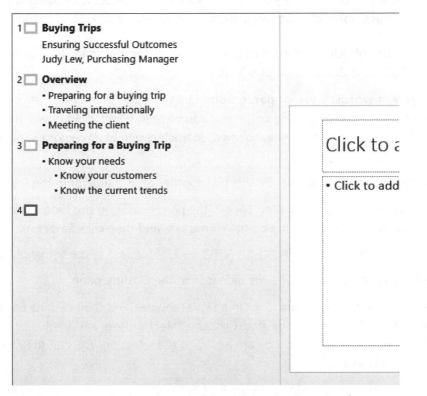

The Outline pane displays the text of the presentation in outline form.

❌ CLEAN UP Close the BuyingTravelA presentation, saving your changes if you want to.

Editing text

After you enter text, you can use standard word processing techniques to change it at any time. You insert new text by clicking where you want to make the insertion and simply entering it. Before you can change existing text, you need to select it by using any of the following techniques, some of which are specific to PowerPoint:

- **Word** Double-click the word to select the word and the space following it. Punctuation following the word is not selected.

- **Adjacent words, lines, or paragraphs** Drag through them. Alternatively, position the cursor at the beginning of the text you want to select, hold down the **Shift** key, and either press an arrow key to select characters one at a time or click at the end of the text you want to select.

- **Bullet point or subpoint** Click its bullet either on the slide or in the **Outline** pane.

- **All the text in a placeholder** Click in the placeholder on the slide, click the **Select** button in the **Editing** group on the **Home** tab, and then click **Select All**.

  KEYBOARD SHORTCUT Press Ctrl+A to select all the text in the active placeholder.

- **All the text on a slide** Click its slide icon in the **Outline** pane.

- **All the objects on a slide** Click in any placeholder, and then click its border, which becomes solid instead of dashed. Click the **Select** button, and then click **Select All**. All the other objects on that slide are added to the selection. You can then work with all the objects as a unit.

  TIP Clicking Select and then Selection Pane displays a pane where you can specify whether particular objects should be displayed or hidden. You might want to hide an object if you're using the slide in similar presentations for two different audiences, one of which needs more detail than the other.

Selected text appears highlighted in the location where you made the selection—that is, either on the slide or in the Outline pane.

To replace a selection, enter the new text. To delete the selection, press either the Delete key or the Backspace key. To move or copy the selected text, you have three options:

- **Drag-and-drop editing** Use this method, which is frequently referred to simply as *dragging*, when you need to move or copy text on the same slide or to a slide that is visible in the Outline pane without scrolling. Start by using any of the methods described previously to select the text. Then point to the selection, hold down the mouse button, drag the text to its new location, and release the mouse button. To copy the selection, hold down the **Ctrl** key while you drag.

■ **Cut, Copy, and Paste buttons** Use this method when you need to move or copy text between two locations that you cannot display at the same time—for example, between slides that are not shown simultaneously in the Outline pane. Also use this method if you need to move or copy text to multiple locations. Select the text, and click the **Cut** or **Copy** button in the **Clipboard** group on the **Home** tab. (The cut or copied item is stored in an area of your computer's memory called the *Microsoft Office Clipboard*, hence the name of the group.) Then reposition the cursor, and click the **Paste** button to insert the selection in its new location. If you click the **Paste** arrow instead of the button, PowerPoint displays a list of different ways to paste the selection.

By using the Paste Options menu, you can specify how you want to paste the cut or copied item.

Pointing to a **Paste Options** button displays a preview of how the cut or copied item will look when pasted into the text in that format, so you can experiment with different ways of pasting until you find the one you want.

SEE ALSO For more information about cut and copied content, see the sidebar "About the Clipboard" later in this chapter.

■ **Keyboard shortcuts** It can be more efficient to press key combinations to cut, copy, and paste selections than to click buttons on the ribbon. The following table shows the main keyboard shortcuts for editing tasks.

Task	Keyboard shortcut
Cut	Ctrl+X
Copy	Ctrl+C
Paste	Ctrl+V
Undo	Ctrl+Z
Repeat/Redo	Ctrl+Y

TIP When moving and copying text in the Outline pane, you can hide bullet points under slide titles so that you can display more of the presentation at one time. Double-click the icon of the slide whose bullet points you want to hide. Double-click again to redisplay the bullet points. To expand or collapse the entire outline at once, right-click the title of a slide, point to Expand or Collapse, and then click Expand All or Collapse All.

If you change your mind about an edit you have made, reverse it by clicking the Undo button on the Quick Access Toolbar. If you undo an action in error, click the Redo button on the Quick Access Toolbar to reverse the change.

To undo multiple actions at the same time, click the Undo arrow and then click the earliest action you want to undo in the list. You can undo actions only in the order in which you performed them—that is, you cannot reverse your fourth previous action without first reversing the three actions that followed it.

TIP The number of actions you can undo is set to 20, but you can change that number by displaying the Backstage view, clicking Options to display the PowerPoint Options dialog box, clicking Advanced, and then in the Editing Options area of the Advanced page, changing the Maximum Number Of Undos setting.

In this exercise, you'll delete and replace words and move bullet points and subpoints in the Outline pane and on slides.

➡ SET UP **You need the BuyingTravelB presentation located in the Chapter02 practice file folder to complete this exercise. Open the presentation, close the Notes pane, switch to Outline view, and then follow the steps.**

1   In the **Outline** pane, in the first bullet on slide **2**, double-click the word **buying**.

    TIP When you select text either in the Outline pane or on the slide, a small toolbar appears. This Mini Toolbar contains buttons for formatting the selected text. Ignore it for now; it won't affect your work. For information about using the Mini Toolbar, see "Changing the alignment, spacing, size, and look of text" in Chapter 4, "Work with slide text."

2   Press the **Delete** key.

3   In the slide **3** title, double-click **Buying**, and then press the **Backspace** key.

    Now let's replace one word with another.

4   In the third bullet point on slide **5**, double-click **good**, and enter **lasting** followed by a space. Notice that the text is replaced in both the **Outline** pane and the **Slide** pane.

Next we'll move a bullet point.

5   On slide **4**, click the bullet to the left of **Know the culture** to select the entire bullet point, including the invisible paragraph mark at the end.

TIP When you want to work with a bullet point or subpoint as a whole, ensure that the invisible paragraph mark at its end is included in the selection. If you drag across the text, you might miss the paragraph mark. As a precaution, hold down the Shift key and press End to be sure that the paragraph mark is part of the selection.

6   On the **Home** tab, in the **Clipboard** group, click the **Cut** button.

KEYBOARD SHORTCUT Press Ctrl+X to cut the selection.

7   Click to the left of the word **Make** in the first bullet point on slide **5**, and then click the **Paste** button to insert the bullet point from slide 4.

KEYBOARD SHORTCUT Press Ctrl+V to paste the contents of the Clipboard.

8   Display slide **3**, and in the **Slide** pane, click the bullet to the left of **Know your needs** to select the bullet point and its subpoints.

9   Drag the selection down and drop it to the left of **Read the Buyer Manual** to move the bullet point and its subpoints as a unit.

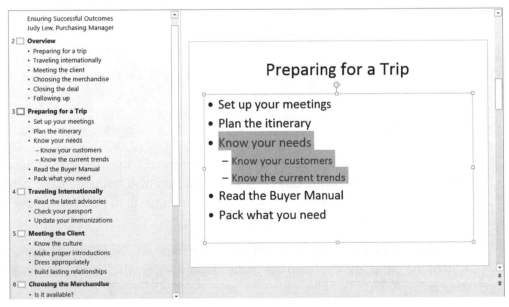

The change is reflected both on the slide and in the Outline pane.

About the Clipboard

You can view the items that have been cut or copied to the Clipboard in the Clipboard pane, which you display by clicking the Clipboard dialog box launcher on the Home tab.

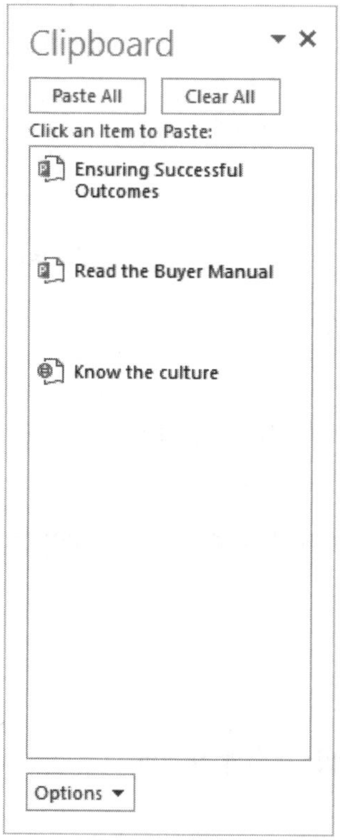

| Clipboard | ▾ ✕ |

| Paste All | Clear All |

Click an Item to Paste:

📄 Ensuring Successful Outcomes

📄 Read the Buyer Manual

📄 Know the culture

| Options ▾ |

The Clipboard stores items that have been cut or copied from any presentation.

To paste an individual item at the cursor, you simply click the item in the Clipboard pane. To paste all the items, click the Paste All button. You can point to an item, click the arrow that appears, and then click Delete to remove it, or you can remove all the items by clicking the Clear All button.

You can control the behavior of the Clipboard pane by clicking Options at the bottom of the pane, and choosing the circumstances under which you want the pane to appear.

Oops, that's not what we meant to do.

10   On the **Quick Access Toolbar**, click the **Undo** button to reverse your last editing action.

KEYBOARD SHORTCUT Press Ctrl+Z to undo the last editing action.

The Redo button appears on the Quick Access Toolbar, to the right of Undo. When you point to the Undo or Redo button, the name in the ScreenTip reflects your last editing action—for example, Redo Drag And Drop.

11   On the **Quick Access Toolbar**, click the **Redo** button to restore the editing action.

KEYBOARD SHORTCUT Press Ctrl+Y to restore the last editing action.

✖ CLEAN UP **Close the BuyingTravelB presentation, saving your changes if you want to.**

Adding and deleting slides

After you create a presentation, you can add a slide by clicking the New Slide button in the Slides group on the Home tab. By default in a new presentation, a slide added after the title slide has the Title And Content layout. Thereafter, each added slide has the layout of the preceding slide. If you want to add a slide with a different layout, simply select the layout from the New Slide gallery, which changes to reflect the layouts available in the template on which the presentation was based.

If you decide you don't want a slide, first select it either in the Thumbnails pane in Normal view, in the Outline pane in Outline view, or in Slide Sorter view, and then press the Delete key. You can also right-click the slide and click Delete Slide. To select a series of slides, click the first slide and hold down the Shift key while clicking the last slide. To select noncontiguous slides, click the first one and hold down the Ctrl key while clicking additional slides.

If you want a slide to have a different layout, you don't have to delete it and then add a new one with the layout you want. Instead, select the new layout from the Layout gallery.

In this exercise, you'll add a slide with the default layout and then add slides with other layouts. You'll delete first a single slide and then a series of slides. Finally, you'll change the layout of a slide.

SET UP You need the ServiceA presentation located in the Chapter02 practice file folder to complete this exercise. Open the presentation, and then follow the steps.

1   On the **Home** tab, in the **Slides** group, click the **New Slide** button (not its arrow) to add a slide with the default **Title and Content** layout.

   KEYBOARD SHORTCUT Press Ctrl+M to add a slide to the presentation.

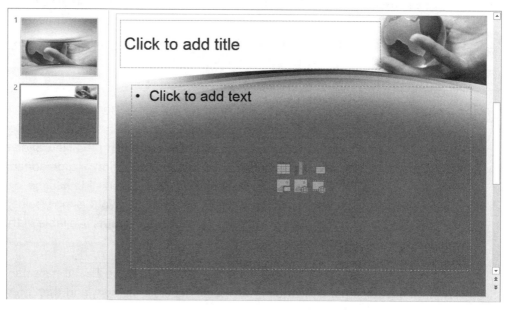

The Title And Content layout accommodates a title and either text or graphic content—a table, chart, diagram, picture, clip art image, or media clip.

TIP You can also add new Title And Content slides by pressing keyboard shortcuts while you're entering text in the Outline pane. For more information, see "Entering text in placeholders" earlier in this chapter.

Now let's add a slide with a non-default layout.

2   In the **Slides** group, click the **New Slide** arrow to display a menu containing the **New Slide** gallery.

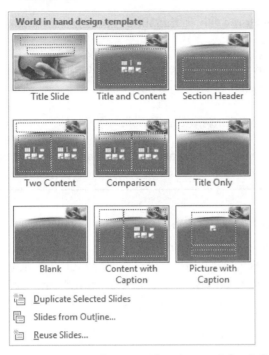

The New Slide gallery provides nine predefined slide layouts for the World In Hand design template, on which this presentation was based.

3   In the gallery, click **Two Content** to add a slide with a title placeholder and two text or graphic content placeholders.

4   Add another slide with the **Two Content** layout by clicking the **New Slide** button in the **Slides** group.

5   Continue adding slides from the **New Slide** gallery, selecting a different layout each time so that you can find out what each one looks like.

When you finish, the presentation contains 10 slides. Let's delete some of them.

6   Scroll to the top of the **Thumbnails** pane. Then right-click slide **3**, and click **Delete Slide**. Notice that PowerPoint renumbers all the subsequent slides.

7   In the **Thumbnails** pane, click slide **5**. Then scroll to the bottom of the pane, hold down the **Shift** key, and click slide **9**.

8   With slides **5** through **9** selected, right-click the selection, and click **Delete Slide**.

The presentation now has four slides. Let's switch the layout of the last slide.

9   With slide **4** selected, on the **Home** tab, in the **Slides** group, click the **Layout** button to display the **Layout** gallery.

> **TIP** This gallery is the same as the New Slide gallery, but it applies the layout you choose to an existing slide instead of adding a new one.

10   In the gallery, click the **Title and Content** thumbnail.

❌ CLEAN UP **Close the ServiceA presentation, saving your changes if you want to.**

Exporting presentation outlines

When you want to use the text from a presentation in another program, you can save the presentation outline as an .rtf (Rich Text Format) file. Many programs, including the Windows and Mac versions of Word and older versions of PowerPoint, can import outlines saved as .rtf files with their formatting intact.

To save a presentation outline as an .rtf file:

1   Display the **Backstage** view, click **Save As**, click **Computer**, and then click **Browse** to open the **Save As** dialog box.

2   In the **File name** box, specify the name of the file.

3   Display **the Save as type** list, and click **Outline/RTF**.

4   Navigate to the folder in which you want to store the outline, and click **Save**.

TIP If your presentation needs to be compatible with assistive technologies, exporting an outline is a good way to identify which content will be accessible and which won't. You can then adjust the presentation's content as necessary.

Importing slides from existing sources

If your presentation will contain information that already exists in a document created in Microsoft Word or another word processing program, you can edit that information into outline format, save it as a Word file or an .rtf file, and then import the outline into a PowerPoint presentation.

For the importing process to work as smoothly as possible, the document must be formatted with heading styles. PowerPoint translates Heading 1 styles into slide titles, Heading 2 styles into bullet points, and Heading 3 styles into subpoints.

If you often include a slide that provides the same basic information in your presentations, you don't have to re-create the slide for each presentation. For example, if you create a slide that shows your company's product development cycle for a new product presentation, you might want to use variations of that same slide in all new product presentations. You can easily tell PowerPoint to reuse a slide from one presentation in a different presentation. The slide assumes the formatting of its new presentation unless you specify otherwise.

Within a presentation, you can duplicate an existing slide to reuse it as the basis for a new slide. You can then customize the duplicated slide instead of having to create it from scratch.

In this exercise, you'll add slides by importing a Word outline. Then you'll reuse a slide from an existing presentation. Finally, you'll duplicate an existing slide.

 SET UP You need the ServiceB and ProjectProcess presentations and the ServiceOutline document located in the Chapter02 practice file folder to complete this exercise. Open the ServiceB presentation, close the Notes pane, and then follow the steps.

1   On the **Home** tab, in the **Slides** group, click the **New Slide** arrow. Then below the gallery in the menu, click **Slides from Outline** to open the **Insert Outline** dialog box, which resembles the **Open** dialog box.

2   With the contents of the **Chapter02** practice file folder displayed, double-click the **ServiceOutline** file to convert the outline into 12 slides.

3   Switch to **Outline** view.

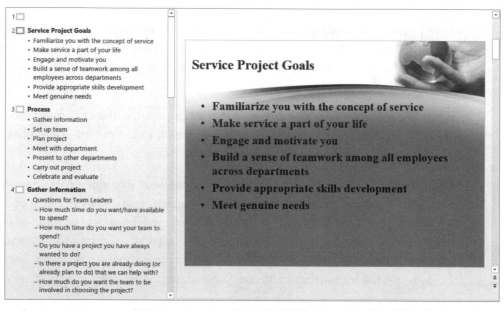

In the presentation, each Heading 1 style is a slide title, each Heading 2 style is a bullet point, and each Heading 3 style is a subpoint.

TIP You can start a new presentation directly from an outline document. From the Open page of the Backstage view, display the Open dialog box, and in the list of file types, click All Files. Then locate and double-click the outline document you want to use.

Now let's reuse a slide from a different presentation.

4   In the **Outline** pane, click the empty slide **1**.

5   On the **Home** tab, in the **Slides** group, click the **New Slide** arrow. Then below the gallery in the menu, click **Reuse Slides** to open the **Reuse Slides** pane on the right side of the screen.

6   In the **Reuse Slides** pane, click **Browse**. Then in the list, click **Browse File** to open the **Browse** dialog box, which resembles the **Open** dialog box.

TIP If your organization uses SharePoint, you and your colleagues can store individual slides or even entire presentations in a slide library so that they are available for use in any presentation. To store a slide in a slide library, publish the slides to the URL of the library from the Share page in the Backstage view. To insert a slide from a slide library into an existing presentation, enter the URL of the library in the Insert Slide From box of the Reuse Slides pane.

7 If the contents of the **Chapter02** practice file folder are not displayed, navigate to that folder. Then double-click **ProjectProcess** to display thumbnails of all the slides in that presentation in the **Reuse Slides** pane.

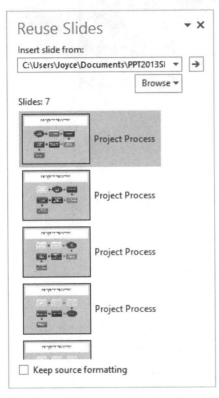

The Reuse Slides pane showing thumbnails of the slides in the ProjectProcess presentation, which display a series of diagrams related to a project workflow.

8 Scroll to the bottom of the **Reuse Slides** pane to display all the available slides.

9   Scroll back to the top of the pane, and click the first thumbnail to insert that slide as slide **2** in the **ServiceB** presentation.

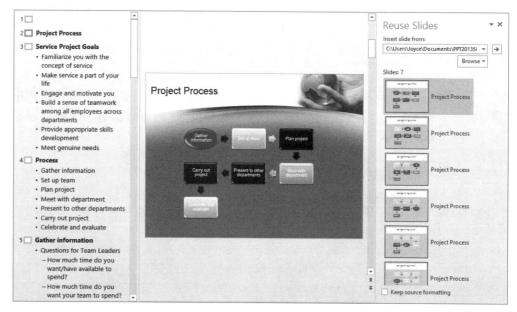

Slide 2 of the ServiceB presentation now displays a diagram from the Projects presentation.

TIP he reused slide takes on the design of the presentation in which it is inserted. If you want the slide to retain the formatting from the source presentation instead, select the Keep Source Formatting check box at the bottom of the Reuse Slides pane.

10   Close the **Reuse Slides** pane.

Let's copy the slide you just inserted.

11   With slide **2** selected in the **Outline** pane, display the **New Slide** gallery. Then click **Duplicate Selected Slides** to insert a new slide **3** identical to slide **2**.

TIP In Normal view, you can right-click the selected slide and then click Duplicate Slide.

You can now modify the existing slide content instead of creating it from scratch.

❌ CLEAN UP Close the ServiceB presentation, saving your changes if you want to.

Key points

- How you start a new presentation depends on whether you need help developing the content, the design, or both.

- You can find many templates that you can customize to meet your needs at *office.microsoft.com*.

- You can enter and edit text on the slide displayed in the Slide pane in Normal view or in the presentation outline in the Outline pane in Outline view.

- You can add as many slides as you want. Most templates provide a variety of ready-made slide layouts to choose from.

- If you change your mind about a slide or its layout, you can delete it or switch to a different layout.

- You can create slides with content already in place by importing an outline document or reusing existing slides. Both methods save time and effort.

2

Chapter at a glance

Divide

Divide presentations into sections,
page 76

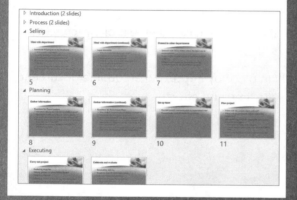

Apply

Apply themes,
page 84

COMPANY MEETING

Florian Stiller

Change

Change the slide background,
page 87

Designing with Color

Wide World Importers

Format

Format text placeholders,
page 96

Solutions

- Windbreaks
- Xeriscaping
- Soil amendment
- Native plants

Work with slides

3

IN THIS CHAPTER, YOU WILL LEARN HOW TO

- Divide presentations into sections.

- Rearrange slides and sections.

- Apply themes.

- Change the slide background.

- Format text placeholders.

When developing a presentation with more than a dozen slides, you can work on subsets of slides by creating sections. Sections are not visible to the audience, but they help you organize your slides logically and format them efficiently. A logical presentation and an overall consistent look, punctuated by variations that add weight exactly where it is needed, can enhance the likelihood that your message will be well received and absorbed by your intended audience.

In this chapter, you'll divide a presentation into sections and will move sections and individual slides to organize them logically. Then you'll apply a theme and its variants to the presentation. You'll also add color and shading to the background of slides and to the background of placeholders.

PRACTICE FILES To complete the exercises in this chapter, you need the practice files contained in the Chapter03 practice file folder. For more information, see "Download the practice files" in this book's Introduction.

Dividing presentations into sections

To make it easier to organize and format a longer presentation, you can divide it into sections. In both Normal view and Slide Sorter view, sections are designated by titles above their slides. They do not appear in other views, and they do not create slides or otherwise interrupt the flow of the presentation.

Because you can hide whole sets of slides under their section titles, the sections make it easier to focus on one part of a presentation at a time. If you are working on a presentation with other people, you can name one section for each person to delineate who is responsible for which slides.

TIP Some templates include a layout for section divider slides. If you divide a long presentation into sections based on topic, you might want to transfer your section titles to these slides to help guide your audience during presentation delivery.

In this exercise, you'll divide a presentation into two sections, adding one in Normal view and the other in Slide Sorter view. After naming the sections, you'll hide their slides and then display first one section and then both sections.

➜ SET UP **You need the CommunityA presentation located in the Chapter03 practice file folder to complete this exercise. Open the presentation, and then follow the steps.**

1   On the **Home** tab, in the **Slides** group, click the **Section** button, and then click **Add Section** to add an **Untitled Section** title before slide **1** in the left pane.

   TROUBLESHOOTING If PowerPoint selects and displays the last slide, scroll back to the top of the Thumbnails pane and click slide 1.

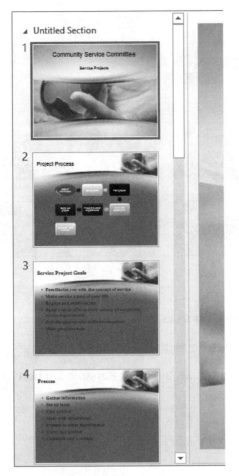

The Thumbnails pane, with the new section title above the first slide in the section.

2   Switch to **Slide Sorter** view, and adjust the zoom percentage to display the 13 slides in the presentation.

3   Click slide **4**. Then click the **Section** button, and click **Add Section** to add an **Untitled Section** title before slide **4**.

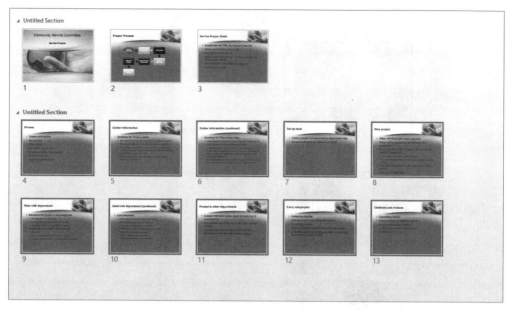

PowerPoint starts a new section and selects its slides.

To make the sections more useful, let's name them.

4   Right-click the second **Untitled Section** title, and click **Rename Section** to open the **Rename Section** dialog box.

In the Rename Section dialog box, the current name is selected in the Section Name box so that you can easily replace it.

5   In the **Section name** box, enter Process, and then click **Rename**.

6   Switch to **Normal** view, scroll to the top of the **Thumbnails** pane, and then click the **Untitled Section** title above slide **1** to select the section title and all the slides in the section.

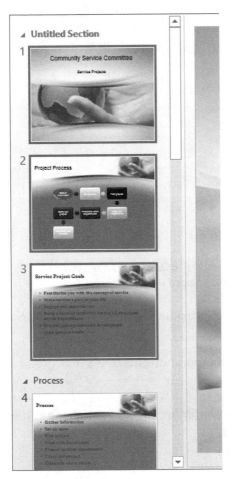

You can select each section of the presentation independently.

7   Display the **Rename Section** dialog box, enter Introduction as the section name, and click **Rename**.

Now let's use sections to view different parts of a presentation.

8   In the **Slides** group, click the **Section** button, and then click **Collapse All** to hide the slides under their section titles.

> ▶ **Introduction (3)**
>
> ▷ Process (10)

You can collapse sections to provide an "outline" of long presentations, with the number of slides in each section displayed in parentheses.

9   In the **Thumbnails** pane, to the left of **Introduction**, click the **Expand Section** arrow to display only the slides in that section.

10 Display all the slides by clicking the **Section** button in the **Slides** group and then clicking **Expand All**.

❌ CLEAN UP **Close the CommunityA presentation, saving your changes if you want to.**

Rearranging slides and sections

After you have added several slides to a presentation, you might want to rearrange their order so that they effectively communicate your message.

TIP You can copy slides from one open presentation to another in Slide Sorter view. First display both presentations in Slide Sorter view, and on the View tab, in the Window group, click the Arrange All button. Then drag slides to copy them from one presentation window to the other.

You can rearrange a presentation in three ways.

- In the **Thumbnails** pane, drag slides up and down to change their order.

- In the **Thumbnails** pane, move entire sections up or down to rearrange the presentation.

- To display more of the presentation at the same time, switch to **Slide Sorter** view, where you can drag slides or sections into the correct order.

In this exercise, you'll work in Normal view and in Slide Sorter view to logically arrange the slides in a presentation. You'll also delete a section you no longer need.

SET UP You need the CommunityB presentation located in the Chapter03 practice file folder to complete this exercise. Open the presentation, and then follow the steps.

1   In the **Thumbnails** pane, click slide **2**. Then drag the selected slide downward until it sits between the **Process** section title and slide **4**, but don't release the mouse button yet. Notice as you drag that the other slides move either up or down to indicate where the selected slide will appear when you release the mouse button.

2   Release the mouse button to move the slide to its new location, and notice that PowerPoint renumbers slides **2** and **3**.

3   To the left of **Introduction** in the first section title, click the black **Collapse Section** arrow. Then repeat this step for the **Process** section.

Even with these two sections collapsed, not all the slides in the Thumbnails pane are visible. Let's move to a view where you can display them all.

4   Switch to **Slide Sorter** view. Then use the **Zoom Slider** at the right end of the status bar to adjust the zoom percentage until all the slides are visible. (We set the zoom percentage to 50 percent.)

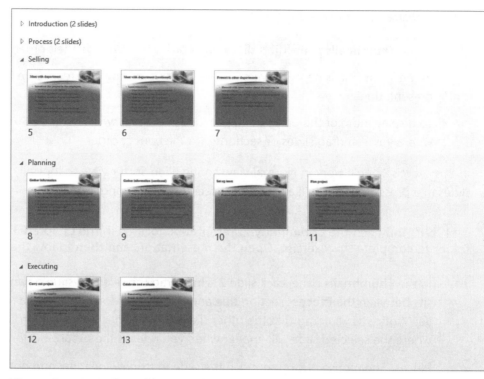

The sections you collapsed in Normal view are still collapsed in Slide Sorter view.

5   In the **Selling** section, click slide **7**, and then drag it to the left until it sits to the left of slide **5**. Notice that PowerPoint renumbers the slides in the section.

Now let's move a section.

6   Right-click the **Planning** section title, and then click **Move Section Up** to move the **Planning** section and all its slides above the **Selling** section.

7   Switch to **Normal** view, expand all the sections in the presentation, and then select slide **1**.

The first two sections could easily be combined into one section, so let's do that next.

8   Remove the second section by clicking the **Process** section title, clicking the **Section** button in the **Slides** group, and clicking **Remove Section**.

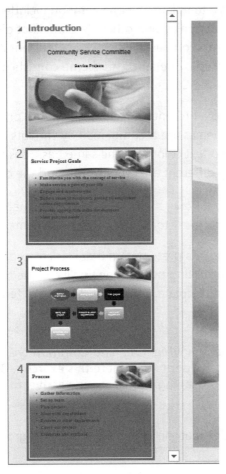

The Introduction section now contains the first four slides.

✖ CLEAN UP Close the CommunityB presentation, saving your changes if you want to.

Applying themes

When you create a presentation based on a template, the presentation includes a theme—a combination of colors, fonts, formatting, graphics, and other elements that gives the presentation a coherent look. Even a presentation based on the Blank Presentation template has a theme; the Office theme is applied by default. This theme consists of a white background, a very basic set of colors, and the Calibri font.

If you want to change the theme applied to a presentation, you can choose one from the Themes gallery on the Design tab. Many themes are accompanied by variants, providing a range of instant choices of background and text color with the same basic design. By using the Live Preview feature, you can easily try different effects until you find the one you want.

SEE ALSO For information about creating your own themes, see "Creating themes, theme colors, and theme fonts" in Chapter 12, "Create custom presentation elements."

In this exercise, you'll first change the theme of a presentation that was created from scratch, using the Blank Presentation template as a starting point. Then you'll change the theme of a presentation that was based on a content template. Finally, you'll apply different theme variants to different sections of a presentation.

➜ SET UP You need the LandscapingA, CompanyMeeting, and CommunityC presentations located in the Chapter03 practice file folder to complete this exercise. Open all three presentations, and then with the LandscapingA presentation active, follow the steps.

1   On slide **1**, click the slide's title. Notice that the slide has a white background with black text in the Calibri font.

2   On the **Design** tab, in the **Themes** group, click the gallery's **More** button to open a menu that contains the entire **Themes** gallery.

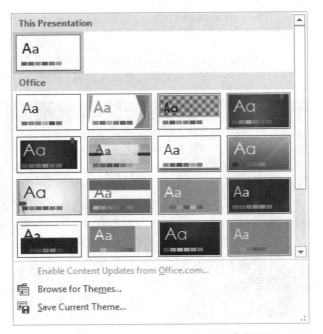

The Themes gallery identifies the current theme and displays all the other available themes. The commands below the gallery enable you to browse for and save themes.

3 In turn, point to each theme thumbnail in the **Office** area of the gallery to display their names in ScreenTips and show a live preview of what the presentation will look like with that theme applied.

4 Click the **Ion** thumbnail to apply that theme to the entire presentation. Notice that the slides now have a dark aqua, gradient background with a red accent in the upper-right corner.

5 With the title still selected, click the **Home** tab. Notice that the title text is now white and in the Century Gothic font.

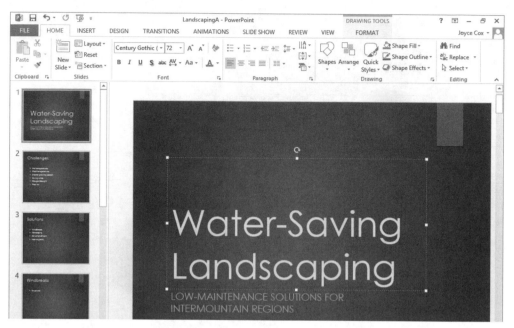

Most built-in themes have a distinctive title slide design that is modified for all the other slide layouts.

Now let's work with a presentation that already has a theme applied to it.

6 On the **View** tab, in the **Window** group, click the **Switch Windows** button, and click **CompanyMeeting**.

7 Display the **Themes** gallery, and then click the **Slice** thumbnail to switch to a design with a bright blue background and text in white and blue Century Gothic.

Good color contrast is important for any presentation, but especially for those that will be delivered on a screen to a roomful of people. Let's look at the variants of the Slice theme to determine whether any of them have better contrast.

8 On the **Design** tab, in the **Variants** group, point to each variant thumbnail in turn to display a live preview of what the presentation will look like with that variant applied.

9 After previewing each variant, click the **Orange** variant at the right end of the group.

Now let's use themes in a presentation that has been divided into sections.

10   On the **View** tab, in the **Window** group, click the **Switch Windows** button, and click **CommunityC**.

11   Switch to **Slide Sorter** view, and adjust the zoom percentage to display all the slides.

12   With slide **1** selected, display the **Themes** gallery from the **Design** tab, and then click the **Retrospect** thumbnail to apply that theme to the entire presentation.

13   Click the **Planning** section title, and in the **Variants** group, click the second variant to apply it to the slides in the **Planning** section.

14   Click the **Selling** section title, and apply the third variant to the slides in that section.

15   Click the **Executing** section title, and click the fourth variant, which makes the slides in that section unreadable.

16   With the **Executing** section title still selected, click the first variant to apply the same theme colors to the slides in the fourth section as those in the first section.

> **TIP** If you like the colors of one theme, the fonts of another, and the effects of another, you can mix and match theme elements. First apply the theme that most closely resembles the look you want. Then in the Variants group, click the More button, and change the colors by clicking the Colors button, the fonts by clicking the Fonts button, or the effects by clicking the Effects button. For more information, see "Creating themes, theme colors, and theme fonts" in Chapter 12, "Create custom presentation elements."

❌ CLEAN UP Close the CommunityC, CompanyMeeting, and LandscapingA presentations, saving your changes if you want to.

Changing the slide background

In PowerPoint, you can customize the background of a slide by adding a solid color, a color gradient, a texture, or even a picture. You make these changes in the Format Background pane, which opens when you click the Format Background button in the Customize group on the Design tab.

In the Format Background pane, you can control the appearance of the color, texture, pattern, or picture applied to the background of the current slide or all slides.

In the Format Background pane, you can click icons to display pages where you can do the following:

- **Fill** Select a solid color, color gradient, picture, texture, or pattern fill, as well as display or hide background graphics and set the color and transparency.

- **Effects** Apply artistic effects to picture or texture fills.

- **Picture** Manipulate the sharpness, brightness, contrast, and color of picture fills.

A color gradient is a visual effect in which a solid color gradually changes from light to dark or dark to light. PowerPoint offers several gradient patterns, each with variations.

If you want something fancier than a solid color or a color gradient, you can give the slide background a texture or pattern. PowerPoint comes with several built-in textures that you can easily apply to the background of slides. If none of these meets your needs, you might want to use a picture of a textured surface. For a dramatic effect, you can even incorporate a picture of your own, although these are best reserved for small areas of the slide rather than the entire background.

In this exercise, you'll shade the background of one slide. Then you'll apply a textured background to all the slides in the presentation.

 SET UP You need the DesignWithColor presentation located in the Chapter03 practice file folder to complete this exercise. Open the presentation, and then follow the steps.

1   On the **Design** tab, in the **Customize** group, click the **Format Background** button to display the **Format Background** pane on the right side of the screen.

2   With the **Fill** page displayed, click **Gradient fill**.

When you select a background option, the Format Background pane changes to show the settings for that option.

3   Adjacent to **Color**, click the **Color** button to display a menu containing two color palettes.

You can select a variation of the colors provided by the current theme or a standard color. Below the palettes are commands for more precise color choices.

4   In the top row of the **Theme Colors** palette, click the eighth swatch (**Purple Accent 4**), which instantly changes the background of slide **1** to a purple gradient.

    TIP To change a theme color throughout a presentation, you need to make the change on the slide master. For information, see "Creating themes, theme colors, and theme fonts" in Chapter 12, "Create custom presentation elements."

    Let's refine the gradient of this title slide background by changing its shape, direction, and color.

5   In the **Format Background** pane, click the **Type** arrow, and then in the list of options, click **Rectangular**. Notice that on the active slide, the purple gradiant changes to reflect this setting.

6   Click the **Direction** button, and then click the rightmost thumbnail (**From Top Left Corner**).

7   In the **Gradient stops** area, click the second handle on the slider (**Stop 2 of 4**), and to the right, click the **Remove gradient stop** button. Then drag the middle handle (**Stop 2 of 3**) to the left until the **Position** setting is **70%**.

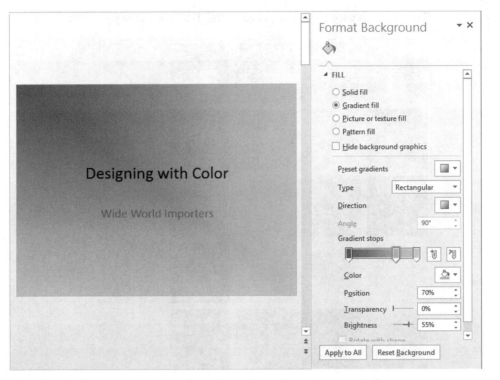

The title slide has a two-tone gradient that radiates from the upper-left corner.

TIP If you want to proof the text of your slides without the clutter of background graphics, clear the Hide Background Graphics check box on the Fill page of the Format Background pane. If you want to print your slides without their color backgrounds, on the Print page of the Backstage view, select the Grayscale or Pure Black And White option.

Now let's fill the background of all the slides with a texture.

8   In the **Format Background** pane, click **Picture or texture fill** to display the settings for that option.

9   Click the **Texture** button to display the **Texture** gallery.

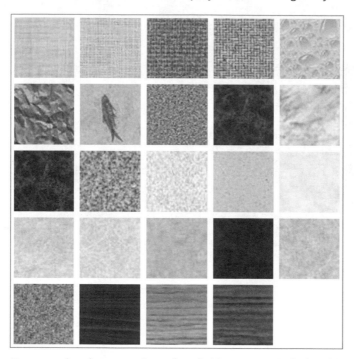

You can select from a variety of available textures, including fabrics, marbles and granites, wood grains, and Formica-like textures in various colors.

10   Click a texture that appeals to you to display slide **1** with that background. Then continue to apply textures, noticing that most of them are too complex, even for a slide with very little text.

11   When you have finished exploring, at the right end of the gallery's top row, click **Water droplets**.

12   In the lower-left corner of the **Format Background** pane, click **Apply to All**. Then close the pane.

The Water Droplets texture has been applied to the background of all the slides.

TIP If you want to add a watermark, such as the word *Draft* or *Confidential*, to the background of your slides, you need to add the text to the background of the slide master. For information about slide masters, see "Viewing and changing slide masters" in Chapter 12, "Create custom presentation elements."

✕ CLEAN UP Close the DesignWithColor presentation, saving your changes if you want to.

Non-theme colors

Although using themes enables you to create presentations with a pleasing design impact, you might want to make an element appear in a color that is not part of the theme. You apply these colors by selecting the element whose color you want to change and then choosing a color from the Standard Colors palette of the associated color menu or by choosing a custom color from the wide spectrum available in the Colors dialog box.

To select a color that is neither part of the theme nor a standard color:

1   Display the appropriate color menu; for example, the menu that appears when you click **Solid Fill**, and then click the **Fill Color** button in the **Format Background** pane.

2   At the bottom of the menu, click **More Colors** to open the **Colors** dialog box.

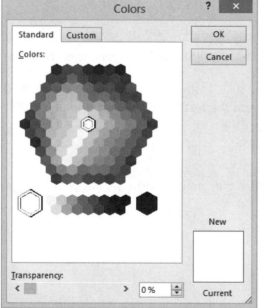

On the Standard page permutations of primary, secondary, and tertiary colors form a hexagonal color wheel.

3   Click a color in the **Colors** wheel, and then click **OK**.

To define a custom color:

1 Display the **Colors** dialog box, and then click the **Custom** tab.

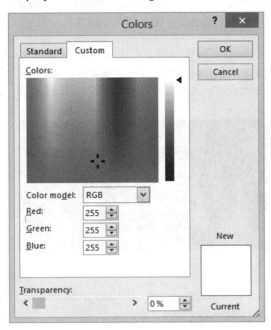

On the Custom page permutations of primary and secondary colors form a spectrum.

2 Click an approximate color in the **Colors** spectrum, and then do one of the following:

- Select the **RGB** color mode, and then precisely define the **Red**, **Green**, and **Blue** settings.

- Select the **HSL** color mode, and then precisely define the **Hue**, **Saturation**, and **Luminescence** settings.

3 Click **OK** to close the **Color** dialog box.

If you want to make a selected element the same color as one that is used elsewhere on the same slide, display the color menu, click Eyedropper, and then click the color you want.

After you use a non-theme or non-standard color, it becomes available in the Recent Colors palette of all color menus. The color remains on the palette even if you change the theme applied to the presentation.

Formatting text placeholders

For a consistent look, you won't usually want to change the formatting of a presentation's text placeholders. However, when you want to draw attention to a slide or one of its elements, you can do so effectively by making specific placeholders stand out.

A text placeholder usually has no border, so when it's not selected, its text appears to float on the slide. When you click the text once, the placeholder has a dashed border. The placeholder is then selected for editing, and you can enter new text or edit existing text.

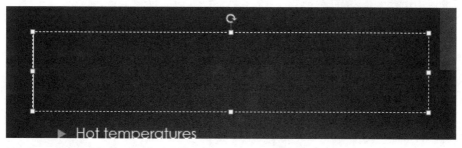

When a placeholder has a dashed border, you can enter or edit text.

Clicking the dashed border changes it to a solid border. You can then manipulate the placeholder as a unit; for example, you can size and move it.

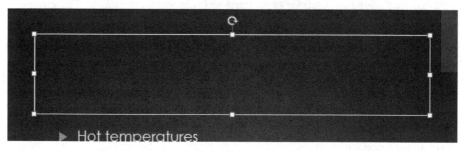

When a placeholder has a solid border, you can manipulate the placeholder.

When a placeholder is selected, the Format tool tab appears on the ribbon, because placeholders are actually text-box shapes that can be manipulated like any other shape.

From the Shape Styles group on this tab, you can format a placeholder in the following ways:

- Fill the background with a color, gradient, texture, pattern, or picture.

- Change the color and style of the shape's outline.

- Apply a style such as a shadow, reflection, or glow.

- Apply a three-dimensional effect.

- Select a predefined shape style that incorporates some or all of the preceding options.

TIP Your changes affect only the selected placeholder, not corresponding placeholders on other slides. If you want to make changes to the same placeholder on every slide, make the adjustments on the presentation's master slide. For more information about working with master slides, see "Viewing and changing slide masters" in Chapter 12, "Create custom presentation elements."

In this exercise, you'll first select a placeholder to review the effect on its border. You'll apply a ready-made style, and then you'll customize the formatting by changing the fill color, adding a border, and applying a special effect.

SET UP You need the LandscapingB presentation located in the Chapter03 practice file folder to complete this exercise. Open the presentation, and then follow the steps.

1   Display slide **3**, and click the slide title to select the placeholder for editing, as indicated by the cursor and dashed border.

     TROUBLESHOOTING If your placeholder border looks solid, try increasing the zoom percentage until the dashes are visible.

2   Point to the border of the placeholder, and when the pointer changes to a four-headed arrow, click once to select the placeholder for manipulation, as indicated by the solid border.

3   On the **Format** tool tab, in the **Shape Styles** group, click the gallery's **More** button to display a menu containing the **Shape Style** gallery

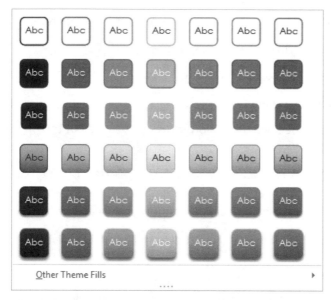

The Shape Style gallery has 42 predefined options.

4   Click the fifth thumbnail in the second row (**Colored Fill - Green, Accent 4**) to fill the placeholder with a light aqua color.

Now let's apply some custom formatting.

5   In the **Shape Styles** group, click the **Shape Fill** button to display a menu containing palettes. Then point to a few color swatches in turn to display a live preview of the effects on the placeholder.

6   Click the fourth swatch in the dark red column (**Dark Red, Accent 1, Darker 25%**) to fill the placeholder with a red that is slightly darker than the accent bar in the upper-right corner.

7   Click the **Shape Fill** button again, and then below the palettes, point to **Gradient** to display a menu containing the **Gradient** gallery.

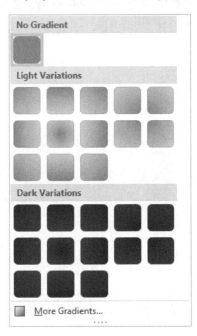

The Gradient gallery offers light and dark versions of gradients in different directions.

8   In the **Dark Variations** area, click the second thumbnail in the third row (**Linear Up**).

Now let's emphasize the border.

9   In the **Shape Styles** group, click the **Shape Outline** button, and then in the **Theme Colors** palette, click the second swatch in the dark teal column (**Dark Teal, Background 2, Lighter 60%**).

10 Click the **Shape Outline** button again. Then below the palettes, point to **Weight**, and in the list, click **3 pt**.

TIP The abbreviation pt stands for *point*. A point is a unit of measurement used in the design and publishing industries. There are 72 points to the inch.

Next let's add an effect to the placeholder.

11   In the **Shape Styles** group, click the **Shape Effects** button to display a gallery of all the types of effects you can apply to the placeholder.

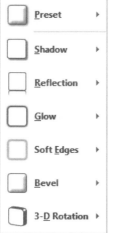

In the Shape Effects gallery, you can select from many possible special effects organized in seven categories: Preset, Shadow, Reflection, Glow, Soft Edges, Bevel, and 3-D Rotation.

12   In turn, display the options for each effect category, and point to a few to display their live previews.

13   When you have finished exploring, point to **Glow**, and then in the **Glow Variations** area of the gallery, click the fifth thumbnail in the last row (**Teal, 18 pt glow, Accent color 5**).

14   Click a blank area of the slide to release the selection so that the effects of your changes to the formatting of the placeholder are more obvious.

You can easily set off placeholders with combinations of color, borders, and effects.

⊗ CLEAN UP Close the LandscapingB presentation, saving your changes if you want to.

Key points

- Grouping slides into sections makes it easy to focus on and format specific parts of the presentation.

- If you need to change the order of slides or sections, you can rearrange them in the Thumbnails pane in Normal view, or in Slide Sorter view.

- Switching from one predefined theme or theme variant to another is an easy way to change the look of an entire presentation. Applying different themes or variants to different sections of a presentation is a good way to signal a change in a major topic.

- To dress up the background of one slide or of all the slides in a presentation, you can apply a solid color, color gradient, texture, pattern, or picture.

- You can change the background, outline, and effect of specific placeholders to make them stand out.

Chapter at a glance

Change

Change the alignment, spacing, size, and look of text, page 104

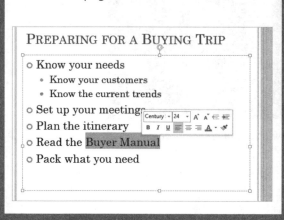

Check

Check spelling and choose the best wording, page 118

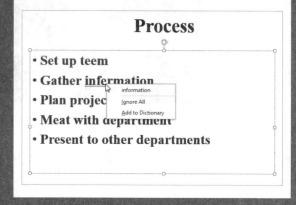

Find

Find and replace text and fonts, page 126

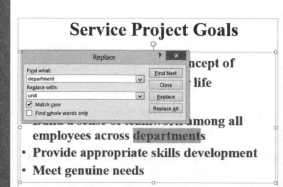

Add

Add text boxes, page 129

Work with slide text 4

IN THIS CHAPTER, YOU WILL LEARN HOW TO

- Change the alignment, spacing, size, and look of text.
- Correct and size text while entering it.
- Check spelling and choose the best wording.
- Find and replace text and fonts.
- Add text boxes.

In later chapters of this book, we show you ways to add fancy effects to electronic presentations so that you can really grab the attention of your audience. But no amount of animation, jazzy colors, and supporting pictures will convey your message if the words on the slides are inadequate to the task.

For most of your presentations, text is the foundation on which you build everything else. Even if you follow the current trend of building presentations that consist primarily of pictures, you still need to make sure that titles and any other words on your slides do their job, and do it well. This chapter shows you various ways to work with text to ensure that the words are accurate, consistent, and appropriately formatted.

In this chapter, you'll format selected text to look the way you want it. You'll use the AutoCorrect feature to help avoid typographical errors and the AutoFit feature to make the words you enter fit in the available space. Then you'll use the spell-checking feature to help detect and correct misspellings and the Thesaurus feature to refine the presentation's language. You'll replace one word with another throughout a presentation by using the Find And Replace feature, which you also use to ensure the consistent use of fonts. Finally, you'll add text boxes to a slide to contain text that appears only on that slide.

PRACTICE FILES To complete the exercises in this chapter, you need the practice files contained in the Chapter04 practice file folder. For more information, see "Download the practice files" in this book's Introduction.

Changing the alignment, spacing, size, and look of text

The alignment and spacing of paragraphs in a presentation's text placeholders are controlled by the template on which the presentation is based. For an individual paragraph, you can change these and other settings, which are collectively called *paragraph formatting*. After clicking anywhere in the paragraph to select it, make changes by using the commands in the Paragraph group on the Home tab, as follows:

- **Lists** Click the **Bullets** arrow to display a gallery of alternative built-in bullet symbols. To remove bullet formatting and create an ordinary paragraph, click **None** in the gallery. To switch to a numbered list, click the **Numbering** arrow, and then click the numbering style you want.

- **Alignment** Click one of the following alignment buttons in the **Paragraph** group on the **Home** tab:

  - Click the **Align Left** button to align text against the placeholder's left edge. Left-alignment is the usual choice for paragraphs.

    KEYBOARD SHORTCUT Press Ctrl+L to left-align text. For a complete list of keyboard shortcuts, see "Keyboard shortcuts" at the end of this book.

  - Click the **Center** button to align text in the middle of the placeholder. Center-alignment is often used for titles and headings.

    KEYBOARD SHORTCUT Press Ctrl+E to center text.

  - Click the **Align Right** button to align text against the placeholder's right edge. Right-alignment isn't used much for titles and bullet points.

    KEYBOARD SHORTCUT Press Ctrl+R to right-align text.

  - Click the **Justify** button to align text against both the left and right edges, adding space between words to fill the line. You might justify a single, non-bulleted paragraph on a slide for a neat look. (This option works only if the paragraph contains more than one line.)

  - Click the **Align Text** button to align text vertically at the top, in the middle, or at the bottom of the placeholder.

- **Line spacing** Click the **Line Spacing** button, and make a selection.

- **Paragraph spacing** Open the **Paragraph** dialog box, either by clicking the **Line Spacing** button and then clicking **Line Spacing Options** at the bottom of the menu, or by clicking the **Paragraph** dialog box launcher. You can then adjust the **Before** and **After** settings for the entire paragraph.

TIP If you want to make multiple changes to a paragraph's formatting, open the Paragraph dialog box so that you can make all the changes in one place. In this dialog box, you can also indent individual bullet points without changing them to subpoints.

In addition to changing the look of paragraphs, you can manipulate the look of individual words by manually applying settings that are collectively called *character formatting*. After selecting the characters you want to format, you make changes by using the commands in the Font group on the Home tab, as follows:

- **Font** Override the font specified by the theme by making a selection in the **Font** box.

  SEE ALSO For information about themes, see "Applying themes" in Chapter 3, "Work with slides."

- **Size** Manually control the size of text by clicking either the **Increase Font Size** button or the **Decrease Font Size** button. Because the effects are immediately evident, using these buttons takes the guesswork out of sizing text. You can also set a precise size in the **Font Size** box.

  KEYBOARD SHORTCUT Press Ctrl+Shift+> or Ctrl+Shift+< to increase or decrease font size.

  TIP If you turn off AutoFit so that you can manually size text, you can drag the handles around a selected placeholder to adjust its size to fit its text. For information about AutoFit, see "Correcting and sizing text while entering it" later in this chapter.

- **Style** Apply text attributes to selected characters by clicking the **Bold**, **Italic**, **Underline**, **Text Shadow**, or **Strikethrough** buttons

  KEYBOARD SHORTCUT Press Ctrl+B to make text bold, Ctrl+I to make it italic, or Ctrl+U to underline it.

- **Color** Change the color of the selected characters by clicking the **Font Color** arrow and then clicking the color you want in the palettes.

4

TIP The colors available in the Theme Colors palette are determined by the theme that is part of the presentation's design. For information about using colors that are not available in the Theme Colors or Standard Colors palette, see the sidebar "Non-theme colors" in Chapter 3, "Work with slides."

- **Case** Change the capitalization of selected words—for example, change small letters to capital letters—by clicking the **Change Case** button and then clicking the case you want.

- **Character spacing** Increase or decrease the space between the characters in a selection by clicking the **Character Spacing** button and then clicking the option you want. You can also click **More Spacing** to display the **Character Spacing** page of the **Font** dialog box, where you can specify the space between characters more precisely.

TIP You can clear all manually applied character formatting, except the Case setting, from a selection by clicking the Clear All Formatting button. (You can also press Ctrl+Spacebar to clear formatting.)

To make it quick and easy to apply the most common paragraph and character formatting, PowerPoint displays the Mini Toolbar when you select text. This toolbar contains buttons from the Font and Paragraph groups on the Home tab, but they're all in one place adjacent to the selection. If you don't want to apply any of the Mini Toolbar formats, simply ignore it and use the ribbon to make the changes you want.

You can quickly make formatting changes by clicking buttons on the Mini Toolbar.

After you have formatted the text on a slide, you might find that you want to adjust the way lines break to achieve a more balanced look. This is often the case with slide titles, but bullet points and regular text can sometimes also benefit from a few manually inserted line breaks. Simply press Shift+Enter to insert a line break at the cursor. This fine-tuning should wait until you have taken care of all other formatting of the slide element, because changing the font, size, and attributes of text can affect how it breaks.

In this exercise, you'll experiment with various types of character formatting and paragraph formatting to achieve the look you want. You'll also insert a few line breaks to balance the text on a slide.

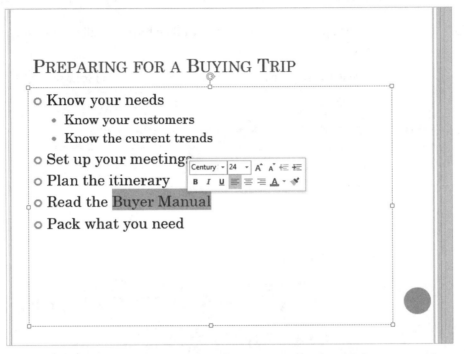

1 Display slide **3**, and in the fourth bullet point, select **Buyer Manual**, noticing that the **Mini Toolbar** appears adjacent to the selection.

The Mini Toolbar contains the tools most frequently used to format characters and paragraphs.

TIP If you move the pointer away from the selection, the Bilingual Dictionary box might also appear. Ignore this box for now. For information about the Bilingual Dictionary, see the sidebar "Researching information and translating text" later in this chapter.

2 On the **Mini Toolbar**, click the **Italic** button to make the words italic.

KEYBOARD SHORTCUT Press Ctrl+I to make selected text italic.

3 Display slide **4**, and on the slide, drag diagonally across the four bullet points to select them.

4   Ignoring the **Mini Toolbar**, on the **Home** tab, in the **Font** group, click the **Font Color** arrow. Then in the **Standard Colors** palette, click the **Red** swatch.

5   Display slide **5**, and click anywhere in the bulleted list. Then in the **Editing** group, click the **Select** button, and click **Select All** to select all the text in the placeholder.

KEYBOARD SHORTCUT Press Ctrl+A to select all the text in a placeholder.

6   In the **Font** group, click the **Increase Font Size** button until the setting in the **Font Size** box is **44**.

KEYBOARD SHORTCUT Press Ctrl+Shift+> to increase the font size.

When bullet points have only a few words, you can increase the font size to make them stand out.

7   In the **Font** group, click the **Clear All Formatting** button to return the font size to
     24 (the original size).

     KEYBOARD SHORTCUT Press Ctrl+Spacebar to clear manual formatting from
     selected text.

     Now let's change some paragraph formatting.

8   Display slide **9**, and select both bullet points.

9   In the **Paragraph** group, click the **Bullets** arrow to display a menu containing the
     Bullets gallery.

The Bullets gallery includes ready-made formats with various bullet characters.
You can click Bullets And Numbering at the bottom of the gallery to create
custom bullets.

10   In the gallery, click **None** to convert the bullet points to regular text paragraphs.

11   With both paragraphs still selected, on the **Home** tab, click the **Paragraph** dialog box
     launcher to open the **Paragraph** dialog box.

In the Paragraph dialog box, you can set alignment, indentation, line spacing, and paragraph spacing all in one place.

12   In the **General** area, change the **Alignment** setting to **Centered**.

13   In the **Spacing** area, enter **0** in the **Before** box, and then increase the **After** setting to **24 pt**.

14   Change the **Line Spacing** setting to **Exactly**, change the **At** setting to **30 pt**, and then click **OK**. Notice that the paragraphs are now centered with space between them, and the lines are farther apart.

      Finally let's make the text in a couple of paragraphs look more balanced by inserting a few line breaks.

15   In the first paragraph, click to the left of the word **only**, and press **Shift+Enter** to insert a line break.

16   Repeat step 15 to insert another line break to the left of the word **that**.

17   In the second paragraph, insert a line break to the left of the word **to** and another to the left of the word **for**.

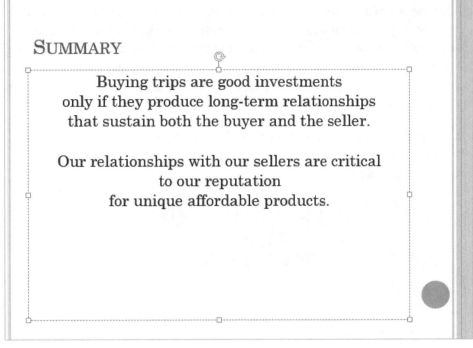

You can use line breaks to balance text and increase readability.

CLEAN UP Close the TripsA presentation, saving your changes if you want to.

Correcting and sizing text while entering it

We all make mistakes while entering text in a presentation. To help ensure that these mistakes don't go uncorrected, PowerPoint uses the AutoCorrect feature to catch and automatically correct many common capitalization and spelling errors. For example, if you enter *teh* instead of *the* or *WHen* instead of *When*, AutoCorrect immediately corrects the entry.

TIP If you don't want an entry to be corrected, click the Undo button on the Quick Access Toolbar when AutoCorrect makes the change.

You can customize AutoCorrect to recognize misspellings you routinely enter or to ignore text you do not want AutoCorrect to change. You can also create your own AutoCorrect substitutions to automate the entry of frequently used text. For example, you might want AutoCorrect to substitute your organization's name when you enter only an abbreviation.

In addition to providing the AutoCorrect feature to correct misspellings, PowerPoint provides the AutoFit feature to size text to fit its placeholder. By default, if you enter more text than will fit in a placeholder, PowerPoint reduces the size of the text so that all the text fits, and displays the AutoFit Options button to the left of the placeholder. Clicking this button displays a list of options that give you control over automatic sizing. For example, you can stop sizing text for the current placeholder while retaining the AutoFit settings for other placeholders.

If you want to change the default AutoFit settings, click Control AutoCorrect Options on the AutoFit Options button's menu to display the AutoFormat As You Type page of the AutoCorrect dialog box.

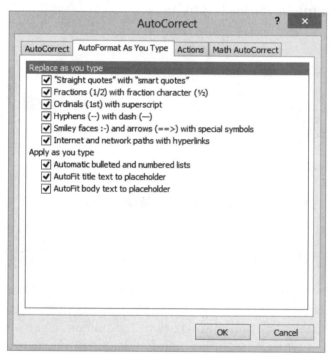

On the AutoFormat As You Type page of the AutoCorrect dialog box, you can clear the AutoFit Title Text To Placeholder and AutoFit Body Text To Placeholder check boxes to stop making text fit in placeholders.

TIP You can also change the AutoFit settings for a placeholder on the Textbox page of the Format Shape pane. The options are Do Not Autofit, Shrink Text On Overflow, and Resize Shape To Fit Text, which resizes the placeholder to fit the text instead of resizing the text to fit the placeholder.

In this exercise, you'll use AutoCorrect to fix a misspelled word, and you'll add an Auto-Correct entry. Then you'll use AutoFit to size text so that it fits within its placeholder, and you'll make a long bulleted list fit on one slide by converting its placeholder to a two-column layout.

SET UP **You need the CommunityServiceA presentation located in the Chapter04 practice file folder to complete this exercise. Open the presentation, and then follow the steps.**

1 Display slide **2**, and click the content placeholder.

2 Being careful for the purposes of this exercise to include the misspellings, enter **Setup teh teem**, press the **Enter** key, and then enter Gather adn analyze data.

3 Notice that almost immediately, AutoCorrect changes *teh* to *the* and *adn* to *and*. Also notice that AutoCorrect does not change *Setup* to *Set up* or *teem* to *team* because both *Setup* and *teem* are legitimate words that are not included in its correction list.

   TIP PowerPoint cannot detect that you have used an incorrect form of a word (the noun *Setup* instead of the verb *Set up*) or a homonym (a word that sounds the same as another word but has a different meaning).

   Now suppose you often misspell the word *assign* as *assine*. Let's add this misspelling to the substitution list so that AutoCorrect will correct it whenever you enter it.

4 Display the **Backstage** view, click **Options**, and in the left pane of the **PowerPoint Options** dialog box, click **Proofing**. Then in the **AutoCorrect options** area, click **AutoCorrect Options** to open the **AutoCorrect** dialog box.

The top part of the AutoCorrect page of the AutoCorrect dialog box lists general rules for correcting errors, such as capitalization mistakes. The lower part contains a huge table of misspellings and the keyboard equivalent of symbols with their replacements.

TROUBLESHOOTING If the AutoCorrect page is not active, click its tab to display its options.

5   In the lower part of the dialog box, scroll through the substitution table. When you enter one of the terms in the first column, PowerPoint automatically substitutes the term from the second column.

6   In the **Replace** box above the table, enter assine, and then press the **Tab** key.

7   In the **With** box, enter assign, and then click **Add**.

8   Close the **AutoCorrect** dialog box, and then close the **PowerPoint Options** dialog box.

9   On slide **2**, with the cursor to the right of the word **data**, press **Enter**. Then enter Assine to a category, and press **Enter**. Notice that PowerPoint changes the word *Assine* to *Assign*, even though you entered the substitution in all lowercase letters.

Let's use AutoCorrect to speed up the entry of a proper name.

10   Display slide **1**, click the subtitle placeholder, and enter Community Service Committee.

11   Select the three words, being sure not to select the blank space, which contains a hidden paragraph mark, after *Committee*. Then press **Ctrl+C** to copy the words to the Clipboard.

12   Open the **PowerPoint Options** dialog box, display the **Proofing** page, and then open the **AutoCorrect** dialog box.

13   In the **Replace** box, enter csc. Then click the **With** box, press **Ctrl+V** to paste in the words you copied to the Clipboard, and click **Add**.

14   Close the **AutoCorrect** dialog box, and then close the **PowerPoint Options** dialog box.

15   Display slide **3**, and click to the left of **Responsibilities**. Then enter csc, and press the **Spacebar**, watching as PowerPoint changes the initials *csc* to *Community Service Committee*.

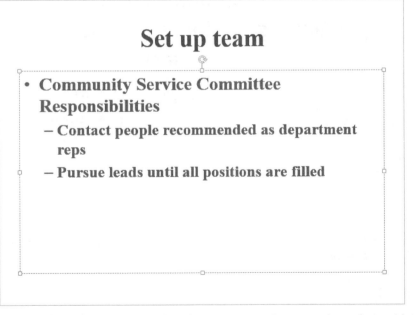

Because you followed the initials with a space, AutoCorrect replaces them with the corresponding entry in the substitution table.

TIP AutoCorrect also recognizes an entry if you follow it with a punctuation mark.

Next let's experiment with AutoFit.

16 Display slide **1**, click at the right end of the title, and notice that the setting in the **Font Size** box in the **Font** group on the **Home** tab is **44**.

17 Enter : (a colon), press **Enter**, and then enter Planning, Selling, and Executing a Project. Notice that AutoFit reduces the size of the title to **40** so that it fits in the title placeholder.

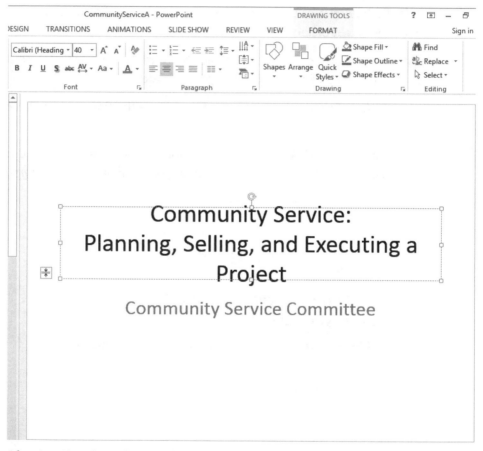

After AutoFit reduces the size of text, the AutoFit Options button appears to the left of the adjusted placeholder.

18   Click the **AutoFit Options** button to display a list of options for the selected title placeholder.

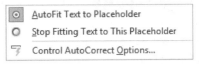

In the AutoFit Options list, you can click Stop Fitting Text To This Placeholder to reverse the size adjustment and prevent future adjustments.

19   Press the **Esc** key to close the list without making a selection.

20   Display slide **8**, click at the right end of the last subpoint, and notice that the font size is **28**.

21   Then press **Enter**, and enter How do we know if we are successful?, noticing that the text size changes to **26**.

22   Click the **AutoFit Options** button to display the list of options for a bulleted list placeholder.

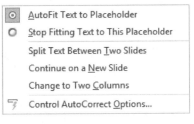

The AutoFit Options list for bullet points includes more options than the one for a title.

23   Click **Change to Two Columns**, and then click a blank area of the slide so that the results are more obvious.

Meet with department (continued)

- **Lead discussion with employees**
  - **What kind of project do we want to do?**
  - **What need do we want to address?**
  - **What are the goals of this project?**
  - **What do we need to do to meet those goals?**

  - Who will perform these tasks?
  - What materials will we need?
  - When will the tasks be performed?
  - How do we stay on schedule?
  - How do we know if we are successful?

The placeholder has been formatted to accommodate a two-column bulleted list.

✖ CLEAN UP If you want, open the AutoCorrect dialog box, and remove the *assine* and *csc* entries from the substitution table. Then close the CommunityServiceA presentation, saving your changes if you want to.

Checking spelling and choosing the best wording

The AutoCorrect feature is useful if you frequently enter the same misspelling. However, most misspellings are the result of erratic finger-positioning errors or memory lapses. You can use one of the following two methods to ensure that the words in your presentations are spelled correctly in spite of these random occurrences.

- By default, the PowerPoint spelling checker checks the spelling of the entire presentation—all slides, outlines, notes pages, and handout pages—against its built-in dictionary. To draw attention to words that are not in its dictionary and that might be misspelled, PowerPoint underlines them with a red wavy underline. You can right-click a word with a red wavy underline to display a menu with a list of possible spellings and actions. You can choose the correct spelling from the menu, tell PowerPoint to ignore the word, or add the word to a supplementary dictionary (explained shortly).

  TIP To turn off this behind-the-scenes spell-checking, open the PowerPoint Options dialog box, click Proofing, and clear the Check Spelling As You Type check box.

- Instead of dealing with potential misspellings while you're creating a presentation, you can check the entire presentation in one session by clicking the **Spelling** button in the **Proofing** group on the **Review** tab. PowerPoint then works its way through the presentation, and if it encounters a word that is not in its dictionary, it displays the word in the **Spelling** pane. After you indicate how PowerPoint should deal with the word, it moves on and displays the next word that is not in its dictionary, and so on.

TIP PowerPoint alerts you to the fact that there are spelling errors in a presentation by placing an X over the spelling indicator at the left end of the status bar.

The English-language version of Microsoft Office 2013 includes English, French, and Spanish dictionaries. If you use a word or phrase from one of these languages, you can mark it so that PowerPoint doesn't flag it as a misspelling.

You cannot make changes to the main dictionary in PowerPoint, but you can add correctly spelled words that are flagged as misspellings to the PowerPoint supplemental dictionary (called *CUSTOM.DIC*). You can also create and use custom dictionaries and use dictionaries from other Microsoft programs.

PowerPoint can check your spelling, but it can't alert you if you're not using the best wording. Language is often contextual—the language you use in a presentation to members of a club is different from the language you use in a business presentation. To make sure you're using words that best convey your meaning in any given context, you can use the Thesaurus feature to look up alternative words, called *synonyms*, for a selected word.

TIP For many words, the quickest way to find a suitable synonym is to right-click the word and point to Synonyms. You can then either click one of the suggested words or click Thesaurus to open the Thesaurus pane.

In this exercise, you'll correct a misspelled word, mark a French phrase so that PowerPoint won't flag it as a misspelling, and check the spelling of an entire presentation. You'll then use the Thesaurus to replace a word with a more appropriate one.

SET UP You need the CommunityServiceB presentation located in the Chapter04 practice file folder to complete this exercise. Open the presentation, and then follow the steps.

1   Display slide **2**, and right-click **infermation**, which PowerPoint has flagged as a possible error with a red wavy underline.

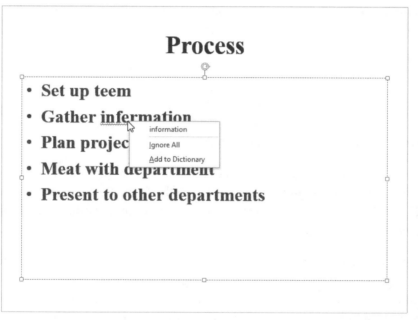

Right-clicking a flagged word displays suggested synonyms and options for correcting it.

2   On the menu, click **information** to replace the misspelled word.

Now let's identify a foreign phrase so that PowerPoint no longer flags it as a misspelling.

3   Display slide **7**, where the French words *Médecins* and *Frontières* have been flagged as possible errors.

4   Select **Médecins Sans Frontières**. Then on the **Review** tab, in the **Language** group, click the **Language** button, and click **Set Proofing Language** to open the **Language** dialog box.

In the Language dialog box, you can mark the selected text with one of a wide selection of languages.

5   To identify *Médecins Sans Frontières* as a French phrase and remove the red wavy underlines, scroll down the list of languages, click **French (France)**, and then click **OK**.

Let's check the spelling of the entire presentation.

6   Click a corner of the slide so that no placeholders are selected, and then press **Home** to move to the first slide in the presentation.

7   On the **Review** tab, in the **Proofing** group, click the **Spelling** button.

KEYBOARD SHORTCUT Press F7 to begin checking the spelling of a presentation.

The spelling checker stops on the word *Persue* and opens the Spelling pane on the right.

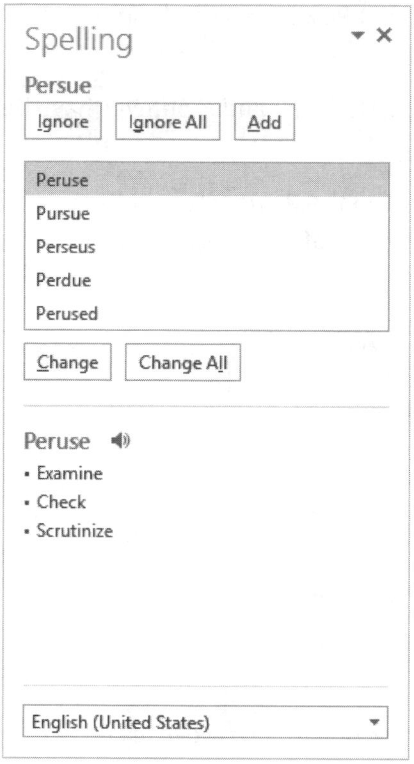

Spelling

Persue

Ignore | Ignore All | Add

Peruse
Pursue
Perseus
Perdue
Perused

Change | Change All

Peruse 🔊
- Examine
- Check
- Scrutinize

English (United States) ▾

In the Spelling pane, the suggested replacements have the same capitalization as the possibly misspelled word.

TIP In the lower part of the Spelling pane, PowerPoint lists a few synonyms for the selected replacement so that you can identify the replacement with the correct meaning. You can also hear the replacement's pronunciation by clicking on the adjacent speaker icon.

8   In the list of suggested replacements, click **Pursue**, and then click **Change**.

The spelling checker replaces *Persue* with the suggested *Pursue* and then stops on the word *CSCom*, suggesting *Como* as the correct spelling. For purposes of this exercise, assume that this is a common abbreviation for *Community Service Committee*.

9   Click **Add** to add the term *CSCom* to the CUSTOM.DIC dictionary.

TIP If you do not want to change a word or add it to the supplemental dictionary, click Ignore or Ignore All. The spelling checker then ignores either just that word or all instances of the word in the presentation during subsequent spell checking sessions.

Next the spelling checker stops on *the* because it is the second of two occurrences of that word.

10   Click **Delete** to delete the duplicated word.

Now the spelling checker identifies *employes* as a misspelling.

11   Change the selected word to **employees**.

TIP If you frequently misspell this word, add the misspelling to the AutoCorrect corrections list.

12   Click **Change** to change *succesful* to **successful**.

13   When a message box tells you that the spelling check is complete, click **OK**.

This presentation still has spelling problems—words that are spelled correctly but that aren't correct in context. We'll leave it to you to proof the slides and correct these errors manually. In the meantime, let's finish the exercise by using the Thesaurus to find a synonym.

14   On slide **1**, select the word **Executing** (but don't select the space following the word).

15   On the **Review** tab, in the **Proofing** group, click the **Thesaurus** button to open the **Thesaurus** pane, which displays a list of synonyms for the selected word.

KEYBOARD SHORTCUT Press Shift+F7 to activate the Thesaurus.

TIP If the pane doesn't show an obvious substitute for the selected word, click a possible replacement word in the Thesaurus list to display synonyms for that word.

In the Thesaurus pane, the synonyms have the same capitalization
as the selected word.

16   Below **Performing**, point to **Completing**, click the arrow that appears, and then click **Insert**.

17   Close the **Thesaurus** pane.

⊗ CLEAN UP To remove *CSCom* from the supplemental dictionary, first display the Proofing page of the PowerPoint Options dialog box, and click Custom Dictionaries. Then with CUSTOM.DIC (Default) highlighted in the Custom Dictionaries dialog box, click Edit Word List. Click CSCom, click Delete, click OK, and close the open dialog boxes. Then close the CommunityServiceB presentation, saving your changes if you want to.

Researching information and translating text

In addition to choosing synonyms, you can access a variety of informational resources and translation tools from the Review tab.

Open the Research pane by clicking the Research button in the Proofing group and then enter a topic in the Search For box, specifying in the box below which service PowerPoint should use to look for information about that topic. Clicking Research Options at the bottom of the Research pane opens the Research Options dialog box, where you can specify which of a predefined set of reference materials and other Internet resources will be available from the service list.

The English language version of PowerPoint comes with the following two translation tools with which you can quickly translate words and phrases, or even entire presentations between English, French, and Spanish:

- When you want to view the translation of a selected word or phrase, point to it to display the **Bilingual Dictionary** box with the translation in the specified language. (The box appears only if the **Mini Translator** is turned on. You turn the **Mini Translator** on or off by clicking the **Translate** button in the **Language** group of the **Review** tab and then clicking **Mini Translator**.) When the **Bilingual Dictionary** box is displayed, click the **Expand** button to open the **Research** pane on the right, where you can change the translation language.

  To change the default language used by the **Mini Translator**, click **Choose Translation Language** on the **Translate** button's menu. Then in the **Translation Language Options** dialog box, select from a list of available languages.

- To obtain the translation of a selected word when the **Mini Translator** is turned off, click the **Translate** button and then click **Translate Selected Text** to open the **Research** pane with the selected word in the **Search for** box. After you specify the language you want, PowerPoint consults the online bilingual dictionary for the language you chose and displays the result. You can also enter a word in the **Search for** box and then click **Start searching** to display the translation.

TIP If you need to use a language other than English, French, or Spanish, you can purchase and install a language pack. For information, search for *language packs* on the Office website.

Finding and replacing text and fonts

If you suspect that you might have used an incorrect word or phrase throughout a presentation—for example, if you have repeatedly used an inaccurate company name—you can click the buttons in the Editing group on the Home tab to do the following:

- To locate each occurrence of a word, part of a word, or a phrase, click the **Find** button to open the **Find** dialog box. Enter the text, and then click **Find Next**. You can specify whether PowerPoint should locate only matches with the exact capitalization, or *case*; in other words, if you specify *person*, you don't want PowerPoint to locate *Person*. You can also tell PowerPoint whether it should locate only matches for the entire text; in other words, if you specify *person*, you don't want PowerPoint to locate *personal*.

- To locate each occurrence of a word, part of a word, or a phrase and replace it with something else, click the **Replace** button to open the **Replace** dialog box. Enter the text you want to find and what you want to replace it with, click **Find Next**, and then click **Replace** to replace the found occurrence or **Replace All** to replace all occurrences. Again, you can specify whether to match capitalization and whole words.

TIP If you are working in the Find dialog box and you want to replace instead of find, click Replace at the bottom of the dialog box to open the Replace dialog box with any settings you have already made intact.

You can also click the Replace arrow, and in the Replace list, click Replace Fonts to open the Replace Font dialog box. Here, you can specify the font you want to change and the font you want PowerPoint to replace it with.

In this exercise, you'll first find and replace a word and then find and replace a font.

SET UP You need the CommunityServiceC presentation located in the Chapter04 practice file folder to complete this exercise. Open the presentation, and then follow the steps.

1   On the **Home** tab, in the **Editing** group, click the **Replace** button to open the **Replace** dialog box.

   KEYBOARD SHORTCUT Press Ctrl+H to open the Replace dialog box.

If you have already used the Find or Replace command, your previous Find What and Replace With entries carry over to this replace operation.

2   In the **Find what** box, enter department, and then press **Tab**.

3   In the **Replace with** box, enter unit.

4   Select the **Match case** check box to locate text that exactly matches the capitalization you specified and replace it with the capitalization you specified.

5   Click **Find Next** to find and select the first instance of *department*, which is in the word *departments* on slide 2.

If you select the Find Whole Words Only check box, PowerPoint does not match this instance.

TIP To move a dialog box so that it doesn't hide the text, drag its title bar.

6   Click **Replace** to replace *departments* with **units**. Then click **Find Next** to locate the next match.

7   Click **Replace All**.

8   When a message box tells you that PowerPoint has finished searching the presentation and changed nine occurrences of *department*, click **OK**. Then close the **Replace** dialog box.

Because you selected Match Case for this replace operation, one occurrence of *Department* has not been changed. We'll leave it to you to change it manually.

Now let's change the font of the entire presentation to make it consistent with the font of the title slide.

9   Click a blank area of the current slide so that no placeholder is selected, and press **Home** to display slide **1**.

10 Click the slide title, and notice that the setting in the **Font** box in the **Font** group is **Calibri (Headings)**.

11 Display slide **2**, and click first the title and then any bullet point, noticing that the font used for these elements is **Times New Roman**.

12 Click a corner of the slide so that no placeholder is selected. Then on the **Home** tab, in the **Editing** group, click the **Replace** arrow, and click **Replace Fonts** to open the **Replace Font** dialog box.

In the Replace Fonts dialog box, the default setting is to replace all instances of the Arial font with the Agency FB font.

13 Display the **Replace** list, which includes only Arial and the two fonts used in the presentation, and then click **Times New Roman**.

14 Display the **With** list, which includes all the fonts available on your computer, and then click **Calibri**.

15 Click **Replace** to change all the Times New Roman text in the presentation to **Calibri**.

> **TIP** The Replace Fonts action changes all slides in the presentation. To change only specific occurrences of a font, first select the text, and then change the font in the Font box.

16 Close the **Replace Font** dialog box.

✖ CLEAN UP **Close the CommunityServiceC presentation, saving your changes if you want to.**

Adding text boxes

> **TIP** The information in text boxes cannot be accessed by some assistive technology devices that make presentations accessible to people with disabilities. If your presentation must be compatible with these devices, avoid putting important information in text boxes.

The size and position of the placeholders on a slide are dictated by the slide's design. Every slide you create with a particular layout of a particular design has the same placeholders in the same locations, and the text you enter in them has the same formatting.

If you want to add text that does not belong in a placeholder—for example, if you want to add a permission-to-use annotation to a graphic—create an independent text box and enter the text there. You can create a text box in two ways:

- Click the **Text Box** button in the **Text** group on the **Insert** tab, click the slide where you want the text box to appear, and then enter the text. The width of the text box expands to fit what you enter on one line.

- Click the **Text Box** button, drag a box where you want the text box to appear, and then enter the text. The box adjusts to the height of one line, but maintains the width you specified. When the text reaches the right boundary of the box, the height of the box expands by one line so that the text can wrap. As you continue entering text, the width of the box stays the same, but the height grows as necessary to accommodate all the text.

By default, a text box has no visible border unless it's selected. As with a placeholder, clicking the text box once surrounds it with a dashed border and selects it for editing; clicking the dashed border surrounds the text box with a solid border and selects it for manipulation. To move the text box, drag its solid border, and to copy it, hold down the Ctrl key while you drag. To change the size of the text box, simply drag the white squares on its border, which are called *sizing handles*. To rotate the text box (and the text in it), drag the grey circle at the top of the text box, which is called the *rotating handle*.

TIP Another way to rotate a single-line text box is to click the Text Direction button in the Paragraph group on the Home tab, and then click the option you want..

If you want to manipulate the text box in more complex ways, you can use commands on the Format tool tab. You can also set options in the Format Shape pane, which appears when you click the Shape Styles dialog box launcher or right-click the text box's border and click Format Shape.

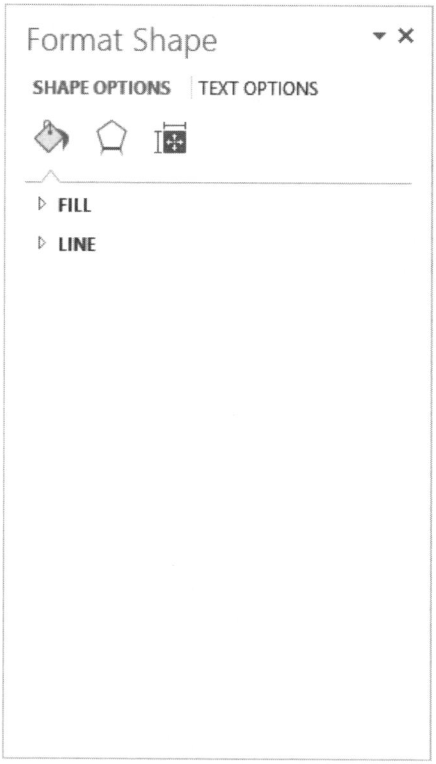

Format Shape

SHAPE OPTIONS TEXT OPTIONS

▷ FILL

▷ LINE

In the Format Shape pane, you can refine both the text-box shape and its text.

In the Format Shape pane, you can click Shape Options icons to display pages where you can do the following:

- **Fill & Line** Change the box's color (**Fill** page) or border (**Line** page).

- **Effects** Apply special effects (**Shadow**, **Reflection**, **Glow**, **Soft Edges**, **3-D Format**, and **3-D Rotation** pages).

- **Size & Properties** Change the box's size (**Size** page) and precisely position it (**Position** page); and enter a title and description to assist with accessibility (**Alt Text** page).

  TIP The page displayed when you click the Size & Properties icon also provides access to the Text Box settings described in the last bullet of the following list.

You can click Text Options icons to display pages where you can do the following:

- **Text Fill & Outline** Change the text's color (**Text Fill** page) or border (**Text Outline** page).

- **Text Effects** Apply special text effects (**Shadow**, **Reflection**, **Glow**, **Soft Edges**, **3-D Format**, and **3-D Rotation** pages).

- **Textbox** Set the alignment, direction, or margins of the text; set the number of columns; and determine whether PowerPoint should shrink the text to fit the box if it won't all fit at the default size (18 points), and whether the text should wrap within the box (**Text Box** page).

The red icon indicates the active settings.

In this exercise, you'll create one text box whose height stays constant while its width increases and another whose width stays constant while its height increases. You'll also manipulate these text boxes by rotating, moving, and putting a border around one of them and by sizing the other.

➜ SET UP You need the TripsB presentation located in the Chapter04 practice file folder to complete this exercise. Open the presentation, and then follow the steps.

1   Display slide **5**, and then click anywhere in the bulleted list to display its placeholder.

2   On the **Insert** tab, in the **Text** group, click the **Text Box** button, and then point below the placeholder for the bulleted list.

3   With the pointer shaped like an upside-down *t*, click the lower-left corner of the slide to create a small, empty text box with a cursor blinking inside it.

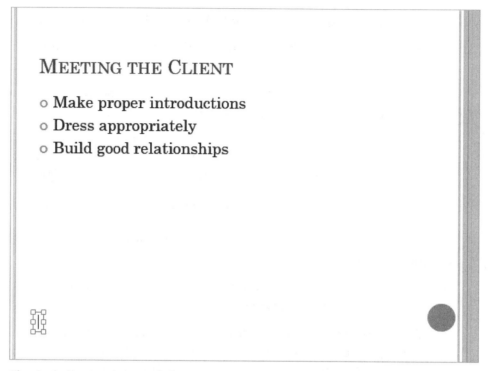

The single-line text box, ready for you to enter text.

4   Enter **Critical to get things off to a good start**. Notice that the width of the text box increases to accommodate the text as you enter it, even expanding beyond the border of the slide if necessary.

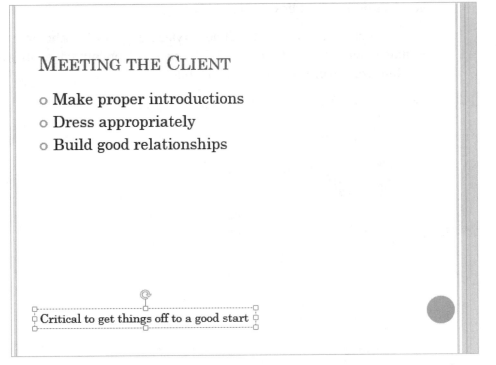

The single-line text box has grown horizontally to accommodate the text you entered.

5   To rotate the text so that it reads vertically instead of horizontally, point to the rotating handle attached to the upper-middle handle of the text box, and drag it 90 degrees clockwise.

TIP You can also rotate a text box by selecting the box for manipulation and then on the Format contextual tab, in the Arrange group, clicking the Rotate Objects button. In the list that appears, select an option to rotate the text box by 90 degrees to the left or right or to flip it horizontally or vertically.

6   Point to the border of the box (not to a handle), and then drag the box up and to the right, until it sits at the right edge of the slide. Release the mouse button when the box is centered on the orange ball and a smart guide tells you that it is aligned with the slide title.

Now let's give the text box a red border.

7 On the **Format** tool tab, click the **Shape Styles** dialog box launcher to open the **Format Shape** pane. Then with the **Fill & Line** shape options page displayed, click the **Line** arrow to display the border options.

8 Click **Solid line** to display those settings.

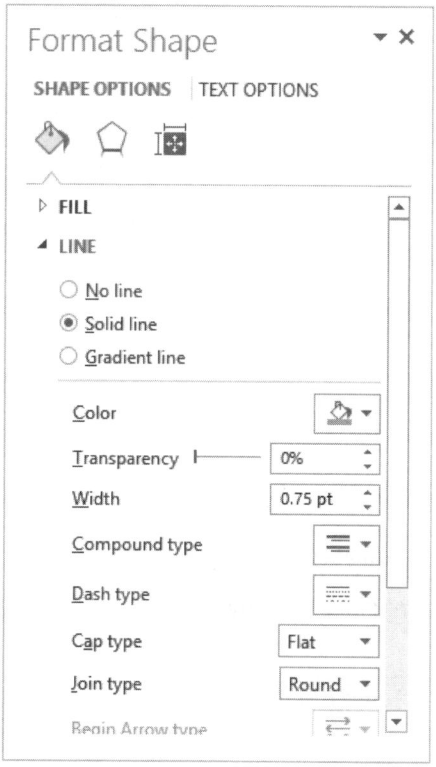

Format Shape ▾ ✕

SHAPE OPTIONS | TEXT OPTIONS

▷ FILL

◢ LINE

○ No line
◉ Solid line
○ Gradient line

Color

Transparency   0%

Width   0.75 pt

Compound type

Dash type

Cap type   Flat

Join type   Round

Begin Arrow type

From the Format Shape pane, you can apply a solid or gradient border.

9 Click the **Color** button, and in the top row of the **Theme Colors** palette, click the red swatch (**Red, Accent 3**). Then close the pane.

10 To display the red border, click a blank area of the slide to deselect the text box.

Next let's add a multi-line text box.

11   Display slide **6**, and then on the **View** tab, in the **Show** group, select the **Ruler** check box to display horizontal and vertical rulers across the top and down the left side of the **Slide** pane.

> **TIP** The 0 mark on each ruler indicates the center of the slide. For clarity, we will refer to marks to the left of 0 on the horizontal (top) ruler or above 0 on the vertical (left) ruler as *negative marks*.

12   On the **Insert** tab, in the **Text** group, click the **Text Box** button. Then on the left side of the area below the bulleted list, drag approximately **2** inches to the right and **0.5** inch down.

13   In the text box, enter **The Buyer Manual has important information about the minimum requirements**. Notice that no matter what height you made the box, it snaps to a standard height when you start to enter text. Then the height of the box increases to accommodate the complete entry.

The multi-line text box has grown vertically to accommodate the text you entered.

14   Click the border of the text box to select it for manipulation. Then drag the solid border to align the text in the box with the bullets, and drag the white sizing handles until the box is two lines high and the same width as the slide title.

15   Click a blank area of the slide to deselect the text box, which has no visible border.

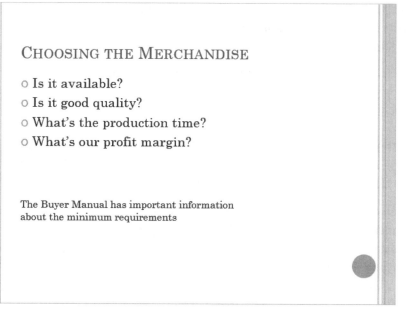

The multi-line text box, after adjusting its position and size.

✖ CLEAN UP Turn off the rulers. Then close the TripsB presentation, saving your changes if you want to.

Changing the default formatting for text boxes

When you create a text box, PowerPoint applies default formatting such as the font, size, and style, in addition to other effects, such as underline, small capitals, and embossing. To save yourself some formatting steps, you can change the default settings for the presentation you are working on.

To save the formatting of a selected text box as the new default, right-click its border, and then click Set As Default Text Box. The next text box you create will have the new default formatting.

Key points

- The formatting of individual paragraphs and characters can easily be changed by using the commands in the Font and Paragraph groups on the Home tab or on the Mini Toolbar.

- PowerPoint provides assistance by correcting common spelling errors and adjusting the size of text so that it fits optimally in its placeholder.

- The spelling checker flags possible misspellings so that you can take care of them as you enter text. Or you can check the spelling of an entire presentation.

- Take advantage of the Find and Replace features to ensure consistent use of terms and fonts throughout a presentation.

- You can place text wherever you want it on a slide by using text boxes.

4

Chapter at a glance

Insert

Insert pictures and clip art images,
page 140

Create

Create diagrams,
page 147

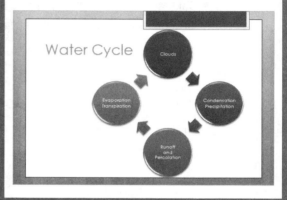

Plot

Plot charts,
page 154

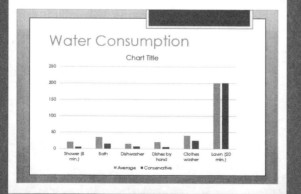

Draw

Draw shapes,
page 162

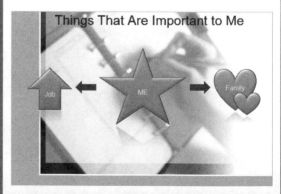

Add simple visual enhancements

5

IN THIS CHAPTER, YOU WILL LEARN HOW TO

- Insert pictures and clip art images.
- Create diagrams.
- Plot charts.
- Draw shapes.
- Add transitions.

With the ready availability of professionally designed templates, presentations have become more visually sophisticated and appealing. The words you use on your slides are no longer enough to guarantee the success of a presentation. These days, presentations are likely to have fewer words and more graphic elements. In fact, many successful presenters dispense with words altogether and use their slides only to graphically reinforce what they say while they deliver their presentations.

The general term *graphics* applies to several kinds of visual enhancements, including pictures, clip art images, diagrams, charts, and shapes. All of these types of graphics are inserted as objects on a slide and can then be sized, moved, and copied. For purposes of this chapter, we also consider transitions from one slide to another as a type of visual enhancement.

TIP Why don't we include tables in this chapter? Their content has to be read like regular text to be understood, so they are not simple visual enhancements. In fact, unless they have only a few rows and columns containing only a few words or numbers, they can be hard to interpret. For information about tables, see Chapter 7, "Present content in tables."

SEE ALSO For information about formatting and otherwise modifying graphics, see Chapter 8, "Fine-tune visual elements."

In this chapter, you'll insert pictures and clip art images. You'll create a diagram and a chart, and you'll draw a simple illustration by using built-in shapes. Finally, you'll change the way slides move on and off the screen during a slide show.

PRACTICE FILES To complete the exercises in this chapter, you need the practice files contained in the Chapter05 practice file folder. For more information, see "Download the practice files" in this book's Introduction.

Inserting pictures and clip art images

You can add images created and saved in other programs, in addition to digital photographs, to your Microsoft PowerPoint 2013 presentations. Collectively, these types of graphics are known as *pictures*. You might want to use pictures to make your slides more attractive and visually interesting, but you are more likely to use pictures to convey information in a way that words cannot. For example, you might display photographs of your company's new products in a presentation to salespeople.

If a slide has a content placeholder, insert a picture that is stored on your computer by clicking the Pictures button in the placeholder. If the slide has no content placeholder, click the Pictures button in the Images group on the Insert tab. Either way, the Insert Picture dialog box opens so that you can locate and insert the picture you want.

In addition to pictures stored on your computer, you can insert pictures from online sources, such as the following:

- **Clip art images stored on the Microsoft Office website** These pictures are license-free and often take the form of professionally designed cartoons, sketches, or symbolic images, but can also include photographs. In a PowerPoint presentation, you can use clip art to illustrate a point you are making, as interesting bullet characters, or to mark pauses in a presentation. For example, you might display a question mark image on a slide to signal a time in which you will answer questions from the audience.

- **Pictures from other websites** Pictures you acquire from the web are often copyrighted, meaning that you cannot use them without the permission of the person who created them. Sometimes owners will grant permission if you give them credit. Professional photographers usually charge a fee to use their work. Always assume that pictures are copyrighted unless the source clearly indicates that they are license-free.

- **Pictures you have stored on Microsoft SkyDrive** These pictures can be uploaded and downloaded easily no matter where you are or what type of device you are using.

To add these types of pictures to a slide, click the Online Pictures button in a content placeholder or the Online Pictures button in the Images group on the Insert tab. Either way, the Insert Pictures pane opens so that you can search for pictures by keyword or browse your SkyDrive folders.

After you have inserted a picture, you can make it larger or smaller and position it anywhere you want on the slide.

TIP You can save PowerPoint slides as pictures that you can insert in other types of documents. Display the Export page of the Backstage view, and click Change File Type. Then click one of the formats listed under Image File Types in the right pane, and click Save As. In the Save As dialog box, specify a name and location, and then click Save. In the message box that appears, click All Slides to save all the slides as images, or click Just This One to save an image of the current slide.

In this exercise, you'll add pictures and clip art images to slides. After inserting them, you'll move and size them to fit their slides.

➜ SET UP You need the WaterLandscapingA presentation and the Penstemon and Agastache pictures located in the Chapter05 practice file folder to complete this exercise. Open the presentation, make sure you have an Internet connection so that you can connect to the Office website, and then follow the steps.

1   Press **End** to move to slide **11**, and delete **<show pictures>**, which removes the content from the content placeholder and redisplays the content buttons.

2   In the content placeholder, click the **Pictures** button to open the **Insert Picture** dialog box.

3   Navigate to the **Chapter05** practice file folder, click the **Penstemon** file, and then click **Insert** to insert the picture in the middle of the content pane.

   TIP If a picture might change, you can ensure that the slide is always up to date by clicking the Insert arrow and then clicking Link To File to insert a link to the picture, or by clicking Insert And Link to both insert the picture and link it to its graphic file.

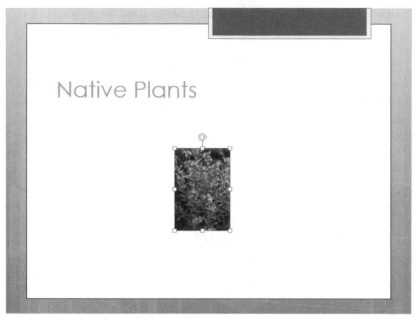

The inserted picture is surrounded by a frame to indicate that it is selected. You can use the handles around the frame to size and rotate the picture.

Let's adjust the position of the picture.

4   If horizontal and vertical rulers are not displayed across the top and down the left side of the **Slide** pane, display them by selecting the **Ruler** check box in the **Show** group on the **View** tab.

5   Point close to the upper-left corner of the picture (but not at the sizing handle), and when a four-headed arrow attached to the pointer appears, drag to the left and down until the picture's upper-left corner is almost level with the **–3.75** inch mark on the horizontal (top) ruler and the **0.5** inch mark on the vertical (left) ruler.

TIP As you drag, red dotted indicators appear on the rulers to show the position of the pointer (not the picture's top and left edges). A vertical dotted line, called a *smart guide*, might appear on the slide to help you align the picture with other elements.

Now let's make the picture bigger.

6   Point to the handle in the upper-right corner of the picture, and drag up and to the right until that corner sits about level with the **–1.5** inch mark on the horizontal ruler and the **1** inch mark on the vertical ruler.

When you drag a corner handle, the picture shrinks or grows proportionally.

TIP Obviously, to make the picture smaller, you would drag in the opposite direction.

Now let's add a picture when there is no content placeholder available.

7 On the **Insert** tab, in the **Images** group, click the **Pictures** button, and then in the **Insert Picture** dialog box, double-click **Agastache**.

8 Point to the **Agastache** picture, and drag upward or downward until a smart guide indicates that the top of this picture is aligned with the top of the adjacent one.

9 Point to the handle in the lower-right corner of the **Agastache** picture, and drag down and to the right until a smart guide indicates that the bottom of this picture is aligned with the bottom of the adjacent one.

10 Click away from the picture to release the selection.

These photographs came from the catalog of the Rugged Country Plants garden center and are used with permission of the owners. Let's identify who owns the copyright.

11   On the **Insert** tab, in the **Text** group, click the **Text Box** button, and then click immediately below the lower-left corner of the **Penstemon** photo.

12   In the text box, enter **Photos courtesy of Rugged Country Plants**. Then select the text, make it **14** points and purple, and click a blank area of the slide.

When you use photos taken by someone else, you should credit the source.

TIP If your presentation needs to be compatible with accessibility tools, instead of using a text box, you should consider adding alt text to each picture to attribute it to its owner. For information about alt text, see the sidebar "Alt text" in Chapter 8, "Fine-tune visual elements."

Now let's add a clip art image on a different slide.

13   Move to slide **4**, and on the **Insert** tab, in the **Images** group, click the **Online Pictures** button to open the **Insert Pictures** window.

14   In the box adjacent to **Office.com Clip Art**, enter **protect**, and click the **Search** button to display thumbnails of clip art images that have the associated keyword *protect* or *protection*.

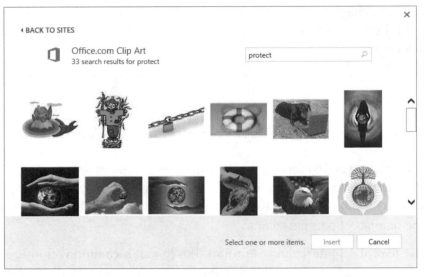

You can find free images of almost any concept by searching the Office website.

15   Scroll down to view all the images that are available, and then click the green and blue drawing of hands protecting a plant to select it.

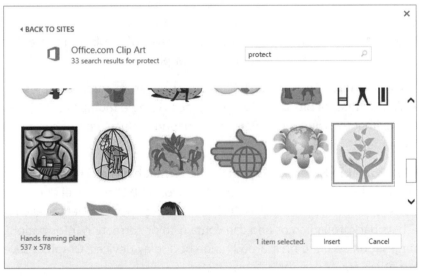

The associated keywords and dimensions of the selected image are displayed in the lower-left corner of the pane.

16   Click **Insert** to both insert the image in the center of the slide and close the Office.com Clip Art pane.

17 Drag the image to the lower-right corner, and then drag the upper-left corner handle until the image occupies about half of the slide. Click a blank area to release the selection.

Graphic formats

You can use picture and clip art files in a variety of formats, including the following:

- **BMP (bitmap)** This format stores graphics as a series of dots, or *pixels*. There are different qualities of BMPs, reflecting the number of bits available per pixel to store information about the graphic—the greater the number of bits, the greater the number of possible colors.

- **GIF (Graphics Interchange Format)** This format is common for images that appear on webpages, because the images can be compressed with no loss of information and groups of them can be animated. GIFs store at most 8 bits per pixel, so they are limited to 256 colors.

- **JPEG (Joint Photographic Experts Group)** This compressed format works well for complex graphics such as scanned photographs. Some information is lost in the compression process, but often the loss is imperceptible to the human eye. Color JPEGs store 24 bits per pixel, so they are capable of displaying more than 16 million colors. Grayscale JPEGs store 8 bits per pixel.

- **TIFF (Tag Image File Format)** This format can store compressed images with a flexible number of bits per pixel. Using tags, a single multipage TIFF file can store several images, along with related information such as type of compression and orientation.

- **PNG (Portable Network Graphic)** This format has the advantages of the GIF format but can store colors with 24, 32. 48, or 64 bits per pixel and grayscales with 1, 2, 4, 8, or 16 bits per pixel. A PNG file can also specify whether each pixel blends with its background color and can contain color correction information so that images look accurate on a broad range of display devices. Graphics saved in this format are smaller, so they display faster.

You can use images to balance the text on a slide.

✖ CLEAN UP Close the WaterLandscapingA presentation, saving your changes if you want to.

Creating diagrams

Sometimes the concepts you want to convey to an audience are best presented in diagrams. You can easily create a dynamic, visually appealing diagram by using SmartArt Graphics, which provide predefined sets of formatting for effortlessly putting together various types of diagrams, such as the following:

- **Process** These visually describe an ordered set of steps to complete a task.
- **Hierarchy** These illustrate the structure of an organization or entity.
- **Cycle** These represent a circular sequence of steps, tasks, or events; or the relationship of a set of steps, tasks, or events to a central, core element.
- **Relationship** These show converging, diverging, overlapping, merging, or containing elements.

TIP You can also create List, Matrix, Pyramid, and Picture diagrams.

On a slide that includes a content placeholder, click the placeholder's Insert SmartArt Graphic button to start the process of creating a diagram. You can also click the SmartArt button in the Illustrations group on the Insert tab to add a diagram to any slide. In either case, you then select the type of diagram and the specific layout you want to create. Clicking OK inserts the diagram with placeholder text that you can replace in an adjacent Text pane.

After you create a diagram, you can move and size it to fit the slide, and change its colors and the look of its shapes to achieve professional-looking results.

TIP If your presentation needs to be compatible with accessibility tools, you should add alt text to your diagrams. For information about alt text, see the sidebar "Alt text" in Chapter 8, "Fine-tune visual elements."

In this exercise, you'll add a cycle diagram to a slide, enter text, and then move and size it. You'll also format its shapes in simple ways.

 SET UP **You need the WaterLandscapingB presentation located in the Chapter05 practice file folder to complete this exercise. Open the presentation, and then with the rulers displayed, follow the steps.**

1   Display slide **6**, and then click the **Insert a SmartArt Graphic** button in the content placeholder to open the **Choose a SmartArt Graphic** dialog box.

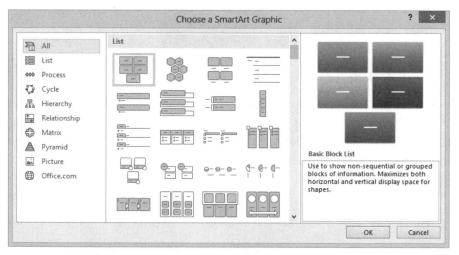

In this Choose A SmartArt Graphic dialog box, all the available layouts are listed in the center pane. A picture and description of the selected layout appear in the right pane.

2   In the left pane, click each layout type in turn to display only the available layouts of that type in the center pane. Then click **Cycle**.

3   In the center pane, click each layout in turn to view its picture and description in the right pane.

4   When you finish exploring, in the top row of the center pane, click the second layout (**Text Cycle**), and then click **OK** to add the structure for a cycle diagram to the slide.

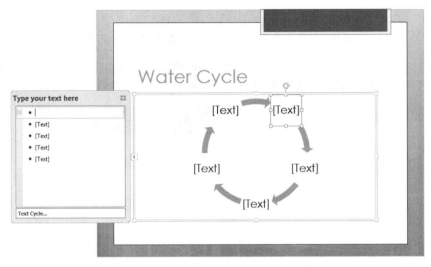

The diagram appears in a frame, with the shapes that will contain text represented as bullet points in the adjacent Text pane.

TIP If the Text pane is not displayed, click the Text Pane button in the Create Graphic group on the Design tool tab to open it.

Let's use the diagram's Text pane to add some descriptive text to its shapes.

5   With the first bullet in the **Text** pane selected, enter Clouds, and then press the **Down Arrow** key to move to the next bullet.

TROUBLESHOOTING Be sure to press the Down Arrow key and not the Enter key. Pressing Enter will add a new bullet point (and a new shape).

6   Pressing **Shift+Enter** after each word to insert a line break, enter Condensation, and, and precipitation. Then press the **Down Arrow** key.

7   Repeat step 6 to add **Runoff, and**, and **percolation**. Then repeat it again to add **Evaporation, and**, and **transpiration**.

8   On the **Design** tool tab, in the **Create Graphic** group, click the **Text Pane** button to close the **Text** pane.

> **TIP** You can also click the Close button in the upper-right corner of the Text pane. To open the Text pane again, you can click the left-pointing arrow on the left side of the diagram's frame.

We don't need the last bullet point, so let's delete its shape from the diagram.

9   In the diagram, select the empty **Text** placeholder shape for manipulation (solid border). Then press the **Delete** key to leave only four sets of text and arrows.

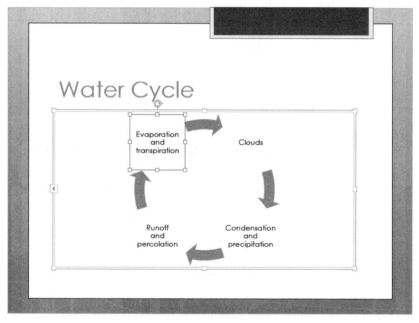

The text and arrow shapes have been resized to fit the available space.

Now let's switch to a different layout.

10   On the **Design** tool tab, in the **Layouts** group, click the gallery's **More** button to view the available **Cycle** diagram layouts. Then click the first thumbnail in the first row (**Basic Cycle**) to switch to that layout.

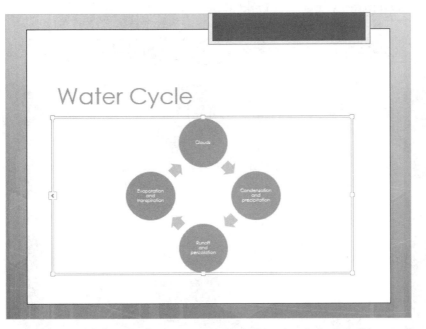

In the Basic Circle layout, the text appears in solid-color circles linked by small arrows.

Next let's size and position the diagram.

11   Point to the white handle in the middle of the right side of the diagram's frame, and drag to the left until the frame is only as wide as the diagram. (Repeat the process as necessary.)

12   Point to a part of the frame where there is no handle, and when a four-headed arrow is attached to the pointer, drag the diagram until it sits in the lower-right corner of the white area of the slide.

13   Point to the handle in the upper-left corner of the frame, and drag up and to the left until the frame sits at about the **−2.5** inch mark on both the horizontal and vertical rulers.

> **TIP** Remember that the 0 mark on both rulers is centered on the slide. You want the 2.5-inch marks to the left of and above the 0 marks.

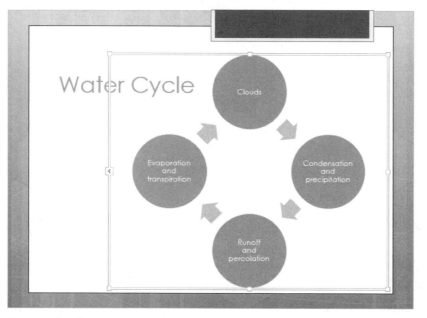

Because the diagram is an independent object, it can sit on top of the empty part of the title placeholder.

Finally, let's format the diagram to make it more dramatic.

14   On the **Design** tool tab, in the **SmartArt Styles** group, click the **Change Colors** button, and then in the **Colorful** area of the gallery, click the second thumbnail (**Colorful Range - Accent Colors 2 to 3**).

15   In the **SmartArt Styles** group, click the **More** button to open a menu that contains the **SmartArt Styles** gallery.

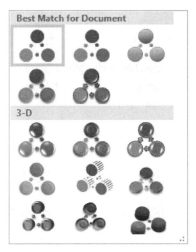

You can apply a two-dimensional or three-dimensional style.

16   In the **3-D** area of the gallery, click the first thumbnail in the first row (**Polished**), and then click outside the frame.

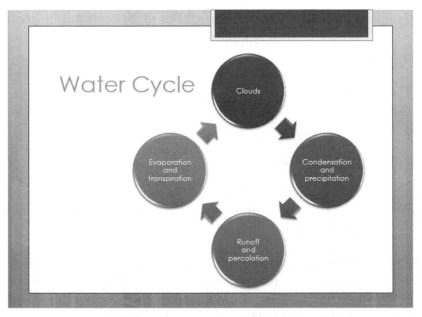

The colors and three-dimensional effect give the diagram pizzazz.

⊗ CLEAN UP Close the WaterLandscapingB presentation, saving your changes if you want to.

Converting existing bullet points into diagrams

You might decide after creating bullet points on a slide that a diagram would more clearly convey your message to your audience. You can easily convert bullet points to a SmartArt diagram with only a few clicks of the mouse button.

To create a diagram from an existing list of bullet points:

1 Click anywhere in the placeholder containing the bullet points you want to convert.

2 Right-click anywhere in the selected placeholder, and point to **Convert to SmartArt**.

3 Do one of the following:

- If the diagram layout you want appears in the gallery, click its thumbnail. (You can pause over a thumbnail to display a live preview of the bulleted list converted to that layout.)

- If the layout you want is not displayed, click **More SmartArt Graphics**. Then in the **Choose a SmartArt Graphic** dialog box, click the layout you want, and click **OK**.

4 Adjust the size, position, and look of the diagram in the usual way.

Plotting charts

For those occasions when you want to display a visual representation of numeric data, you can add a chart to a slide. Trends that might not be obvious from looking at the numbers themselves are more obvious in a chart.

On a slide that includes a content placeholder, you can click the placeholder's Insert Chart button to start the process of creating a chart. You can also click the Chart button in the Illustrations Group on the Insert tab to add a chart to any slide. In either case, you then select the type of chart you want. When you click OK, a sample chart of the selected type is inserted in the current slide. An associated Microsoft Excel worksheet containing the data plotted in the sample chart is displayed in a separate window. You use this worksheet to enter the data you want to plot, following the pattern illustrated by the sample data.

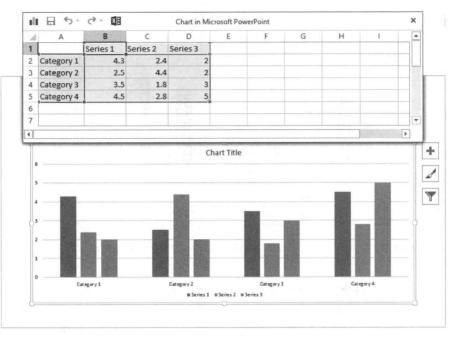

The sample data in the worksheet is plotted as a column chart on the slide.

The Excel worksheet is composed of rows and columns of cells that contain values, which in charting terminology are called *data points*. Collectively, a set of data points is called a *data series*. Each worksheet cell is identified by an address consisting of its column letter and row number—for example, A2. A range of cells is identified by the address of the cell in the upper-left corner and the address of the cell in the lower-right corner, separated by a colon—for example, A2:D5.

When you replace the sample data in the worksheet, the results are immediately plotted in the chart on the slide. Each data point in a data series is represented graphically in the chart by a data marker. The data is plotted against an x-axis—also called the *category axis*—and a y-axis—also called the *value axis*. (Three-dimensional charts also have a z-axis—also called the *series axis*.) Tick-mark labels along each axis identify the categories, values, or series in the chart. A legend provides a key for identifying the data series.

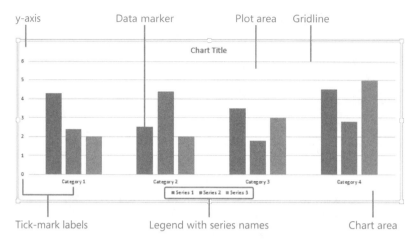

The major elements of a chart. Not all types of charts display all the elements. For example, a pie chart has no axes or tick-mark labels.

To enter data in a cell of the Excel worksheet, first click the cell to select it. You can select an entire column by clicking the column header—the box containing a letter at the top of each column—and an entire row by clicking the row header—the box containing a number at the left end of each row. You can select the entire worksheet by clicking the Select All button—the box at the junction of the column and row headers.

Having selected a cell, you enter data by typing it directly. However, if the data already exists in an Excel worksheet or a Microsoft Access or Microsoft Word table, you don't have to retype it. You can copy the data from its source program and paste it into the Excel worksheet that is associated with the chart.

After you've plotted the data in the chart, you can move and size the chart to suit the space available on the slide. At any time, you can edit the data—both the values and the column and row headings—and PowerPoint then replots the chart to reflect your changes.

In this exercise, you'll create a chart by pasting existing data into the associated Excel worksheet. You'll then size the chart and edit its data.

SET UP You need the WaterConsumption workbook and the WaterLandscapingC presentation located in the Chapter05 practice file folder to complete this exercise. From File Explorer (Windows Explorer in Windows 7), open the WaterConsumption workbook in Excel by double-clicking the workbook's file name. Then open the WaterLandscapingC presentation, and follow the steps.

1   Display slide **7**, and then in the content placeholder, click the **Insert Chart** button to open the **Insert Chart** dialog box.

In the Insert Chart dialog box, you can choose from many types of charts.

2   In the left pane, click **Line** to display the line-chart variations in the right pane. Then click each of the other chart types in the left pane to view their variations.

SEE ALSO For information about creating pie charts, see the sidebar "Pie charts" in Chapter 8, "Fine-tune visual elements."

3   Click **Column**, and then with the first column-chart variation (**Clustered Column**) selected, click **OK** to insert a sample column chart and open its associated Excel worksheet containing the plotted data.

4   From the **Windows Taskbar**, activate the **WaterConsumption** worksheet. Then in the worksheet, select all the cells in the range A3:C13 by pointing to cell **A3** and dragging down and to the right to cell **C13**.

5　　On the Excel **Home** tab, in the **Clipboard** group, click the **Copy** button.

6　　From the **Windows Taskbar**, activate the Water**LandscapingC** presentation. Then in the worksheet, right-click cell **A1**.

7　　Under **Paste Options** in the menu, click **Paste**. Notice that when you paste the data into the worksheet, PowerPoint immediately replots the chart.

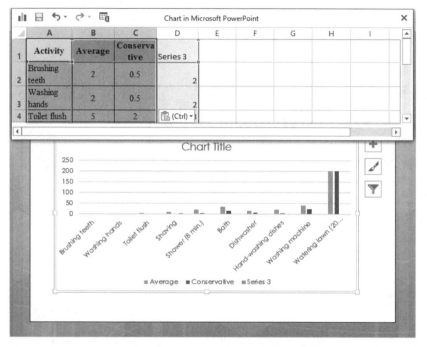

The copied data overwrites the data in columns A, B, and C, but the original data still exists in column D (Series 3).

In the worksheet, pale blue shading and a blue border indicate that the plotted data range includes the Series 3 column. Let's exclude that column so that only the Activity, Average, and Conservative columns are plotted.

8　　In the worksheet, scroll the window until row **11** (the last row containing data) appears. Then in the lower-right corner of the cell in the **Series 3** column and row **11**, drag the handle to the left, releasing it when the cells in the **Series 3** column are no longer shaded.

9   Close the worksheet associated with the chart, and then close the
     WaterConsumption workbook.

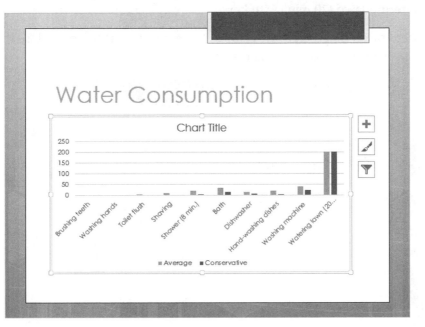

The pasted Water Consumption data has been plotted as a clustered column chart.

Now let's make the chart bigger.

10   Point to the white handle in the middle of the bottom of the frame, and drag down-
     ward until the frame sits at the bottom of the white area of the slide. Then drag the
     top of the frame until it almost touches the *p* in the title.

     The chart area is still not big enough to display all of the category labels. Let's edit
     the labels to make them fit the available space.

11   On the **Design** tool tab, in the **Data** group, click the **Edit Data** button to open the
     associated Excel worksheet.

     TIP By default, the chart is plotted based on the series in the columns of the work-
     sheet, which are identified in the legend. If you want to base the chart on the series
     in the rows instead, click the chart to select it, and then click the Switch Row/Column
     button in the Data group on the Design tool tab. The worksheet must be open for
     the button to be active.

12   Scroll the worksheet, click cell **A9**, enter Dishes by hand, and press the **Enter** key. Then in cell **A10**, enter Clothes washer, and press **Enter**. Finally in cell **A11**, replace **Watering lawn (20 min.)** with Lawn (20 min.), and press **Enter**.

13   After PowerPoint replots the chart with the new category labels, close the Excel worksheet. Then click outside the chart frame.

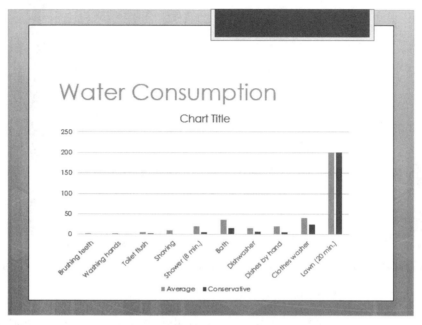

All the category labels now fit in the chart area.

Now let's focus temporarily on the categories with the largest water consumption.

14   Point to the blank area of the chart to the right of the title, and when the **Chart Area** ScreenTip appears, click to activate the chart area.

15   To the right of the chart's frame, click the **Chart Filters** button (the bottom button) to open the **Chart Filters** pane, where all the series and all the categories are selected.

16   In the **Categories** area, point to each category in turn, noticing that, in the chart, all the other categories are dimmed to highlight the one you are pointing to.

17   Clear the check boxes of **Brushing teeth**, **Washing hands**, **Toilet flush**, and **Shaving**. Then at the bottom of the **Chart Filters** pane, click **Apply** to replot the data with only the selected categories.

The chart now plots only the six categories that have the largest water consumption.

18   Click the **Chart Filters** button to close the **Chart Filters** pane.

    SEE ALSO For information about working with the other two buttons to the right of the chart, see "Formatting charts" in Chapter 8, "Fine-tune visual elements."

❌ CLEAN UP Close the WaterLandscapingC presentation, saving your changes if you want to.

Drawing shapes

To emphasize the key points in your presentation, you might want to include shapes in addition to text. PowerPoint provides tools for creating several types of shapes, including stars, banners, boxes, lines, circles, and squares. With a little imagination, you'll soon discover ways to create drawings by combining shapes.

To create a shape in PowerPoint, click the Shapes button in the Illustrations group on the Insert tab. Then click the shape you want to insert, and drag across the slide.

TIP To draw a circle or a square, click the Oval shape or a Rectangle shape, and hold down the Shift key while you drag.

After you draw the shape, it is surrounded by a set of handles, indicating that it is selected. (You can click a shape at any time to select it.) The handles serve the following purposes:

- Drag the white sizing handles to change the size of a shape.

- If a shape has a yellow adjustment handle, the shape is adjustable. You can use this handle to alter the appearance of the shape without changing its size.

- Drag the rotating handle to adjust the angle of rotation of a shape.

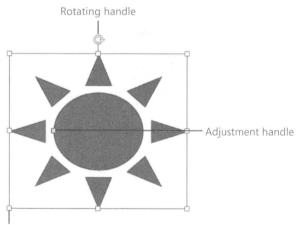

You can use the three types of handles to manipulate the shape in various ways.

You can copy or cut a selected shape or multiple shapes and then paste the shapes else-where in the same presentation, in another presentation, or in any Office program. To move a shape from one location to another on the same slide, simply drag it. To create a copy of a selected shape, drag it while holding down the Ctrl key, or click the Copy arrow in the Clipboard group on the Home tab and then click Duplicate.

After drawing a shape, you can modify it by using the commands on the Format tool tab that appears when a shape is selected. For example, you can:

- Add text to a shape. PowerPoint centers the text as you enter it, and the text becomes part of the shape.
- Change the size and color of the shape and its border.
- Apply special effects, such as making the shape look three-dimensional.

Having made changes to one shape, you can easily apply the same attributes to another shape by clicking the shape that has the desired attributes, clicking the Format Painter button in the Clipboard group on the Home tab, and then clicking the shape to which you want to copy the attributes. (Any adjustments you made with the adjustment handle are not copied.) If you want to apply the attributes of a shape to all future shapes you draw on the slides of the active presentation, right-click the shape and then click Set As Default Shape.

When you have multiple shapes on a slide, you can group them so that you can copy, move, and format them as a unit. You can change the attributes of an individual shape—for ex-ample, its color, size, or location—without ungrouping the shapes. If you do ungroup them, you can regroup the same shapes by selecting one of them and then clicking Regroup in the Group list.

In this exercise, you'll draw several shapes, add text to them, and change their colors. Then you'll duplicate and copy a shape and switch one shape for another.

SET UP You need the JournalingA presentation located in the Chapter05 practice file folder to complete this exercise. Open the presentation, and then follow the steps.

1   Display slide **5**, and on the **Insert** tab, in the **Illustrations** group, click the **Shapes** button to display the **Shapes** gallery.

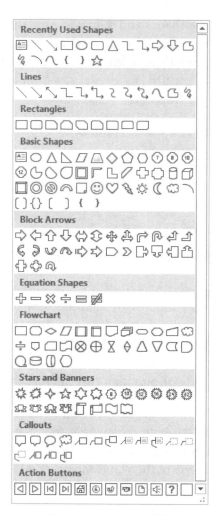

In the Shapes gallery, the different types of shapes are grouped by category.

2   In the **Stars and Banners** category of the gallery, click the **5-Point Star** shape, and then drag the crosshair pointer in the middle of the slide to draw a star shape that spans the shadow of the hand in the background graphic.

TIP If you click a shape button and then change your mind about drawing the shape, you can release the shape by pressing the Esc key.

You can draw a shape anywhere on the slide.

3   On the **Format** tool tab, in the **Insert Shapes** group, click the gallery's **More** button. Then in the **Shapes** gallery, in the **Block Arrows** category, click the **Right Arrow** shape, and draw a small arrow to the right of the star.

Instead of drawing another arrow, let's copy this one to ensure a consistent size and shape.

4   With the arrow shape still selected, hold down the **Ctrl** key, and drag a copy of the arrow to the left of the star. Release the shape when the smart guides indicate that it is aligned with the right one.

TROUBLESHOOTING Be sure to release the mouse button before you release the Ctrl key. Otherwise you'll move the shape instead of copying it.

Let's make this arrow face the other way.

5   With the left shape still selected, in the **Arrange** group, click the **Rotate Objects** button, and then click **Flip Horizontal**.

TIP You can rotate or flip any type of image. Rotating turns a shape 90 degrees to the right or left; flipping turns a shape 180 degrees horizontally or vertically. You can also rotate a shape to any degree by dragging the rotating handle.

6   Adjacent to the left arrow, add a scroll shape, and then adjacent to the right arrow, add a heart shape. Notice that all the shapes have the same outline and interior colors.

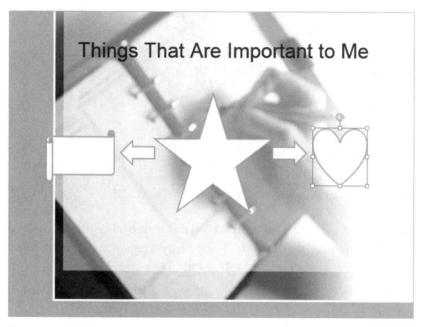

You can build a picture with the shapes available in the Shapes gallery.

7   With the heart selected, on the **Home** tab, in the **Clipboard** group, click the **Copy** arrow (not the button). Then in the list of options, click **Duplicate** to paste a copy of the shape on top of the original.

Let's make the second heart smaller than the first.

8   Point to the handle in the upper-left corner of the shape, and drag down and to the right.

Next let's add some text to the shapes.

9   On the **Format** tool tab, in the **Insert Shapes** group, click the **Draw a Text Box** button to the right of the gallery. Then click the center of the star, and enter ME. (Don't worry that the text is barely visible; you'll fix that in a later step.)

SEE ALSO For information about working with text boxes, see "Adding text boxes" in Chapter 4, "Work with slide text."

10   Repeat step 9 to add the word Education to the scroll shape and Family to the heart shape. Then resize the shapes as necessary to make all the words fit on one line.

The shapes look somewhat flat and uninteresting. Let's make them livelier with a special effect.

11   Click the scroll shape (don't click the text), hold down the **Shift** key, click the star shape, and then click the two hearts.

12   With all four shapes selected, in the **Shape Styles** group, click the gallery's **More** button to display the **Shape Styles** gallery.

5

13   Point to several thumbnails to display live previews of their effects, and then click the last thumbnail in the last row (**Intense Effect – Light Blue, Accent 6**).

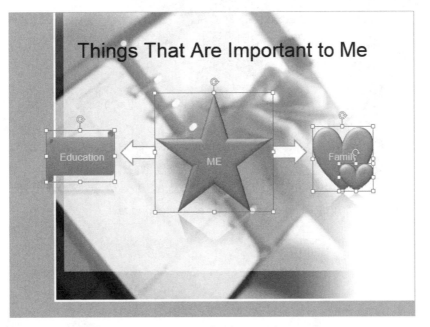

The text stands out after you change the shape style.

Suppose you have completed your education and have entered the workforce. Let's change the scroll shape to reflect your current status.

14   Click a blank area of the slide to release the selection, and then click the scroll shape (don't click its text).

15   On the **Format** tool tab, in the **Insert Shapes** group, click the **Edit Shape** button to the right of the gallery. Then point to **Change Shape**, and in the **Block Arrows** category of the gallery, click the third shape (**Up Arrow**).

16   In the up arrow shape, double-click **Education**, and enter Job. Then adjust the size and position of the shape so that it balances with the other shapes on the slide. (Use the smart guides to help align the shapes.).

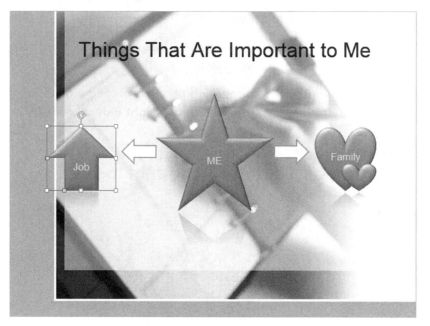

You can tell a story by using a combination of shapes and text.

SEE ALSO For information about precisely arranging shapes, see "Arranging graphics" in Chapter 8, "Fine-tune visual elements."

Connecting shapes

If you want to show a relationship between two shapes, you can connect them with a line by joining special handles called *connection points*.

To connect shapes:

1   On the **Insert** tab, in the **Illustrations** group, click the **Shapes** button. Then in the **Shapes** gallery, in the **Lines** category, click one of the **Connector** shapes.

2   Point to the first shape, and when a set of small black connection points appears, point to a connection point, and then drag over to the other shape (don't release the mouse button).

3   When connection points appear on the other shape, point to a connection point, and release the mouse button.

The connector joins two connection points.

TROUBLESHOOTING Green handles appear at each end of the line when the shapes are connected. If a white handle appears instead of a green one, the shapes are not connected. Click the Undo button on the Quick Access Toolbar to remove the connection line, and then redraw it.

After you have drawn the connector, you can adjust its shape by dragging the yellow adjustment handle and format it by changing its color and weight. If you move a connected shape, the connector moves with it, maintaining the relationship between the shapes.

Next we'll group the shapes together as one object so that we can format them all at the same time.

17 Select all the shapes on the slide. Then on the **Format** tool tab, in the **Arrange** group, click the **Group Objects** button, and in the list, click **Group**.

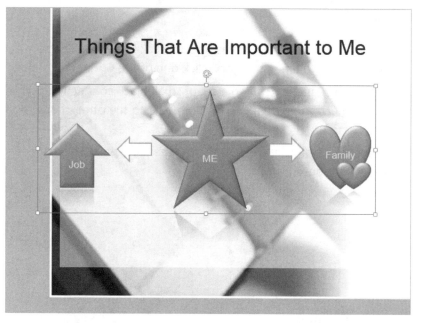

When shapes are grouped, one set of handles surrounds the entire group.

18 With the group selected (as indicated by the single set of handles), in the **Shape Styles** group, click the **Shape Outline** button, and then in the **Standard Colors** palette, click the last color swatch (**Purple**).

19 Move the entire group by pointing to any of its shapes, and when the pointer has a four-headed arrow attached to it, drag the group until the shapes are centered and balanced with the slide title.

Even though the shapes are grouped, let's change the attributes of just one of its shapes.

20   Double-click the left arrow. In the **Shape Styles** group, click the **Shape Fill** button, and change the arrow's color to purple.

21   With the left arrow still selected, on the **Home** tab, in the **Clipboard** group, click the **Format Painter** button, and then click the right arrow to make it purple.

      Let's finish by ungrouping the shapes.

22   Click away from the selected shape, and then click any shape to select the group.

23   On the **Format** tool tab, in the **Arrange** group, click the **Group Objects** button, and then click **Ungroup**.

❌ CLEAN UP Close the JournalingA presentation, saving your changes if you want to.

Adding transitions

5

When you deliver a presentation, you can move from slide to slide by clicking the mouse button or you can have PowerPoint replace one slide with the next at predetermined intervals. To avoid abrupt breaks between slides, you can use transitions to control the way slides move on and off the screen. Each slide can have only one transition. You can set the transition for one slide at a time, for a group of slides, or for an entire presentation.

PowerPoint comes with the following categories of built-in transition effects:

- **Subtle** This category includes fades, wipes, and a shutter-like effect.

- **Exciting** This category includes more dramatic effects such as checkerboards, ripples, turning, and zooming.

- **Dynamic Content** This category holds the background of the slides still and applies a dynamic effect to the title and other content, such as rotating or flying onto the slide.

In addition to selecting the type of transition, you can specify the following:

- The sound
- The speed
- When the transition occurs (called the *slide timing*)

SEE ALSO For information about slide timings, see "Rehearsing presentations" in Chapter 13, "Prepare for delivery."

In this exercise, you'll apply a transition to a single slide and then apply the same transition to all the slides in the presentation. You'll also add sound to the transition and set the transition speed.

SET UP You need the JournalingB presentation located in the Chapter05 practice file folder to complete this exercise. Open the presentation, and then follow the steps.

1   Display slide **2** in **Normal** view. Then on the **Transitions** tab, in the **Transition to This Slide** group, click each thumbnail that is visible in the gallery to view its effects.

2   To the right of the gallery, point to the scroll down arrow, and notice that a ScreenTip tells you there are eight rows of thumbnails in this gallery.

3   Click the scroll down arrow, and continue previewing the effects of each transition.

4   When you have finished exploring, click the **More** button to display the gallery, and then click the **Cover** thumbnail in the **Subtle** category.

    PowerPoint demonstrates the Cover transition effect on slide 2 and indicates that the transition has been applied by placing an animation symbol below the slide number in the Thumbnails pane. (There is no indication on the slide itself.)

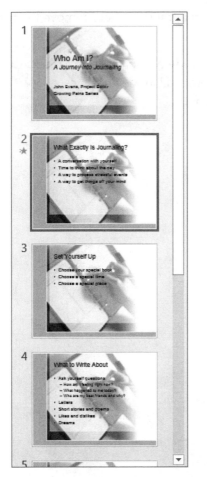

You have applied an animation to one slide.

5   In the **Transition to This Slide** group, click the **Effect Options** button, and then click **From Top-Left**.

Let's add this transition to all the slides in the presentation.

6   In the **Timing** group, click the **Apply To All** button.

7   In the **Thumbnails** pane, click the animation symbol below slide **3** to display the effect of the **Cover** transition from slide **2** to slide **3**.

To be able to start the slide show without a transition, let's remove the transition from the title slide.

8   Display slide **1**. In the **Transition to This Slide** group, click the **More** button to display the gallery, and then click the **None** thumbnail in the **Subtle** category. Notice that slide **1** no longer has an animation symbol.

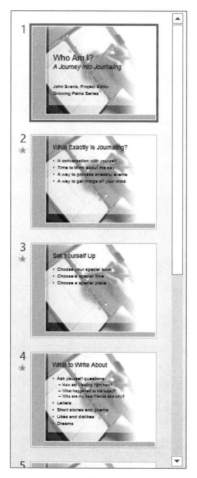

Because you will usually start a presentation with the title slide displayed,
there is no need for a transition on this slide.

Before we go any further, let's preview the results so far.

9   On the **View Shortcuts** toolbar at the right end of the status bar, click the **Reading View** button to display slide **1** in that view.

10   At the bottom of the screen, click the **Next** button repeatedly to show the transitions of the first few slides, and then press **Esc** to return to **Normal** view.

Now let's add sound and specify the duration of the transitions.

11   Switch to **Slide Sorter** view. Then select all the slides that have transitions by clicking slide **2**, holding down the **Shift** key, and clicking slide **7**.

12   In the **Timing** group, click the **Sound** arrow, and then click **Wind**.

> **TIP** If you want to associate a sound file of your own with a slide transition, click Other Sound at the bottom of the Sound menu. Then in the Add Audio dialog box, find and select the sound file you want to use, and click Open.

13   In the **Timing** group, click the **Duration** up arrow until the duration is set to **02.00**.

14   In the **Preview** group, click the **Preview** button to preview the transition effect in **Slide Sorter** view. Then if you want, preview it again in **Reading** view.

❌ CLEAN UP Close the JournalingB presentation, saving your changes if you want to.

Key points

- Using pictures you don't own without permission, especially for business purposes, can breach the copyright of the owner. Limited use for non-commercial purposes is usually allowed as long as you acknowledge the source.

- Thousands of free clip art images are available to help you add visual interest to your slides.

- With SmartArt, you can create a variety of professional-looking diagrams with a few mouse clicks.

- Charts present numeric data in an easy-to-grasp visual format. You can choose from 11 types with many variations.

- Shapes can add interest to a slide and draw attention to key concepts. However, they can become tiresome and produce an amateurish effect if they are overused.

- Avoid abrupt transitions by having one slide smoothly replace another. You can control the transition type, its speed, and when it takes place.

Chapter at a glance

Set up

Set up presentations for delivery,
page 178

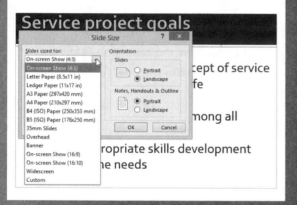

Preview

Preview and print presentations,
page 184

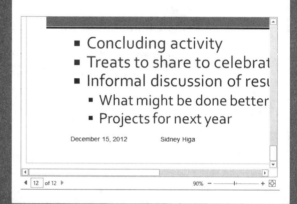

Prepare

Prepare speaker notes and handouts,
page 189

Deliver

Deliver presentations,
page 204

Review and deliver presentations

6

IN THIS CHAPTER, YOU WILL LEARN HOW TO

- Set up presentations for delivery.

- Preview and print presentations.

- Prepare speaker notes and handouts.

- Finalize presentations.

- Deliver presentations.

Before exposing a new presentation to the eyes of the world, you should check a few settings and proof the text of the slides, preferably on paper, where typographic errors seem to stand out much better than they do on the screen. When you are satisfied that the presentation is complete, you can prepare for your moment in the spotlight by creating speaker notes. You might also want to create handouts to give to your audience, to remind them later of your presentation's message.

When all these tasks are complete, you should remove extraneous information before declaring the presentation final.

If you will deliver the presentation from your computer as an electronic slide show, it pays to become familiar with the tools available in Slide Show view, where the slide occupies the entire screen. You navigate through slides by clicking the mouse button or by pressing the Arrow keys, moving forward and backward one slide at a time or jumping to specific slides as the needs of your audience dictate. During the slide show, you can mark slides with an on-screen pen or highlighter to emphasize a point.

In this chapter, you'll set up a slide show for delivery, preview a presentation, and print selected slides. You'll prepare speaker notes to assist in your presentation delivery and create handouts so that the audience can record key points. You'll also remove the properties attached to a presentation and prevent other people from making further changes to it. Finally, you'll deliver a presentation, including marking up slides.

Setting up presentations for delivery

In the old days, presentations were delivered by speakers with few supporting materials. Little by little, "visual aids" such as white board drawings or flip charts on easels were added, and eventually, savvy speakers began accompanying their presentations with 35mm slides or transparencies projected onto screens. To accommodate these speakers, early versions of PowerPoint included output formats optimized for slides of various sizes, including 35mm slides and the acetate sheets used with overhead projectors.

Technology has evolved to the point where most presentations are now delivered electronically. When you create a new presentation based on the Blank Presentation template or any of the PowerPoint design templates, the slides are sized for a widescreen monitor because the likelihood is that you will be delivering the presentation with a portable computer and a projection device designed for this format. With the default Widescreen setting, slides are oriented horizontally with a width-to-height ratio of 16:9 (13.333 by 7.5 inches).

If you do not know whether your presentation will be displayed on a portable computer or a desktop computer—for example, if the presentation will be viewed online—you might want to use the Standard size for your slides. Simply click the Slide Size button in the Customize group of the Design tab, and then click Standard to give your slides a width-to-height ratio of 4:3 (10 by 7.5 inches).

TIP It is a lot more efficient to set the slide size of the presentation before you begin developing your content so that you place elements appropriately. If you decide to use a different size, you can change it; but you will have to check and if necessary adjust every slide to ensure that its content still appears as you want it.

If the Widescreen and Standard formats don't suit your needs, you can click Custom Slide Size at the bottom of the Slide Size menu and select from the following slide sizes in the Slide Size dialog box:

- **Letter Paper** For a presentation printed on 8.5-by-11-inch US letter-size paper

- **Ledger Paper** For a presentation printed on 11-by-17-inch legal-size paper

- **A3 Paper, A4 Paper, B4 (ISO) Paper, B5 (ISO) Paper** For a presentation printed on paper of various international sizes

- **35mm Slides** For 35mm slides to be used in a carousel with a projector

- **Overhead** For transparencies for an overhead projector

- **Banner** For a banner for a webpage

- **On-screen Show** For an electronic slide show on screens of various aspects: 4:3 (the Standard format), 16:9 (the Widescreen format), or 16:10

- **Custom** For slides that are a nonstandard size

If you want the same identifying information to appear at the bottom of every slide, you can insert it in a footer. You can specify the date and time, the slide number, and custom text in the Header And Footer dialog box, which shows a preview of where the specified items will appear on the slide.

If you are going to deliver a presentation before an audience and will control the progression of slides manually, the default settings will work well. However, provided the slides have been assigned advancement times on the Transitions tab, you can set up the presentation to run automatically, either once or continuously. For example, you might want to set up a product demonstration slide show in a store or at a tradeshow so that it runs automatically, looping until someone stops it. All it takes is a few settings in the Set Up Show dialog box.

In this exercise, you'll experiment with slide size. Then you'll add footer information to every slide in a presentation. Finally you'll turn the presentation into a self-running slide show.

SET UP You need the ServiceProjectsA presentation located in the Chapter06 practice file folder to complete this exercise. Open the presentation, and then follow the steps.

1 Display slide **2**. Then on the **Design** tab, in the **Customize** group, click the **Slide Size** button and click **Widescreen**. Notice that the slide expands horizontally and the bullet point text no longer needs to wrap to fit the slide.

2 Click the **Slide Size** button again, and then click **Standard**.

Because you are reducing the width of the slides, PowerPoint needs to know how to adjust the content.

3 Click the **Ensure Fit** image or button. Notice that PowerPoint restores the original slide size but reduces the text size so that the bullet point text continues to fit without wrapping.

4 On the **Quick Access Toolbar**, click the **Undo** button. Then on the **Design** tab, click the **Slide Size** button, and click **Standard** again. This time, click **Maximize** in the instruction box to return the slide to its original size and content arrangement.

Let's take a look at the other available sizes.

5 Click the **Slide Size** button, and click **Custom Slide Size** to open the **Slide Size** dialog box. Then display the **Slides sized for** list.

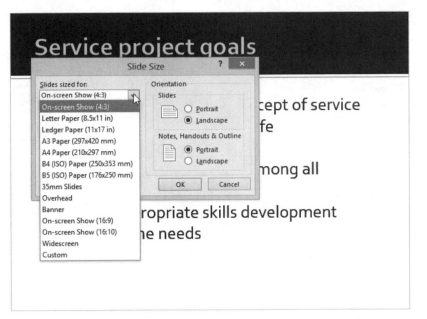

The Slide Size dialog box provides several slide sizes suitable for printing and alternative presentation delivery methods.

> **TIP** In the Slide Size dialog box, you can change the slide orientation so that it is taller than it is wide. For example, you might want to do this to compare two presentations side by side in Reading view.

6   Click **Banner**, which changes the **Width** setting to **8** inches and the **Height** setting to **1** inch.

> **TIP** The Banner format is useful if you want to design a presentation that will display in a frame across the top or bottom of a webpage. Obviously, the current presentation with its long title and many bulleted lists is not suitable for the Banner format. If you want to create a banner, be sure to set the format before you begin developing the content of your presentation so that you choose words and graphics that fit within the space available.

7   Click **Cancel** to close the **Slide Size** dialog box without changing the current settings.

Now let's add information to the slide's footer.

8   On the **Insert** tab, in the **Text** group, click the **Header & Footer** button to open the **Header and Footer** dialog box with the **Slide** page displayed.

By default, the slides in this presentation do not display footer information.

9   In the **Include on slide** area, select the **Date and time** check box. Then click **Fixed**. Although it is not very visible on the thumbnail in the **Preview** area, notice that the date will appear in the lower-left corner of the slide.

TIP By default, the Fixed date is initially set to the current date in *mm/dd/yyyy* format. You can replace this date with any date you want in any format you want. If you want the date to be updated every time you open the presentation file, click Update Automatically instead of Fixed. You can then display the Update Automatically list to choose the format for the date and/or time. You can also select a different language and calendar type.

10 Select the **Slide number** check box, and notice on the thumbnail that the slide number will appear in the lower-right corner.

11 Select the **Footer** check box, and then enter your name in the text box below the check box.

12 Select the **Don't show on title slide** check box, and click **Apply to All**.

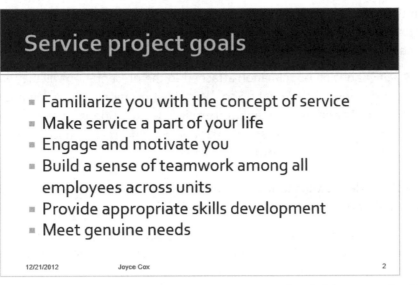

Slide 2 shows the footer information you have entered for all slides except the title slide.

Next we'll set up the slide show so that it runs automatically.

13   On the **Slide Show** tab, in the **Set Up** group, click the **Set Up Slide Show** button to open the **Set Up Show** dialog box.

By default, the presentation is set for presenter delivery and to include all slides.

14   In the **Show type** area, click **Browsed at a kiosk (full screen)**. Notice in the **Show options** area that the **Loop continuously until 'Esc'** check box is now selected and unavailable so that you cannot clear it. Then click **OK**.

> **TIP** Any narration or animation attached to the presentation will play with the presentation unless you select the Show Without Narration or Show Without Animation check box. For information about narration, see the sidebar "Recording presentations" in Chapter 13, "Prepare for delivery." For information about animation, see Chapter 10, "Add animations, audio, and videos."

15   Display slide **1**, switch to **Reading** view, and watch as the presentation runs, using the transition effects and timings applied to its slides.

> **SEE ALSO** For information about transitions, see "Adding transitions" in Chapter 5, "Add simple visual enhancements." For information about slide timings, see "Rehearsing presentations" in Chapter 13, "Prepare for delivery."

16   When the presentation starts again at slide **1**, press **Esc** to stop the slide show and return to **Normal** view.

If you want to run this slide show unattended, navigate to the folder where it is stored, double-click it, and switch to **Slide Show** view. Press **Esc** to stop the slide show at any time.

❌ CLEAN UP   Close the ServiceProjectsA presentation, saving your changes if you want to.

Previewing and printing presentations

Even if you plan to deliver your presentation electronically, you might want to print the slides to proof them for typographical errors and stylistic inconsistencies. Before you print, you can preview how the slides will look on paper. You perform this type of preview on the Print page of the Backstage view, where the presentation's slides appear in the right pane.

You can change your print settings from the Print page of the Backstage view.

To move among the slides, click the Next Page or Previous Page button in the lower-left corner of the right pane. To zoom in on part of a slide, click the Zoom In button on the Zoom Slider in the lower-right corner. Click the Zoom To Page button to fit the slide to the pane.

If you will print a color presentation on a monochrome printer, you can preview in grayscale or black and white to verify that the text is legible against the background.

TIP In Normal view, you can preview how your slides will look when printed on a mono-chrome printer by clicking either the Grayscale button or the Black And White button in the Color/Grayscale group on the View tab.

When you're ready to print, you don't have to leave the Backstage view. You can simply click the Print button to print one copy of each slide on the default printer.

If the default settings aren't what you want, you can make the following changes on the Print page:

- **Number of copies** Click the arrows to adjust the **Copies** setting.

- **Which printer** If you have more than one printer available, specify the printer you want to use and set its properties (such as paper source and image compression).

- **Which slides to print** You can print all the slides, the selected slides, or the current slide. To print only specific slides, click the **Slides** box, and enter the slide numbers and ranges separated by commas (no spaces). For example, enter 1,5,10-12 to print slides 1, 5, 10, 11, and 12.

- **What to print** From the **Print Layout** gallery, specify whether to print slides (one per page), notes pages (one half-size slide per page with space for notes), or an outline. You can also print handouts, specifying the number of slides that print on each page (1, 2, 3, 4, 6, or 9) and their order.

You can select what to print from the Print Layout gallery.

- **Whether to frame slides** Click this option at the bottom of the **Print Layout** menu to put a frame around the slides on the printed page.

- **Whether to scale slides** If you haven't set the size of the slides to match the size of the paper in the printer, click **Scale to Fit Paper** to have PowerPoint automatically reduce or increase the size of the slides to fit the paper when you print.

  SEE ALSO For information about setting the size of slides, see "Setting up presentations for delivery" earlier in this chapter.

- **Print quality** Click this option if you want the highest quality printed output.

- **Print comments and ink markup** Click this option if electronic or handwritten notes are attached to the presentation and you want to review them along with the slides.

  SEE ALSO For information about adding comments to slides, see "Collaborating with other people" in Chapter 11, "Share and review presentations." For information about marking up slides, see "Delivering presentations" later in this chapter.

- **Collate multiple copies** If you're printing multiple copies of a presentation, specify whether complete copies should be printed one at a time.

- **Color range** Specify whether the presentation should be printed in color (color on a color printer and grayscale on a monochrome printer), grayscale (on either a color or a monochrome printer), or pure black and white (no gray on either a color or a monochrome printer).

- **Edit the header or footer** Click the **Edit Header & Footer** link to open the **Header and Footer** dialog box.

  SEE ALSO For information about adding footers to slides, see "Setting up presentations for delivery" earlier in this chapter.

In this exercise, you'll preview a presentation in grayscale, select a printer, and print a selection of slides.

→ SET UP You need the ServiceProjectsB presentation located in the Chapter06 practice file folder to complete this exercise. Open the presentation, and then follow the steps.

1   Display the **Backstage** view, and then click **Print**. Notice that the right side of the **Print** page displays the first slide as it will print with the current settings.

2   In the **Settings** area, click **Color**, and then click **Grayscale** to display the previewed slide in black, white, and shades of gray.

3   Click the **Next Page** button to move through the slides, until slide **12** is displayed.

Let's magnify the slide to make it easier to examine the date in the footer.

4   On the **Zoom Slider**, click the **Zoom In** button several times, and then use the scroll bars that appear to scroll the lower-left corner into view.

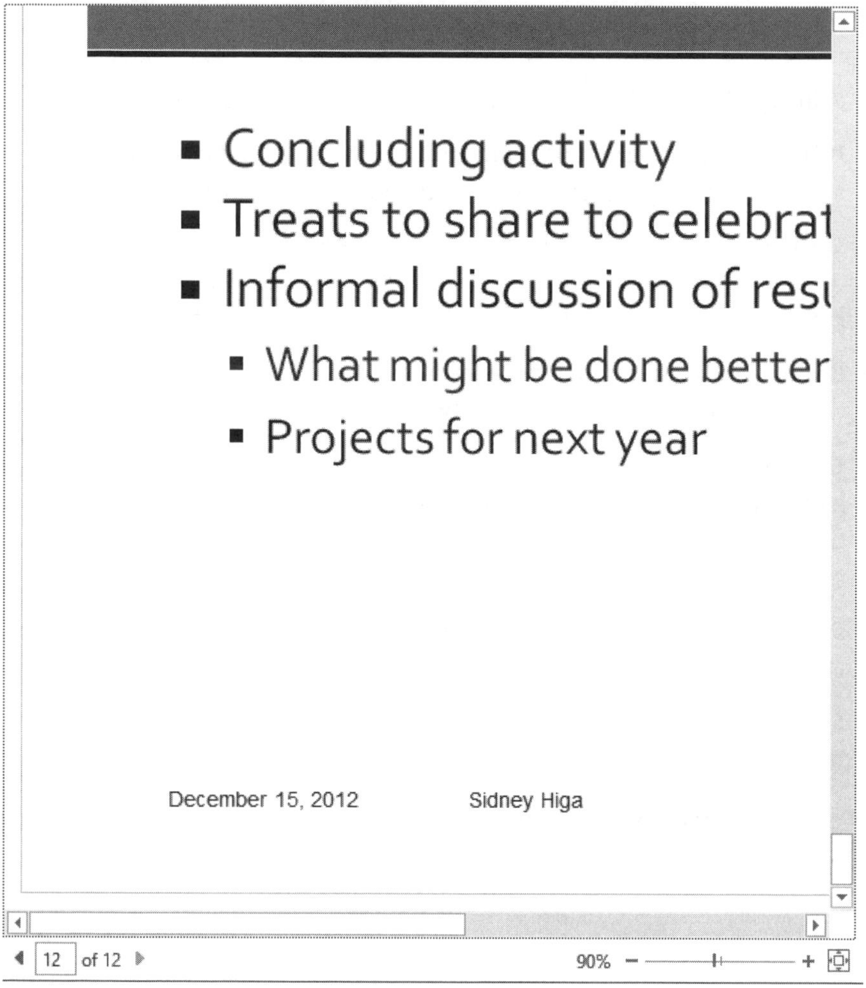

- Concluding activity
- Treats to share to celebrat
- Informal discussion of resu
  - What might be done better
  - Projects for next year

December 15, 2012   Sidney Higa

12 of 12   90%

You can use the Zoom Slider to zoom in on parts of a slide.

5   Click the **Zoom to Page** button to return to the original zoom percentage.

Now let's adjust the print settings.

6   In the middle pane, click the setting for your printer to display a list of all the printers installed on your computer. Then in the list, click the printer you want to use.

TIP After choosing a printer, you can customize its settings for this particular print operation by clicking Printer Properties to open the Properties dialog box. For example, if the printer you have selected has duplex capabilities, you might want to specify that it should print slides on both sides of the page.

7   In the **Settings** area, in the **Slides** box, enter **1-3,5**, and then press **Tab**. Notice that in the right pane, PowerPoint displays a preview of slide **1**. Below the preview, the slide indicator changes to **1 of 4**, and you can now preview only the selected slides.

8   Click **Full Page Slides**, and on the **Print Layout** menu, click **Frame Slides**.

9   At the top of the pane, click the **Print** button to print slides **1**, **2**, **3**, and **5** with frames in shades of gray on the selected printer.

❌ CLEAN UP **Close the ServiceProjectsB presentation, saving your changes if you want to.**

Preparing speaker notes and handouts

If you will be delivering your presentation before a live audience, you will probably want speaker notes to guide you. Each slide in a PowerPoint presentation has a corresponding notes page. As you create a slide, you can open the Notes pane and enter notes that relate to the slide's content. If you want to include something other than text in your speaker notes, switch to Notes Page view by clicking the Notes Page button in the Presentation Views group on the View tab, and create the notes there. When your notes are complete, you can print them to help you rehearse the delivery of the presentation.

TIP In Presenter view, you can display your notes on one monitor while you display the slides to your audience on another monitor. For information about Presenter view, see the sidebar "Setting up Presenter view" later in this chapter.

As a courtesy for your audience, you might want to supply handouts showing the presentation's slides so that people can take notes. Printing handouts requires a few decisions, such as which of the nine available layouts you want to use and whether you want to add headers and footers. Otherwise, you don't need to do anything special to create simple handouts.

TIP The layout of PowerPoint notes pages and handouts is controlled by templates called the *notes master* and the *handout master.* Usually, you'll find that the default masters are more than adequate, but if you want to make changes, you can. For information about customizing masters, see "Viewing and changing slide masters" in Chapter 12, "Create custom presentation elements."

In this exercise, you'll enter speaker notes for some slides in the Notes pane. Then you'll switch to Notes Page view and insert a graphic into one note and a diagram into another. Finally, you'll print both speaker notes and handouts.

SET UP You need the Harmony presentation and the YinYang graphic located in the Chapter06 practice file folder to complete this exercise. Open the presentation, display the Notes pane, and then follow the steps.

1   With slide **1** displayed, drag the border between the **Slide** pane and the **Notes** pane upward to enlarge the **Notes** pane.

2   Click anywhere in the **Notes** pane, enter Welcome and introductions, and then press the **Enter** key.

3   On separate lines, enter Logistics and Establish knowledge level.

4   Display slide **2**, and in the **Notes** pane, enter Talk about the main concepts.

5   Display slide **3**, and in the **Notes** pane, enter Complementary energies. Then press **Enter** twice.

   Now let's add a picture to the note.

6   On the **View** tab, in the **Presentation Views** group, click the **Notes Page** button to display slide **3** in **Notes Page** view, where the entire notes page fits in the window.

7   On the **Insert** tab, in the **Images** group, click the **Pictures** button.

8   In the **Insert Picture** dialog box, navigate to the **Chapter06** practice file folder, and then double-click the **YinYang** graphic.

9   Drag the image down below the note you entered in step 5, using the smart guide to align the image with the slide.

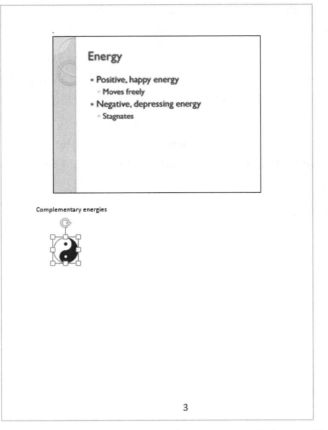

You can add images to your speaker notes to remind yourself of concepts you want to cover while the slide is displayed.

While we are in Notes Page view, let's add a diagram to the note for the next slide, showing visually the concepts to be emphasized during the presentation.

10   At the bottom of the scroll bar, click the **Next Slide** button to display slide **4**. Then click the border around the text placeholder to select it, and press **Delete**.

11   On the **Insert** tab, in the **Illustrations** group, click the **SmartArt** button. In the left pane of the **Choose a SmartArt Graphic** dialog box, click **Hierarchy**, and then in the middle pane, double-click the second thumbnail in the fourth row (**Hierarchy List**).

SEE ALSO For information about how to work with SmartArt diagrams, see "Creating diagrams" in Chapter 5, "Add simple visual enhancements," and "Customizing diagrams" in Chapter 8, "Fine-tune visual elements."

Don't worry about the placement of the diagram until it has all its shapes and text. Let's complete that aspect of this hierarchy diagram now.

12 Open the **Text** pane, and with the cursor in the first placeholder in the hierarchy, enter the following, pressing the **Down Arrow** key or the **Enter** key as indicated to create two sets of shapes, each with a primary shape and four subordinate shapes.

Focus (Down Arrow)

Health (Down Arrow)

Creativity (Enter)

Relationships (Enter)

Community (Down Arrow)

Follow (Down Arrow)

Knowledge (Down Arrow)

Career (Enter)

Fame (Enter)

Fortune

TIP If you can't read the notes at this zoom percentage, you might want to click the Zoom In button on the Zoom Slider in the lower-right corner of the window.

13 Close the **Text** pane, and then move and size the diagram to fit in the space below the slide.

14 Use the formatting options available in the **SmartArt Styles** group on the **Design** tool tab to format the diagram any way you want. (We used the **Moderate Effect** style and the **Colored Fill – Accent 3** colors.)

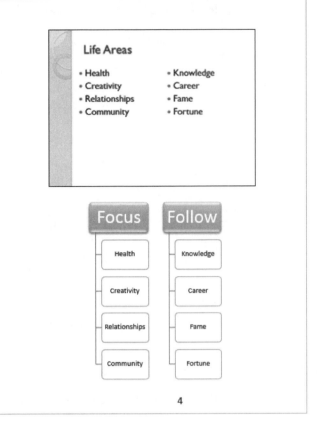

Diagrams can give you an at-a-glance reminder of important concepts.

15 Switch to **Normal** view, and notice that the diagram on slide **4** is not visible in the **Notes** pane in this view.

16 Display slide **3**, and notice that the **YinYang** graphic is not visible in this view either.

You might have noticed that in Notes Page view, the pages display page numbers but no other header or footer information. Let's add headers and footers to the notes.

17 Switch to **Notes Page** view, and then on the **Insert** tab, in the **Text** group, click the **Header & Footer** button to open the **Header and Footer** dialog box with the **Notes and Handouts** page displayed.

On the Notes And Handouts page, you can insert a header and a footer that will appear at the top or bottom of your speaker notes.

18 Select the **Date and time** check box, and then click **Fixed**.

19 Select the **Header** check box, and then in the text box, enter Harmony in Your Home.

20 Select the **Footer** check box, and then in the text box, enter Wide World Importers.

21 Click **Apply to All**.

Finally, let's print speaker notes for our own use and handouts for the audience.

22 Switch to **Normal** view, and display the **Print** page of the **Backstage** view. Then in the **Settings** area, click **Full Page Slides**, and in the **Print Layout** area, click **Notes Pages**.

23 If you want to proof the speaker notes, click the **Slides** box, enter 1-4, and then click the **Print** button.

24   Display slide **1**, and if necessary, display the **Print** page of the **Backstage** view again. In the **Settings** area, click **Notes Pages**, and in the **Handouts** area of the gallery, click **3 Slides**.

Harmony in Your Home   December 15, 2012

Harmony in Your Home

Wide World Importers

Principles
• Let energy flow
• Enhance life areas
• Set goals
• Create balance

Energy
• Positive, happy energy
  • Moves freely
• Negative, depressing energy
  • Stagnates

World Wide Importers   1

When you print three slides per page, PowerPoint adds lines for notes to the right of each slide image.

25   If you want, change the **Slides** setting to **1-3**, and then click the **Print** button to print the first page of handouts.

❌ CLEAN UP Close the Harmony presentation, saving your changes if you want to.

Enhanced handouts

If you want to provide audience handouts that include notes as well as pictures of the slides, you can send the presentation to a Microsoft Word document and then develop the handout content in Word.

To create handouts in Word:

1   Display the **Export** page of the **Backstage** view, and click **Create Handouts**.

2   In the right pane, click the **Create Handouts** button to open the **Send to Microsoft Word** dialog box.

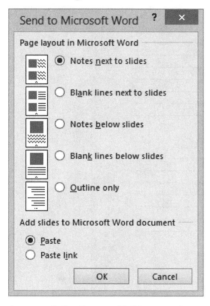

In two of the five available page layouts, you can enter notes along with the pictures of the slides.

3   Click the notes layout you want.

4   If the slide content might change, in the **Add slides to Microsoft Word document** area, click **Paste link**.

5   Click **OK**.

    Word starts and opens a document formatted for the layout you selected. (If you selected Outline Only, the presentation's text appears in the document as a structured list.) You can then add any notes you want to be part of your handouts.

Easy note-taking

If you want your audience to be able to take digital notes in OneNote during your presentation, make the presentation file available ahead of time. Then when your start your delivery, audience members can follow along, taking notes in OneNote.

To take notes in OneNote that are linked to a presentation's slides:

1 Open the presentation file, and on the **Review** tab, in the **OneNote** group, click the **Linked Notes** button to start OneNote.

2 If necessary, designate where your notes should be stored. A OneNote page opens on the right side of the screen, and the presentation's slides are displayed on the left side.

3 Name the OneNote page, and then with the first slide selected in the **Thumbnails** pane of the PowerPoint window, take any notes you want.

4 When the presenter moves to the next slide, do the same, taking notes that are linked to that slide.

5 As the presenter moves through the slides, follow along taking linked notes as appropriate.

6 When you review your notes later, click the **Powerpoint** icon to the left of each note to display the linked slide.

6

Finalizing presentations

These days, many presentations are delivered electronically as email attachments or from a website. As you develop a presentation, it can accumulate information that you might not want in the final version, such as the names of people who worked on the presentation, comments that reviewers have added to the file, or hidden text about status and assumptions. If your presentation file will never leave your computer, you don't have to worry that it might contain something that shouldn't be available to other people. However, if the presentation file is going to be shared with other people, you will want to remove this identifying and tracking information before you distribute the presentation.

To examine some of the information attached to a presentation, display the presentation's properties on the Info page of the Backstage view. You can change or remove some properties in the Properties pane, or you can open the Document Panel or the Properties dialog box by clicking Properties at the top of the pane and clicking the option you want. However, to automate the process of finding and removing all extraneous and confidential information, PowerPoint provides a tool called the *Document Inspector*.

You can use the Document Inspector to identify and remove six types of information.

TIP When rearranging the objects on a slide, you might drag an object to one side while you decide whether to include it. The Off-Slide Content option in the Document Inspector dialog box detects any stray content that you might have overlooked. The Document Inspector also looks for invisible content on the slide. This is content you might have hidden by displaying the Selection pane and then clearing the object's check box. (To display this pane, click the Select button in the Editing group on the Home tab, and then click Selection Pane.)

After you run the Document Inspector, a summary of its search results is displayed, and you have the option of removing all the items found in each category.

PowerPoint also includes two other finalizing tools:

■ **Check Accessibility** This tool checks for presentation elements and formatting that might be difficult for people with certain kinds of disabilities to view or that might not be compatible with assistive technologies. It reports its findings and offers suggestions for fixing any potential issues.

■ **Check Compatibility** This tool checks for the use of features not supported in earlier versions of PowerPoint. It presents a list of features that might be lost or degraded if you save the presentation in an earlier PowerPoint file format.

After you have handled extraneous information and accessibility and compatibility issues, you can mark a presentation as final and make its file read-only so that other people know that they should not make changes to this released presentation. This process does not lock the presentation, however; if you want to make additional changes to the presentation, you can easily turn off the final status.

In this exercise, you'll examine the properties attached to a presentation, remove personal information from the file, and then mark the presentation as final.

➔ SET UP You need the MeetingA presentation located in the Chapter06 practice file folder to complete this exercise. Open the presentation, and then follow the steps.

1   Display the **Info** page of the **Backstage** view, and in the **Properties** area of the right pane, examine the standard properties associated with this presentation.

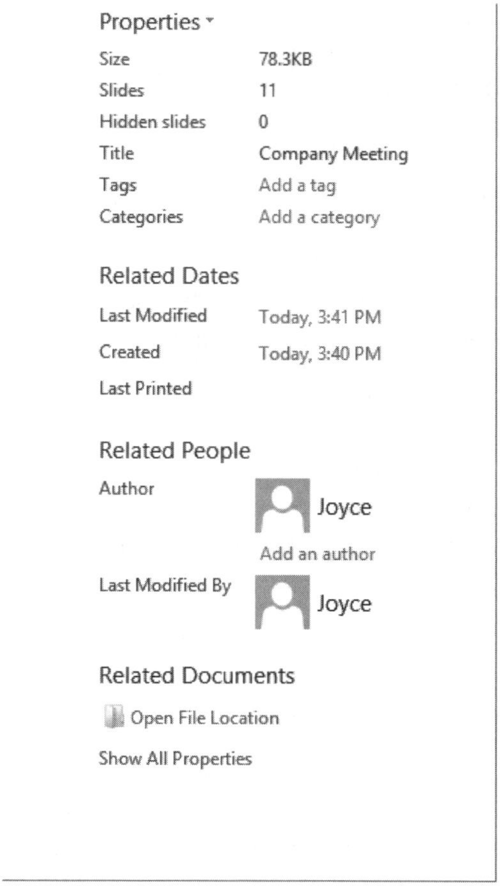

Properties ▾

Size	78.3KB
Slides	11
Hidden slides	0
Title	Company Meeting
Tags	Add a tag
Categories	Add a category

Related Dates

Last Modified	Today, 3:41 PM
Created	Today, 3:40 PM
Last Printed	

Related People

Author

Joyce

Add an author

Last Modified By

Joyce

Related Documents

Open File Location

Show All Properties

PowerPoint controls some of the properties, such as the size and dates; you can add and change others, such as the assigned categories and authors.

2 At the bottom of the **Properties** pane, click **Show All Properties** to expand the pane. Let's change some of these properties.

3 To the right of **Status**, click **Add text**, and enter Done.

4   At the top of the pane, click **Properties**, and in the list, click **Advanced Properties**. Then in the **MeetingA Properties** dialog box, click the **Summary** tab.

MeetingA Properties	?	✕

General **Summary** Statistics Contents Custom

Title: Company Meeting

Subject:

Author: Joyce

Manager:

Company:

Category:

Keywords:

Comments:

Hyperlink
base:

Template: MeetingA

☑ Save preview picture

OK   Cancel

The Summary page of the Properties dialog box includes in a convenient format some of the properties you might want to change.

5   Click in the **Subject** box, enter Morale event, and then click **OK**.

6   Save your changes to the presentation.

Now let's check whether the presentation contains personal or confidential information.

7   Display the **Info** page of the **Backstage** view, and to the left of **Inspect Presentation**, click **Check for Issues**. In the list of inspection tools, click **Inspect Document** to open the **Document Inspector**.

6

8   Clear the **Task Pane Apps** and **Custom XML Data** check boxes. Then with the **Comments and Annotations, Document Properties and Personal Information, Invisible On-Slide Content**, and **Presentation Notes** check boxes selected, click **Inspect**.

The Document Inspector reports that this presentation includes properties that you might not want others to be able to view.

9   To the right of **Document Properties and Personal Information**, click **Remove All**.

10   Close the **Document Inspector**, and notice that all the properties have been cleared from the **Properties** pane.

Now let's finalize the presentation.

11   On the **Info** page, click **Protect Presentation**, and then click **Mark as Final**.

12   When a message tells you that the presentation will be marked as final and then saved, click **OK** in the message box. Then click **OK** in the confirmation box.

13   Notice that the title bar indicates that the presentation is read-only, that the ribbon is collapsed to hide its buttons, and that the Information bar below the ribbon indicates that the presentation is final.

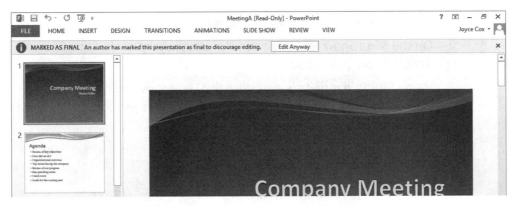

Marking a presentation as final discourages but does not prevent editing.

14   Click the **Home** tab to display its commands, most of which are inactive. Then click away from the ribbon to hide its buttons again.

15   On the title slide, click the title, double-click the word **Company**, and then press the **Delete** key.

Nothing happens. You cannot change any of the objects on the slides unless you click the Edit Anyway button in the Information bar to remove the presentation's final status.

❌ CLEAN UP Close the MeetingA presentation.

Setting up Presenter view

If your computer can support two monitors, or if you will be presenting a slide show from your computer through a projector, you might want to check out Presenter view. In this view, you can control the presentation on one monitor while the audience views the slides in Slide Show view on the delivery monitor or the projector screen.

To deliver a presentation on one monitor and use Presenter view on another:

1 Open the presentation you want to set up.

2 On the **Slide Show** tab, in the **Set Up** group, click **Set Up Slide Show** to open the **Set Up Show** dialog box.

3 In the **Multiple monitors** area, click the **Slide show monitor** arrow, and then in the list, click the name of the monitor you want to use to show the slides to your audience.

> **TROUBLESHOOTING** The settings in the Multiple Monitors area are active only if your computer is set up to use multiple monitors.

4 Select the **Use Presenter View** check box, and then click **OK**.

5 On the **Slide Show** tab, in the **Start Slide Show** group, click the **From Beginning** button.

The title slide is displayed full screen on the delivery monitor, and **Presenter** view is displayed on the control monitor. As the presenter, you can view details about what slide or bullet point is coming next, refer to your speaker notes, jump directly to any slide, black out the screen during a pause in the presentation, and keep track of the time.

6 On the control monitor, use the **Presenter** view tools to control the presentation.

Delivering presentations

To deliver a presentation to an audience, you start by displaying the first slide full screen. Then depending on how you have set up the presentation, you can either click the mouse button without moving the mouse to display the slides in sequence, or you can allow PowerPoint to display the slides according to the timings you have set on the Transitions tab.

SEE ALSO For information about slide timings, see "Adding transitions" in Chapter 5, "Add simple visual enhancements," and "Rehearsing presentations" in Chapter 13, "Prepare for delivery."

If you need to move to a slide other than the next one or the previous one, you can move the mouse pointer to display an inconspicuous toolbar in the lower-left corner of the slide.

- Key spending areas
- Head count
- Goals for the coming year

The six buttons on the toolbar provide various tools that can enhance the delivery of a presentation.

You can use four of the buttons on this toolbar to move among slides in the following ways:

- To move to the previous slide, click the first button (**Previous**).

- To move to the next slide, click the second button (**Next**).

- To jump to a slide out of sequence, click the fourth button (**See All Slides**), and then click the thumbnail of the slide you want.

- To jump to the last viewed slide, click the sixth button (**Slide Show Options**), and then click **Last Viewed**.

- To end the presentation, click the sixth button, and then click End Show.

KEYBOARD SHORTCUTS To display a list of keyboard shortcuts for carrying out presentation tasks, click the sixth button on the toolbar (or right-click the screen), and then click Help. For example, you can press the Spacebar, the Down Arrow key, or the Right Arrow key to move to the next slide; press the Page Up key or the Left Arrow key to move to the previous slide; and press the Esc key to end the presentation. For a complete list of keyboard shortcuts, see "Keyboard shortcuts" at the end of this book.

During a presentation, you can reinforce your message by pointing to slide elements with a laser pointer, drawing on the slides with an electronic "pen," or changing the background behind text with a highlighter. Simply click the third button (Pointer Options) on the toolbar, click the tool you want, and then begin pointing, drawing, or highlighting. The laser pointer and pen colors are determined by settings in the Set Up Show dialog box, but during the presentation you can use a pen with a different color by clicking the Pointer Options button, and then selecting a color from the palette at the bottom of the Pointer Options menu.

In addition to using a laser pointer to draw attention to slide elements, you can shine a spotlight on a specific area of the slide by clicking the fifth button on the toolbar and then moving the spotlight over the dimmed slide. Clicking the spotlight zooms in on the highlighted part of the slide.

If you need to pause a manually controlled presentation to address a question from the audience or explain a point not covered by a slide, click the sixth button and select an option to display a black or white screen during the diversion. If you need to temporarily halt a presentation controlled by slide timings, click the sixth button and click Pause.

When you want to stop using a tool you have launched from the toolbar, simply press the Esc key to resume the presentation.

In this exercise, you'll move around in a presentation in various ways while delivering it. You'll also use a pen tool to mark up one slide, change the color of the markup, and then mark up another slide.

 SET UP **You need the MeetingB presentation located in the Chapter06 practice file folder to complete this exercise. Open the presentation, and then follow the steps.**

1   With slide **1** displayed in **Normal** view, on the **View Shortcuts** toolbar, click the **Slide Show** button to switch to **Slide Show** view, where the title slide appears full-screen.

2   Click the mouse button to advance to slide **2**, whose contents rotates onto the screen with a dynamic content transition.

3   Press the **Left Arrow** key to move back to the previous slide, and then press the **Right Arrow** key to display the next slide.

4   Move the mouse to display the pointer, and notice the shadow toolbar that is barely visible in the lower-left corner.

TROUBLESHOOTING If the navigation toolbar doesn't seem to appear, move the pointer to the lower-left corner of the screen and move it slowly to the right. The six toolbar buttons should become visible in turn. If they don't, press the Esc key to end the slide show. Then display the Backstage view, and click Options. In the PowerPoint Options dialog box, click Advanced, and in the Slide Show area, select the Show Pop-up Toolbar check box, and click OK.

5   On the toolbar, click the second button from the left (**Next**) to display slide **3**.

6   Right-click anywhere on the screen, and then click **Previous** to redisplay slide **2**.

Now let's display a slide out of sequence.

7   Display the toolbar, click the fourth button from the left (**See All Slides**), and then in the thumbnail display, click slide **6**.

8   Display the toolbar, click the sixth button from the left (**Slide Show Options**) button, and then click **Last Viewed** to display slide **2**.

9   Use various navigation methods to display various slides in the presentation until you are comfortable moving around.

10 Right-click anywhere on the screen, and then click **End Show**.

TIP If you click all the way through to the end of the presentation, PowerPoint displays a black slide to indicate that the next click will return you to the previous view. If you do not want the black slide to appear at the end of a presentation, open the PowerPoint Options dialog box, and click Advanced. Then in the Slide Show area, clear the End With Black Slide check box, and click OK. Clicking while the last slide is displayed will then return you to the previous view.

Let's use a few techniques to draw attention to the content of the slides.

11 In **Normal** view, display slide **3**, and then switch to **Slide Show** view.

12 Right-click anywhere on the screen, point to **Pointer Options**, and click **Laser Pointer**. Move the pointer over the text to test how you might use this tool, and then press the **Esc** key to stop using it.

13 Display the toolbar, and click the fifth button from the left (**Zoom In**). Move the spotlight over the bulleted list, and then press **Esc** to stop using this tool.

14   Right-click anywhere on the screen, point to **Pointer Options**, and click **Highlighter**. Then on the slide, highlight the words **unique** and **successful**.

TIP When the pen or highlighter tool is active in Slide Show view, clicking the mouse button does not advance the slide show to the next slide. You need to switch back to the regular pointer to use the mouse to advance the slide.

15   Right-click anywhere on the screen, point to **Pointer Options**, and click **Pen**. Then on the slide, below the word **shared**, draw a line in the default color specified in the **Set Up Show** dialog box.

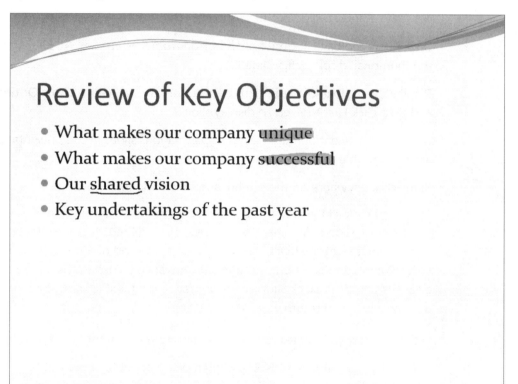

You can emphasize a point with the highlighter or pen.

16   Right-click the screen, point to **Pointer Options**, and then click **Erase All Ink on Slide**.

TROUBLESHOOTING If the ink doesn't completely disappear, move to the next slide and then move back again.

17   Press the **Spacebar** to move to the next slide.

18   Display the toolbar, click the third button from the left (**Pointer Options**), and then in the palette, click the **Dark Red** swatch.

19   Draw a line below the word **overview**.

20   Press the **Esc** key to stop using the pen tool, and then click the mouse button to advance to the next slide.

21   Press **Esc** to stop the presentation.

22   When a message asks whether you want to keep your ink annotations, click **Discard**.

❌ CLEAN UP Close the MeetingB presentation.

Key points

6

- For efficiency, set up your presentation in its intended output format before you begin adding content.

- To proof a presentation on paper, you can print it in color, grayscale, or black and white, depending on the capabilities of your printer.

- You can easily create speaker notes to facilitate presentation delivery, or print handouts for your audience.

- Finalizing a presentation ensures that it doesn't contain personal or confidential information and that people know not to make further changes.

- Knowing how to use all the toolbar buttons, commands, and keyboard shortcuts to move around in Slide Show view is important for smooth presentation delivery.

- To emphasize a point during a presentation, you can point to and spotlight slide content. You can also mark up slides by using a pen in various colors or by using a highlighter.

Presentation enhancements

Chapter at a glance

Insert

Insert tables,
page 213

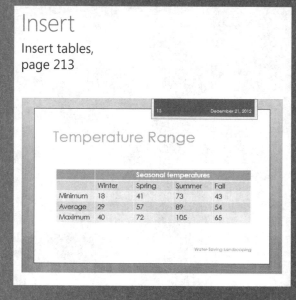

Format

Format tables,
page 218

Embed

Embed and update Excel worksheets,
page 221

Present content in tables   7

IN THIS CHAPTER, YOU WILL LEARN HOW TO

- Insert tables.

- Format tables.

- Embed and update Excel worksheets.

Often you will want to bolster the argument you are making in a Microsoft PowerPoint 2013 presentation with facts and figures that are best presented in a table. Tables condense information into highly structured row and column grid formats so that identifying categories or individual items and making comparisons is easier. You can place a table on any PowerPoint slide, whether or not it includes a content placeholder.

If the tabular information already exists—for example, as a Microsoft Excel worksheet—you can copy and paste it into a PowerPoint table. If you want to preserve formulas, it's best to embed the worksheet as an object in the PowerPoint slide.

In this chapter, you'll insert and format a table on one PowerPoint slide and then embed and manipulate an Excel worksheet.

PRACTICE FILES To complete the exercises in this chapter, you need the practice files contained in the Chapter07 practice file folder. For more information, see "Download the practice files" in this book's Introduction.

Inserting tables

When you want to present a lot of data in an organized and easy-to-read format, a table is often your best choice. On a slide that includes a content placeholder, you can click the placeholder's Insert Table button to start the process of creating a table. On any slide, click the Table button in the Tables group on the Insert tab to add a table outside a placeholder.

TIP The use of tables has become a common way to design and organize webpages. You might be tempted to use tables to design and organize slides in the same way, especially for widescreen format presentations. However, if producing presentations that are compatible with assistive technologies is important, bear in mind that information presented in tables is not accessible.

After you specify the number of columns and rows you want in the table, PowerPoint creates the table structure, which consists of a two-dimensional organization of rows and columns. The box at the intersection of each row and column is called a *cell*. Often the first row is used for column headings, and the leftmost column is used for row headings.

You work with tables in PowerPoint in much the same way as you work with tables in Microsoft Word. (If the table you want to use already exists in a Word document, you can copy and paste that table into a PowerPoint slide, rather than re-creating it.)

To enter information in the table, first click a cell and then enter the data. You move the cursor from cell to cell by pressing the Tab key. Pressing Tab in the last cell of the last row inserts a new row at the bottom of the table. If you need a new row elsewhere, you can insert a row above or below the row containing the cursor or insert a column to the left or right by clicking the corresponding buttons in the Rows & Columns group of the Layout tool tab. If you no longer need a column or row, you can remove it by clicking the Delete button in the Rows & Columns group and then clicking Delete Columns or Delete Rows.

You can click the Merge Cells button in the Merge group of the Layout tab to merge (combine) selected cells into one cell that spans two or more columns or rows. Another way to merge cells is by clicking the Eraser button in the Draw Borders group on the Design tool tab, and then dragging the eraser across the border between two cells.

If you want to split a single cell into two or more cells, either select the cell and then click the Split Cells button in the Merge group on the Layout tab, or click the Draw Table button in the Draw Borders group on the Design tab and then draw a cell border with the pencil.

TIP If you don't already have a table on a slide, you can click the Table arrow and click Draw Table to activate the pencil. You can then drag cells the size and shape you need to create the table.

In this exercise, you'll create a table, enter text in its cells, insert a row, and merge cells.

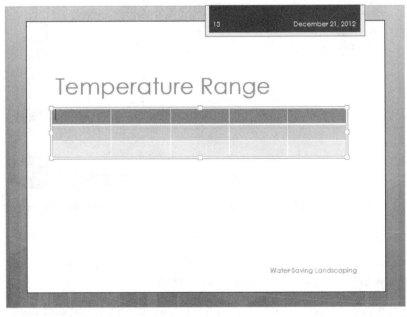

SET UP You need the WaterSavingA presentation located in the Chapter07 practice file folder to complete this exercise. Open the presentation, and then follow the steps.

1 Display slide **13**, which has the **Title And Content** layout.

2 In the content placeholder, click the **Insert Table** button to open the **Insert Table** dialog box.

In the Insert Table dialog box, you specify the number of columns and rows the table should initially contain.

3 Leave the setting in the **Number of columns** box at **5**, but change the setting in the **Number of rows** box to 3.

4 Click **OK** to insert a blank table with five columns and three rows.

By default, the heading row is shaded and the remaining rows are banded with subtle shades of the same color.

5   Click the first cell of the second column, enter Winter, press **Tab**, enter Spring, press **Tab**, enter Summer, and press **Tab**. Then enter Fall, and press **Tab** again to move the cursor to the first cell of the second row.

6   Enter the following, pressing **Tab** after each entry:

| Minimum | 18 | 41 | 73 | 43 |
| Average | 29 | 57 | 89 | 54 |

Notice that when you press Tab after the last entry, PowerPoint adds a new row to the table.

7   Enter the following, pressing **Tab** after each entry except the last:

| Maximum | 40 | 72 | 105 | 65 |

The banding in the rows below the heading row makes the information easier to read.

Let's add a new row above the headings.

8   Click anywhere in the heading row, and then on the **Layout** tool tab, in the **Rows & Columns** group, click the **Insert Above** button.

9   Click the second cell in the new row, hold down the **Shift** key, and then press the **Right Arrow** key three times.

10　　With four cells selected, in the **Merge** group, click the **Merge Cells** button.

11　　In the merged cell, enter **Seasonal temperatures**.

12　　Without moving the cursor, in the **Alignment** group, click the **Center** button.

KEYBOARD SHORTCUT Press Ctrl+E to center text. For a complete list of keyboard shortcuts, see "Keyboard shortcuts" at the end of this book.

Now let's move the table.

13　　Point to the frame of the table (but not to a sizing handle). Then drag the table downward so that it sits in about the center of the space between the title and the footer.

14　　Click a blank area of the slide to deactivate the table.

The table has no frame when it is inactive.

❌ CLEAN UP Close the WaterSavingA presentation, saving your changes if you want to.

Formatting tables

You can format an entire table in addition to individual cells by using the commands on the Design and Format tool tabs, which appear when a table is active. For example, you can use buttons on the Design tool tab to switch to a different table style, instantly changing the look of the text and cells to make key information stand out. If you want, you can also format individual words and individual cells.

In this exercise, you'll apply a different table style, and format a row and individual cells.

→ **SET UP You need the WaterSavingB presentation located in the Chapter07 practice file folder to complete this exercise. Open the presentation, and then follow the steps.**

1   Display slide **13**, and click anywhere in the table to activate it.

2   On the **Design** tool tab, in the **Table Style Options** group, clear the **Banded Rows** check box to make all rows except the title row the same color.

3   In the **Table Style Options** group, select the **First Column** check box to make that column and its text the same colors as the title.

		13	December 21, 2012

Temperature Range

	Seasonal temperatures			
	Winter	Spring	Summer	Fall
Minimum	18	41	73	43
Average	29	57	89	54
Maximum	40	72	105	65

Water-Saving Landscaping

Two formatting adjustments have completely changed the look of the table.

4   In the **Table Styles** group, click the **More** button to display a menu containing the **Table Styles** gallery.

An orange selection frame surrounds the thumbnail of the applied style.

5   Drag the bottom border of the gallery upward until the table is visible.

6   Point to various table styles to preview their effects on the table, and then in the **Medium** area, click the fifth thumbnail in the second row (**Medium Style 2 - Accent 4**).

Now let's experiment by formatting individual cells.

7   Drag across the cells containing the **Winter**, **Spring**, **Summer**, and **Fall** headings to select them.

8   On the **Design** tool tab, in the **Table Styles** group, click the **Shading** arrow, and then in the **Theme Colors** palette, click the green swatch at the top of the third column (**Light Green, Background 2**).

9   Click the cell containing **105**, click the **Shading** arrow, and then in the **Theme Colors** palette, click the orange swatch at the top of the seventh column (**Orange, Accent 3**).

10 Click the cell containing **18**, click the **Shading** arrow, and below the palettes in the menu, click **More Fill Colors**. Then on the **Standard** page of the **Colors** dialog box, click a pale blue color near the center of the color wheel, and click **OK**.

11 Select **Seasonal Temperatures**, and then in the **WordArt Styles** group, click the **Quick Styles** button to display its gallery. Then click the fifth thumbnail in the third row (**Fill – Light Green, Background 2, Inner Shadow**).

12 Repeat step 11 to format **Minimum**, **Average**, and **Maximum**.

    Let's add a border to the table.

13 On the **Layout** tool tab, in the **Table** group, click the **Select** button, and then click **Select Table**.

14 On the **Design** tool tab, in the **Table Styles** group, click the **Borders** arrow, and then click **Outside Borders**. Click anywhere on the slide, outside the table, to review your changes.

    After experimenting, let's try a simpler look. We'll apply a table style to clear the cell formatting but leave the text effects applied to the top row and first column.

15 Click anywhere in the table, and display the **Table Styles** gallery. Then, in the **Medium** area, click the third thumbnail in the second row (**Medium Style 2 – Accent 2**).

A simple approach makes the column and row headings stand out.

✖ CLEAN UP Close the WaterSavingB presentation, saving your changes if you want to.

Embedding and updating Excel worksheets

The table capabilities of PowerPoint are perfectly adequate for the display of simple information that is unlikely to change during the useful life of the presentation. However, if your data involves calculations or is likely to require updating, you'll probably want to maintain the information in an Excel worksheet. You can then either embed the worksheet in a slide or link the slide to the worksheet.

Embedded objects and linked objects differ in the following ways:

- An embedded object maintains a direct connection to its original program, known as the *source program*. After you insert an embedded object, you can easily edit it by double-clicking it, which opens the program in which it was originally created. Be aware that embedding an object increases the presentation's file size, because PowerPoint has to store not only the data itself but also information about how to display the data.

- A linked object is a representation on a slide of information that is still stored in the original document, known as the *source document*. If you edit the source document in the source program after inserting a linked object, PowerPoint updates the slide's representation of the object. Because PowerPoint stores only the data needed to display the information, linking results in a smaller file size than embedding.

  TIP Always make modifications to the source document, not to the linked object on the slide. Any changes you make to the linked object will be overwritten the next time you open the presentation, because PowerPoint will update the linked object to reflect the information in the source document.

For example, suppose a sales manager stores past sales information and future sales projections in Excel worksheets. On one slide in a presentation, she might embed the past sales information, because it is unlikely to change. On another slide, she might link the future sales projections, because she is still in the process of fine-tuning them. As she updates the sales projections worksheet, the linked table in the PowerPoint presentation automatically updates as well.

In this exercise, you'll embed an Excel worksheet and then update and format the content of the embedded object.

SET UP You need the MayMeeting presentation and the NewEquipment workbook located in the Chapter07 practice file folder to complete this exercise. Open the presentation, and then follow the steps.

1. Display slide **9**, and then on the **Insert** tab, in the **Text** group, click the **Object** button to open the **Insert Object** dialog box.

You can create any of the objects in the Object Type list from within PowerPoint.

2   Click **Create from file**, and then click **Browse** to open the **Browse** dialog box, which is similar to the **Open** dialog box.

3   Navigate to the **Chapter07** practice file folder, and double-click the **NewEquipment** workbook to return to the **Insert Object** dialog box.

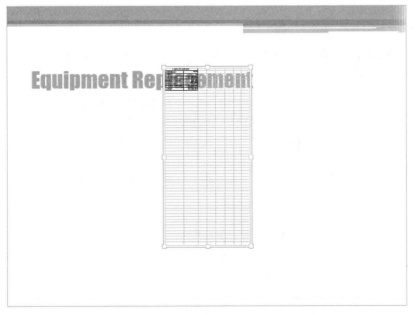

To link rather than embed the workbook, select the Link check box.

4   To embed the data from the first worksheet of the specified workbook in the active slide, click **OK**.

The Excel worksheet object is inserted in the center of the slide.

5   Double-click the worksheet object to open it in an Excel window within PowerPoint.

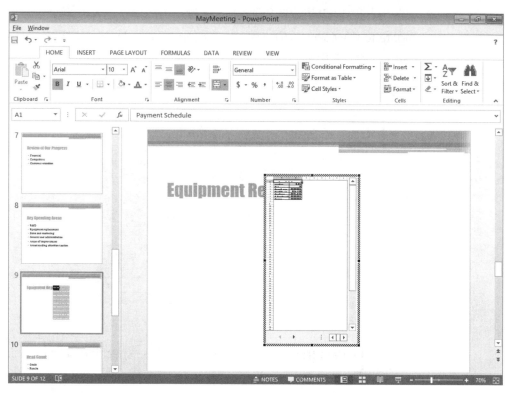

When you double-click an embedded worksheet, the Excel ribbon replaces the PowerPoint ribbon, and a formula bar appears above the Thumbnails and Slide panes.

Let's exclude blank rows and columns from the object, enlarge the object, and center it on the slide.

6   Drag the black handles in the middle of the bottom and right sides of the frame around the Excel worksheet until the object's window is just big enough to contain the active part of the worksheet.

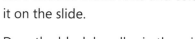

The frame just fits the data.

7   Click outside the object's window to return to PowerPoint. Then point to the lower-right corner of the object, and drag down and to the right to enlarge it.

> **TROUBLESHOOTING** Be sure to point to the corner so that you drag the sizing handle, even if the sizing handle is not visible. If you drag the frame, you'll move the object instead of sizing it. If that happens, click the Undo button, and try again.

8   Point to the frame (not to a handle), and drag the worksheet object down and to the left so that it is centered horizontally on the slide.

Now let's try to update the object's data.

9   Double-click the worksheet object to display it in an Excel window.

The worksheet object contains two columns labeled A and B and eight numbered rows.

You can reference each cell by its column letter followed by its row number (for example, A1). You can reference a block of cells by the cell in its upper-left corner and the cell in its lower-right corner, separated by a colon (for example, A1:C3).

10   Click cell **B2**, and notice in the **Number** group that the cell's contents are formatted as a percentage.

11   Click each of the other cells in column **B** in turn, and notice the contents of the formula bar (the box to the right of **fx** above the slide) and the format in the **Number** group.

12   Click cell **B2**, enter **6**, and then press the **Enter** key. Notice that Excel uses formulas in cells **B5**, **B6**, and **B8** to calculate the new cost of the equipment loan. The amount in cell **B5** changed to **$17,208**, the amount in **B6** changed to **$619,494**, and the amount in cell **B8** changed to **$1,180,506**. These changes affect only the object on the slide; the data in the original Excel worksheet has not changed.

Let's format a few cells to make it easier to read the data.

13   Select cell **A1**, which is merged with cell **B1**, and then on the Excel **Home** tab, in the **Font** group, click the **Fill Color** arrow. Then in the **Theme Colors** palette, click the third swatch in the green column (**Olive Green, Accent 3, Lighter 60%**).

14   Point to cell **A2**, and drag down to cell **A8**. Then click the **Fill Color** button to shade the selected cells with the active color.

15   Click a blank area of the slide to close Excel and redisplay the object on the slide in PowerPoint.

16   Click the blank area again to deactivate the object.

Equipment Replacement

Payment Schedule	
Interest Rate	6.0%
Years	10
Loan Amount	$1,550,000
Monthly Payment	$17,208
Cost of Loan	$619,494
10-Year Lease Cost	$1,800,000
Savings	$1,180,506

In the embedded worksheet, the interest rate is now 6 percent and the top row and first column are shaded to make them stand out.

✖ CLEAN UP Close the MayMeeting presentation, saving your changes if you want to.

Key points

- Use a table to organize information neatly in rows and columns.

- You can customize and format individual cells as well as the entire table.

- If the information you need already exists in an Excel worksheet, you can embed the worksheet in a slide. Double-clicking the worksheet object opens it in Excel so that you can edit it.

- If the information in the Excel worksheet is likely to change, you can link the slide to the source worksheet so that the slide is updated if the worksheet changes.

7

Chapter at a glance

Edit

Edit pictures,
page 229

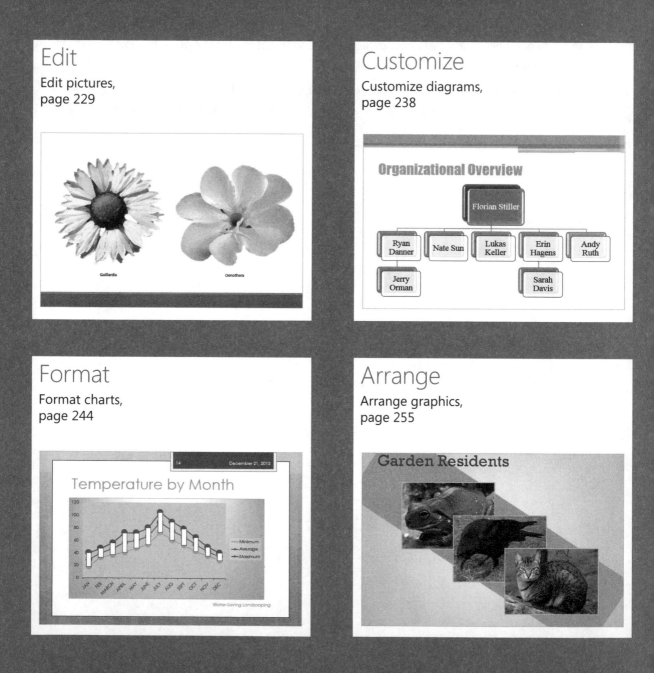

Customize

Customize diagrams,
page 238

Format

Format charts,
page 244

Arrange

Arrange graphics,
page 255

Fine-tune visual elements 8

IN THIS CHAPTER, YOU WILL LEARN HOW TO

- Edit pictures.

- Customize diagrams.

- Format charts.

- Arrange graphics.

In Chapter 5, "Add simple visual enhancements," you were introduced to the primary ways you can use graphic elements to convey information or dress up your slides. You inserted pictures and a clip art image, created a diagram, plotted data in a chart, drew shapes, and eased the transition from one slide to another by using a graphic effect. These simple techniques might be all you need to enhance your presentations. But if you need to manipulate graphic elements to produce more dramatic effects, you can push the Microsoft PowerPoint 2013 capabilities further to get just the result you are looking for.

In this chapter, you'll create a photo album and insert and manipulate photographs. Next, you'll manipulate diagram shapes to customize an organization chart. Then you'll format a chart and save it as a template. Finally, you'll use various techniques to arrange graphics.

PRACTICE FILES To complete the exercises in this chapter, you need the practice files contained in the Chapter08 practice file folder. For more information, see "Download the practice files" in this book's Introduction.

Editing pictures

From time to time in this book, we have alluded to the modern trend away from slides with bullet points and toward presentations that include more graphics. Successful presenters have learned that most people can't listen to a presentation while they are reading slides. So these presenters make sure most of their slides display graphics that represent the point they are making, giving the audience something to look at while they focus on what is being said. PowerPoint gives you the tools you need to create graphic-intensive rather than text-intensive presentations.

When you want to display a dynamic array of pictures in a presentation, you can use a photo album template to do the initial layout and then customize the album by adding frames of different shapes, in addition to captions.

TIP To integrate the slide layouts from a photo album template into a more traditional presentation, create the photo album and then import its slides into the other presentation by clicking Reuse Slides at the bottom of the New Slide gallery. For information about reusing slides, see "Adding slides from existing sources" in Chapter 2, "Create presentations."

After you insert any picture into a presentation, you can modify it by using the commands on the Format tool tab. For example, you can do the following:

- Remove the background by designating either the areas you want to keep or those you want to remove.

- Sharpen or soften the picture, or change its brightness or contrast.

- Enhance the picture's color.

- Make one of the picture's colors transparent.

- Choose an effect, such as Pencil Sketch or Paint Strokes.

- Apply effects such as shadows, reflections, and borders; or apply combinations of these effects.

- Add a border consisting of one or more solid or dashed lines of whatever width and color you choose.

- Rotate the picture to any angle, either by dragging the rotating handle or by choosing a rotating or flipping option.

- Crop away the parts of the picture that you don't want to show on the slide. (The picture itself is not altered—parts of it are simply covered up.)

- Minimize the presentation's file size by specifying the optimum resolution for where or how the presentation will be viewed—for example, on a webpage or printed page. You can also delete cropped areas of a picture to reduce file size.

In this exercise, you'll create a photo album displaying pictures of native plants. You'll crop and resize the pictures, remove their backgrounds, apply artistic effects, and add captions. You'll also reuse a slide from another photo album, and apply a theme.

SET UP You need the NativePlants presentation and the NativePlant1 through NativePlant8 photographs located in the Chapter08 practice file folder to complete this exercise. Open a new blank presentation, and then follow the steps.

1   On the **Insert** tab, in the **Images** group, click the **Photo Album** button to open the **Photo Album** dialog box.

2   In the **Insert picture from** area, click **File/Disk** to open the **Insert New Pictures** dialog box.

3   Navigate to the **Chapter08** practice file folder, click **NativePlant1**, hold down the **Ctrl** key, and click **NativePlant3**, **NativePlant4**, and **NativePlant5**. Then click **Insert** to redisplay the **Photo Album** dialog box with the four files you selected in the **Pictures in album** list.

In the Photo Album dialog box, you can click each photo in turn to view it in the Preview box.

4   In the **Pictures in album** list, select the check box to the left of **NativePlant4**, and click the **Move Up** button to make it the second photo. Then clear the check box.

5   Preview the photos in turn by clicking each name in the **Pictures in album** list. Then make the four photos more even in tone by selecting the check box of any photo whose contrast or brightness you want to adjust and clicking the **Contrast** and **Brightness** buttons.

TIP Your contrast and brightness adjustments affect only the photo displayed in the Preview box. You can also adjust the photo's angle of rotation in this dialog box.

6   In the **Album Layout** area, display the **Picture layout** list, and click **2 pictures**.

7   Display the **Frame shape** list, and click **Rounded Rectangle**. Then click **Create** to create a presentation called **Photo Album** that contains a title slide and two other slides, each containing two photos.

8   On the **Design** tab, in the **Themes** group, click the white **Office Theme** thumbnail to make the photos show up against a white background.

9   Save the presentation as **My Photo Album**.

Let's crop, size, and position the photos.

10   Display slide **2**, and click the photo on the left. Then on the **Format** tool tab, in the **Size** group, click the **Crop** arrow. In the list, point to **Aspect Ratio**, and then in the **Portrait area**, click **2:3** to center a "window" over the photo, sized to the proportions you specified.

Cropping handles surround the active area so that if you want, you can adjust the built-in aspect ratio.

11 Click a blank area of the slide to accept the suggested cropping of the photo.

12 Click the photo on the right, and repeat the cropping process in steps 10 and 11.

13 In turn, select each photo, and drag the upper-left and bottom-right corner handles until the photos occupy the majority of the space on the slide.

TIP When you are sizing the photo on the right, release the mouse button when the smart guide appears, letting you know that the photo is aligned with the photo on the left.

14 Display slide **3**, and crop the photo on the left to **Square**, **1:1**. Then point inside the crop window, and drag to the left to center the cropping window on the flower while maintaining its size.

The image of the flower is centered in the crop window.

15 Click the photo on the right, and in the **Size** group, use the down arrow to reduce the **Shape Height** setting to **3"**. Then crop the photo to **Square**, **1:1**, adjusting the crop window so that all of the flower is showing.

16 Enlarge and align the photos so that they occupy the entire width of the slide.

17 Click a blank area of the slide to release the selection. Then save the photo album.

8

Cropping enables you to focus attention on the significant parts of photographs.

Now let's add captions to all the pictures. To do so, you need to edit the photo album.

18   On the **Insert** tab, in the **Images** group, click the **Photo Album** arrow, and then click **Edit Photo Album** to open the **Edit Photo Album** dialog box, which is the same as the **Photo Album** dialog box.

19   In the **Picture Options** area, select the **Captions below ALL pictures** check box, and then click **Update** to add a text box containing the file name below each photo.

    TIP PowerPoint adjusts the size of the photos as necessary to accommodate the text boxes.

20   On slides **2** and **3**, replace the file names with the following captions:

NativePlant1	Achillea
NativePlant4	Hedysarum
NativePlant3	Gaillardia
NativePlant5	Oenothera

Next let's remove the backgrounds of the two photos on slide 3.

21   Click the left photo, which selects the caption box, and then click again to select the photo. On the **Format** tool tab, in the **Adjust** group, click the **Remove Background** button to display the **Background Removal** tool tab and mark the areas of the photo that will be removed.

The thumbnail in the Thumbnails pane shows what the flower will look like after its background is removed.

22   Drag the handles on the frame surrounding the flower until the entire flower is visible within the frame. Then on the **Background Removal** tool tab, in the **Close** group, click the **Keep Changes** button.

23   Repeat steps 17 and 18 to remove the background of the photo on the right. Then click a blank area of the slide to review the results.

Gaillardia   Oenothera

The flowers stand out vividly against the plain slide background.

Let's experiment with some artistic effects.

24   Select the photo on the left, and then on the **Format** tool tab, in the **Adjust** group, click the **Artistic Effects** button to display a menu containing the **Artistic Effects** gallery.

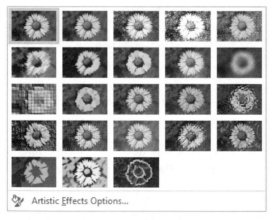

You can choose from a wide variety of effects in the Artistic Effects gallery.

25   Point to each thumbnail in turn to display a live preview of the photo with the effect applied. Then click the third thumbnail in the second row (**Paint Brush**), which makes the photo resemble a painting.

26   Repeat steps 23 and 24 for the photo on the right.

Finally, let's replace the title with the title slide layout from a different photo album.

27   Click slide **1**, and on the **Home** tab, in the **Slides** group, click the **New Slide** arrow, and at the bottom of the menu, click **Reuse Slides** to open the **Reuse Slides** pane.

28   In the pane, click **Browse**, click **Browse File**, and browse to the **Chapter08** practice file folder. Then double-click the **NativePlants** presentation, which contains one slide.

   TIP This slide was based on one from the Contemporary Photo Album template available from the New page of the Backstage view.

29   In the **Reuse Slides** pane, click **Slide 1** to insert it after the title slide of the **My Photo Album** presentation. Then close the pane.

30   Delete the original title slide. Then to showcase the photos, apply the **Retrospect** theme to the photo album.

The photo album's theme should reflect the subject matter and set off but not compete with the photographs.

❌ CLEAN UP Save the My Photo Album presentation, and then close it.

Alt text

Alt (alternate) text is a description associated with a graphic object that enables people with vision or other impairments to determine what the object is. You attach alt text to objects to improve the accessibility of presentations that will be viewed on the screen without a presenter.

To attach alt text to a graphic object:

1   Select the object, and on the **Format** tool tab, click the **Format Shape** dialog box launcher to display the **Format** pane corresponding to the type of object selected.
2   In the **Format** pane, click the **Size & Properties** icon to display that page, and then click **Alt Text**.
3   Enter a title and description for the graphic object, and then close the pane.

If you need to attach alt text to a graphic object that has several components, such as a diagram, standard practice is to attach text to each component. An easier method is to use the screen clipping tool to create an image of the entire object and then insert that image in place of the object. That way, you can attach alt text only once. For information about using the screen clipping tool, see "Capturing screen clippings" in Chapter 9, "Add other enhancements."

Customizing diagrams

We've already shown you how to use SmartArt to create a diagram, and we've shown you how to move and size it and apply simple formatting. But many diagrams involve different levels of information and benefit from more sophisticated formatting techniques. After you create a basic diagram, you can customize it at any time by using the commands on the Design and Format tool tabs.

Use the commands on the Design tool tab to make changes such as the following:

- Add and change the hierarchy of shapes.

    TIP You can remove a shape by selecting it and then pressing the Delete key. You can also rearrange shapes by dragging them.

- Switch to a different layout of the same type or a different type.

   TIP If some of the text in the original diagram doesn't fit in the new layout, that text is not shown. However, it is retained so that you don't have to re-enter it if you change the layout again.

Use the commands on the Format tool tab to customize individual shapes in the following ways:

- Change an individual shape—for example, change a square to a star to make it stand out.

- Apply a built-in shape style.

- Change the color, outline, or effect of a selected shape.

- Format the text in a shape.

TIP If you customize a diagram and then decide you preferred the original version, you can revert to the original by clicking the Reset Graphic button in the Reset group on the Design tool tab.

In this exercise, you'll customize an organization chart by adding subordinate shapes. You'll change the layout of the chart as a whole and then change the color, size, and text of individual shapes.

➔ SET UP You need the JuneMeeting presentation located in the Chapter08 practice file folder to complete this exercise. Open the presentation, and then follow the steps.

1 Display slide **5**, click the diagram to activate it, and then select the **Ryan Danner** shape for manipulation.

2 On the **Design** tool tab, in the **Create Graphic** group, click the **Add Shape** arrow, and then click **Add Shape Below**.

3 Open the **Text** pane, and to the right of the new bullet symbol, enter Jerry Orman as the third-level bullet point.

4 Press **Enter** to add a duplicate shape at the same level in the hierarchy.

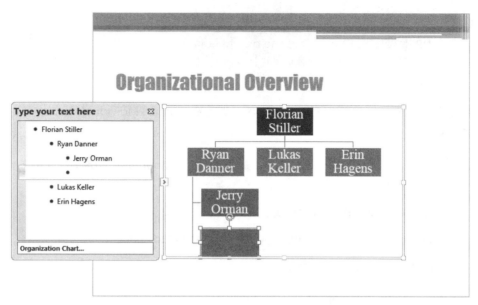

The colors of the shapes in the diagram reflect the theme color scheme.

TROUBLESHOOTING Our instructions assume you are entering text in the Text pane. Pressing Enter in a diagram shape enters a new paragraph in the same shape instead of creating a new shape.

5   Enter **Nate Sun**.

6   In the **Text** pane, click to the right of **Erin Hagens**, press **Enter** to add a new shape at the same level, press **Tab** to make the new shape subordinate, and then enter **Sarah Davis**.

7   In the diagram, select the **Florian Stiller** shape for manipulation, click the **Add Shape** arrow in the **Create Graphic** group, and then click **Add Assistant**.

8   In the **Text** pane, click to the right of the new arrow bullet symbol, and enter **Andy Ruth**. Then close the **Text** pane.

9   In the diagram, select the **Nate Sun** shape for manipulation, and then in the **Create Graphic** group, click the **Promote** button to move the selected shape up one level in the hierarchy.

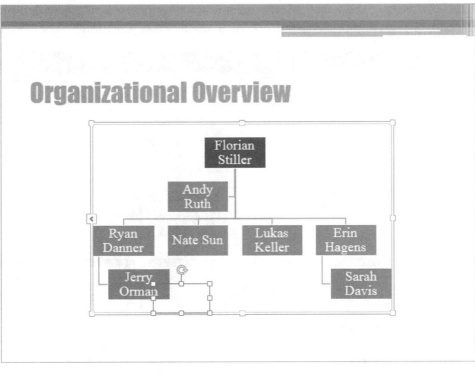

Nate Sun is now a peer of his former manager.

TROUBLESHOOTING Don't worry if your chart still shows the box and handles in the former location of the Nate Sun shape. They will disappear when you work on a different shape.

10 Drag the handles around the frame of the expanded diagram until it fills the available space on the slide.

Now let's switch to a different diagram layout and style.

11 On the **Design** tool tab, display the **Layouts** gallery, and point to each thumbnail in turn to show a live preview of the various layout options for an organization chart. Then click the second thumbnail in the second row (**Hierarchy**).

TIP Some of the layouts allow you to insert pictures of people in addition to their names.

12 Display the **SmartArt Styles** gallery, and after previewing the available styles, in the **3-D** area, click the last thumbnail in the first row (**Cartoon**).

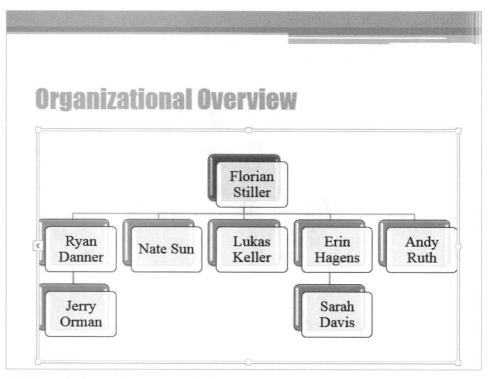

The Hierarchy layout does not provide for assistants, so the Andy Ruth shape now appears on the same level as the four managers.

Let's turn our attention to some of the individual shapes, which can be enhanced with formatting.

13 Andy Ruth is an assistant, not a manager, so select his background shape, and on the **Format** tool tab, in the **Shape Styles** group, click the **Shape Fill** button. Then in the **Theme Colors** palette, click the tan swatch (**Tan, Text 2**).

14 Select the **Florian Stiller** shape for manipulation, and then in the **Shapes** group, click the **Larger** button four times.

15   In the **Shape Styles** group, click the **Shape Fill** button, and then in the **Theme Colors** palette, click the fourth swatch in the fifth column (**Gray-50%, Accent 1, Lighter 40%**)

16   To make the text in the shape a contrasting color, in the **WordArt Styles** group, click the **Text Fill** button and in the **Theme Colors** palette, click the **White, Background 1** swatch.

17   Click outside the diagram frame to display the final result.

You can use shape size and color, in addition to text color, to clarify a hierarchy diagram.

❌ CLEAN UP Close the JuneMeeting presentation, saving your changes if you want to.

Formatting charts

You already know how to plot data in simple charts and how to edit that data in the associated Microsoft Excel worksheet. Often, you will need nothing more than these basic techniques to be able to convey your numeric data in a visual format. However, for those times when you need more than a basic chart, PowerPoint provides formatting capabilities that enable you to produce just the effect you want.

If you decide that the type of chart you selected doesn't adequately depict the most important characteristics of your data, you can change the type at any time. There are 10 chart types, each with two-dimensional and three-dimensional variations, and you can customize each aspect of each variation. Common chart types include the following:

- **Column charts**   Use to show how values change over time.
- **Bar charts**   Use to show the values of several items at one point in time.
- **Line graphs**   Use to show erratic changes in values over time.
- **Pie charts**   Use to show how parts relate to the whole.

If you don't want to spend a lot of time on a chart, you can apply the predefined combinations of formatting from the Chart Layouts and Chart Styles groups on the Design tool tab to create sophisticated charts with a minimum of effort. You can also click the Chart Styles button to the right of a selected chart to switch to a different predefined set of formatting and a different color scheme.

If you want to add an element to a chart, including trend lines, bars, and other lines, you can either click the Add Chart Element button in the Chart Layouts group on the Design tab, or you can click the Chart Elements button to the right of a selected chart and then make your selection from the Chart Elements pane.

Finally, if you want more control over the appearance of your chart, you can use the commands on the Format tool tab. It is worth exploring these options so that you know how to do the following:

- Add shapes.

- Format individual elements such as titles, axes, data labels, and gridlines.

- Customize the walls and floor or otherwise manipulate a three-dimensional chart.

- Customize the look of shapes.

- Add and format fancy text (WordArt).

- Arrange objects precisely.

- Precisely control the overall size of the chart.

You can double-click almost any chart element to change its attributes. For example, you can double-click an axis to display the Format Axis pane, where you can change the scale, tick marks, label position, line style, and other aspects of the axis. If you have trouble double-clicking some of the smaller chart elements, select the element you want to format from the Chart Elements list in the Current Selection group on the Format tool tab, and then click the Format Selection button in the same group to display the Format pane for the selection.

If you make extensive modifications to the design of a chart, you might want to save it as a template. Then when you want to plot similar data in the future, you can avoid having to repeat all the changes by applying the template as a custom chart type.

In this exercise, you'll modify the appearance of a chart by changing its chart type and style. You'll change the color of the plot area and the color of two data series. You'll then hide gridlines and change the layout to display titles and a datasheet. After adding an annotation in a text box, you'll save the chart as a template.

8

SET UP You need the SavingWater presentation located in the Chapter08 practice file folder to complete this exercise. Open the presentation, and then follow the steps.

1 Display slide **14**, and click the blank area above the chart legend to activate the chart without selecting any of its elements.

   TROUBLESHOOTING Be sure to click a blank area inside the chart frame. Clicking any of its elements will activate that element, not the chart as a whole.

2 On the **Design** tool tab, in the **Type** group, click the **Change Chart Type** button to open the **Change Chart Type** dialog box.

In the Change Chart Type dialog box, each chart category provides several different design options.

3   To change the column chart to a line chart, click **Line** in the right pane, and then double-click the fourth thumbnail (**Line with Markers**).

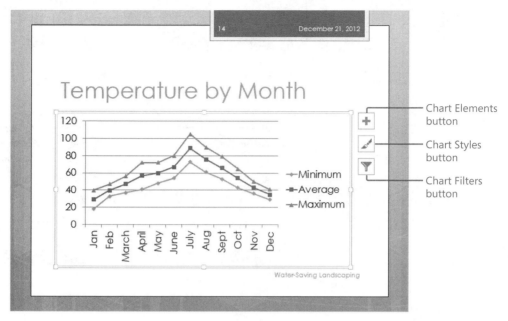

The temperature data plotted as a line chart.

The three buttons to the right of the chart area provide easy ways to add an element to or remove an element from the chart (**Chart Elements**), display thumbnails of pre-defined styles and color combinations (**Chart Styles**), and hide or display categories and series (**Chart Filters**).

SEE ALSO For information about the Chart Filters button, see "Plotting charts" in Chapter 5, "Add simple visual enhancements."

4   To the right of the chart, click the **Chart Styles** button to open the **Chart Styles** pane with the **Style** page displayed.

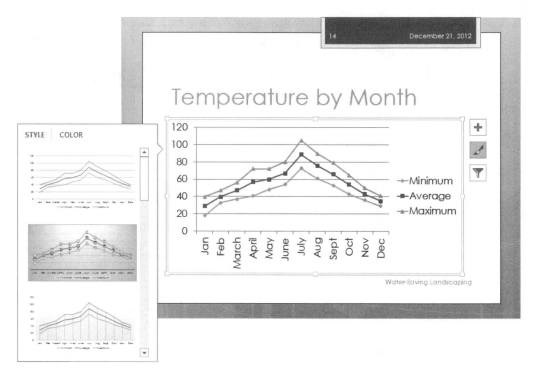

By making a selection from the Chart Styles pane, you can quickly switch to a different background or data marker style.

5   In the pane, click the second thumbnail (**Style 2**). Notice that the chart background is now shaded with a blue gradient, the value axis has disappeared, and the data points are now represented as circles containing their values.

6   At the top of the **Chart Styles** pane, click **Color**, and in the **Colorful** area, click any color in the fourth row. Then click the **Chart Styles** button to close the pane.

     Let's change the color of the plot area, which is the area between the axes that contains the data markers. (PowerPoint treats this area as a shape.)

7   Move the pointer over the chart, and when a ScreenTip indicates you are pointing to the plot area, click to select it.

8   On the **Format** tool tab, in the **Shape Styles** group, click the **Shape Fill** button, and in the menu, click **Eyedropper**.

9   Move the **Eyedropper** over the upper-left corner of the slide, and click to transfer the color under the Eyedropper to the selected plot area. Then click away from the chart.

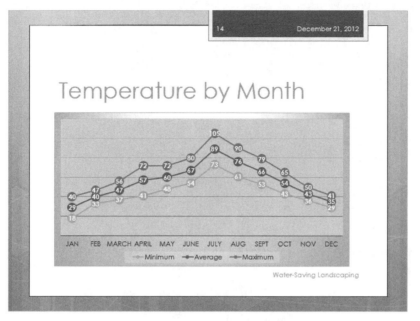

The line chart with customized data markers and plot area.

TIP To change several aspects of the plot area, right-click the area and then click Format Plot Area to open the Format Plot Area pane. You can then change the fill, border, and special effects in one location.

Now let's change the color of one of the data series and then remove the horizontal gridlines from the chart.

10   Select the chart. Then on the **Format** tool tab, in the **Current Selection** group, click the **Chart Elements** arrow, and in the list, click **Series "Maximum"** to select all the data points of that series.

11   In the **Current Selection** group, click the **Format Selection** button to open the **Format Data Series** pane, and then click the **Fill & Line** icon to display the **Line** page.

You can change several aspects of the selected data series on the pages of this pane.

TROUBLESHOOTING If the Marker page is displayed, click Line to display that page.

12   On the **Line** page, click **Solid line**. Then click the **Outline color** button, and in the **Standard Colors** palette, click the first swatch (**Dark Red**).

13   Click **Marker** to display the **Marker** page, and then if the **Fill** options are not expanded, click **Fill**.

14   Click **Solid Fill**, and then change the color to the same dark red.

15   Repeat step 14 for the marker border color, and then close the **Format Data Series** pane.

Suppose we want to draw more attention to the legend by moving it to the top or side of the chart. To do this, we need to select a different layout.

16 On the **Design** tool tab, in the **Chart Layouts** group, click the **Quick Layout** button to display the **Quick Layout** gallery.

You can quickly change the layout of the chart by selecting one of the predefined options.

17 Point to each thumbnail in turn to display its live preview, and then click the last thumbnail in the last row (**Layout 12**).

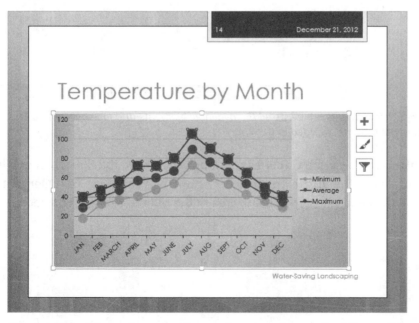

The chart now has a value axis, values no longer appear on the data markers, and the legend is positioned to the right of the chart.

TIP When you don't have a lot of data, choosing a layout that includes a datasheet—a table with all the values plotted in the chart—can clarify without adding clutter. In this case, we have too much data to add a datasheet.

18 To the right of the slide, click the **Chart Elements** button to open the **Chart Elements** pane.

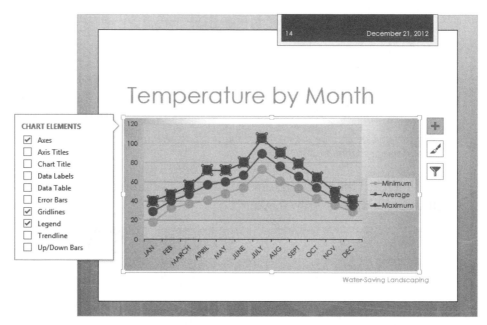

The Chart Elements pane lists all the available elements and indicates with a check mark those elements that are included in this chart.

19 In the pane, clear the **Gridlines** check box to remove the horizontal gridlines from the chart. Select the **Up/Down Bars** check box. Then click the **Chart Elements** button to close the pane, and click a blank area of the slide to release the selection.

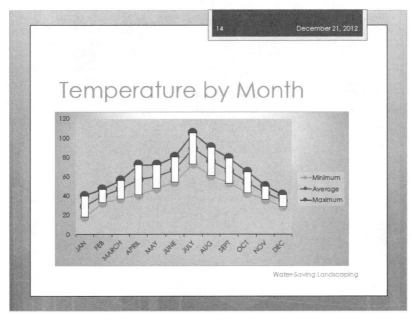

You have customized the chart to visually emphasize the seasonal variations.

In case we want to create a similarly formatted chart in the future, let's save this chart as a custom chart type.

20   Click a blank area of the chart. Then right-click the chart, and click **Save as Template** to open the **Save Chart Template** dialog box with the contents of your **Charts** folder (a subfolder of your **Templates** folder) displayed.

> **TROUBLESHOOTING** If the Charts folder does not appear in the Address bar, navigate to the AppData\Roaming\Microsoft\Templates\Charts folder in your user profile.

21   Save the custom chart type with the name Temperature By Month.

22   On the **Design** tool tab, in the **Type** group, click the **Change Chart Type** button, and in the left pane of the **Change Chart Type** dialog box, click **Templates** to display the template you just created.

8

In the future, you can click the custom template to create a chart with the same layout and formatting.

TIP To delete a custom chart type, click Manage Templates in the lower-left corner of the Change Chart Type dialog box, and then when File Explorer opens with your Charts folder displayed, right-click the template and click Delete. Close File Explorer, and then close the Change Chart Type dialog box.

23   Close the dialog box.

✖ CLEAN UP If you don't want to keep the chart template, delete it by following the directions in the preceding tip. Then close the SavingWater presentation, saving your changes if you want to.

Pie charts

Unlike, column, bar, and line charts, which plot at least two series of data points, pie charts plot just one series, with each data point, or *slice*, reflecting a fraction of the whole series. If you plot a multi-series chart and then change the chart type to a pie chart, PowerPoint hides all but the first series, retaining the hidden information in case you change back to a chart type capable of showing more than one series. You can switch to a different series by clicking the Chart Filters button to the right of the chart, selecting the series you want in the Series area of the Chart Filters pane, and clicking Apply.

When you plot a pie chart, you can use an effective formatting option that is not available with multi-series chart types. To draw attention to individual data points, you can "explode" the pie by dragging individual slides away from the center. Or you can double-click a slice to select it and display the Format Data Point pane, where you can set a precise Angle Of First Slice and Point Explosion percentage. For a really dynamic effect, you can animate the slices so that they move when you click the mouse button during presentation delivery.

TIP You can draw attention to the series in any chart by animating them. Start by animating the entire chart; for example, you might apply the Pulse effect. Then click the Effect Options button and click By Series to animate each series in turn. Alternatively, you can animate each category or even individual data points. For information about animation, see Chapter 10, "Add animations, audio, and videos."

8

Arranging graphics

After inserting pictures or drawing shapes in the approximate locations you want them on a slide, you can align them and change their stacking order by clicking the buttons in the Arrange group on the Format tool tab.

Clicking the Align Objects button in the Arrange group gives you access to commands for aligning individual or multiple graphics in several ways. For example, you can:

- Align graphics vertically by the left or right edges or centerline, or horizontally by the top or bottom edges or centerline.

- Distribute graphics evenly within their current space, either horizontally or vertically.

- Align graphics relative to the slide that contains them or to other selected objects.

TIP If you added pictures to a slide by clicking the Picture button in the Images group on the Insert tab, you can group them and then align and position them as a group the same way you would group shapes. However, if you have added them by clicking the Insert Picture From File button in a content placeholder, you cannot group them. For information about grouping shapes, see "Drawing shapes" in Chapter 5, "Add simple visual enhancements."

When graphics overlap each other, they are stacked. The stacking order is determined by the order in which you inserted the graphics. You can change the order by selecting a graphic and then clicking the Bring Forward or Send Backward button to move the graphic forward or backward in the stack one graphic at a time. To move the selected graphic to the top of the stack, click the Bring Forward arrow and then click Bring To Front in the list; to move it to the bottom, click the Send Backward arrow and then click Send To Back in the list.

TIP If you can't select a graphic because it is covered by others in the stack, click the Selection Pane button, and then in the Selection pane, select the graphic you want. To deliberately hide an object that you want to keep but not display on a slide, click the object's eye icon.

If your presentation must be compatible with assistive technology devices that make presentations accessible to people with disabilities, you should check the order assigned to objects in the Selection pane to ensure that they are in a logical tab or reading order. If necessary, adjust the order by using the Bring Forward or Send Backward arrows.

In this exercise, you'll align graphics in various ways, change their stacking order, and position them with the help of gridlines and guides.

SET UP You need the NaturalGardening presentation located in the Chapter08 practice file folder to complete this exercise. Open the presentation, and then follow the steps.

1   On slide **1**, select the three photos.

2   On the **Format** tool tab, in the **Arrange** group, click the **Align Objects** button, and then in the list, click **Distribute Vertically**. Notice that the middle photo moves down so that it is the same distance below the left photo as it is above the right one.

3   In the **Arrange** group, click the **Align Objects** button, and then click **Align Center**, which moves all the photos horizontally to the center of the slide.

Centering the photos stacks them so that you can no longer discern what the two lower ones are.

Let's experiment with the stacking order.

4   Click away from the stack to release the selection, and then click the obscured photo of the crow.

5   In the **Arrange** group, click the **Bring Forward** arrow, and then click **Bring to Front**, which obscures the middle photo.

Now let's try bringing the hidden middle photo forward in the stacking order.

6   In the **Arrange** group, click the **Selection Pane** button to open the **Selection** pane.

In the Selection pane, the top and middle photos are designated as content placeholders because they were inserted into placeholders.

7   In the **Selection** pane, click **Content Placeholder 10**, and then close the pane.

8   With the obscured middle photo selected, click the **Bring Forward** button in the **Arrange** group.

Enough experimenting. Let's make sure the photos are evenly stacked and spaced by using gridlines and guides.

9   On the **View** tab, in the **Show** group, select the **Gridlines** check box to display a faint dotted grid on the slide.

10   Drag the selected cat photo to the right and down, so that its right and bottom borders align with the first gridlines from the right and bottom edges of the slide.

11   Drag the crow photo so that its right and bottom borders align with the second gridlines from the right and bottom edges of the slide.

12 Drag the frog photo so that its right and bottom borders align with the third gridline from the right and bottom edges of the slide.

Gridlines make it easier to visually align multiple graphics.

13 On the **View** tab, click the **Show** dialog box launcher to open the **Grid and Guides** dialog box.

In the Grid And Guides dialog box, you specify the size of the grid and other options that control alignment tools.

14   In the **Grid settings** area, clear the **Display grid on screen** check box to turn off the grid.

15   In the **Guide settings** area, select the **Display drawing guides on screen** check box, and then click **OK**.

16   Point to the vertical guide (away from any text or objects), and drag it to the left, releasing it when the accompanying ScreenTip reads **3.50**. Then point outside the slide to the horizontal guide, and drag it down until its ScreenTip reads **0.50**.

      TROUBLESHOOTING If you move an object on the slide instead of a guide, click the Undo button, and then point outside the slide to drag the guide. If the slide occupies the entire Slide pane so that you can't point outside the slide, reduce the zoom percentage.

      TIP The ScreenTips show in inches how far each guide is from the 0 mark in the center of the slide. As you drag, numbers are skipped because the Snap Objects To Grid check box is selected in the Grid And Guides dialog box. This option snaps guides and graphics to the grid even when it is not displayed. You can turn off this option and set the spacing of the grid in the Grid And Guides dialog box.

17   Point to the selected frog photo, and drag it up and to the left until its left and bottom borders align with the guides.

18   Select all the photos. Then on the **Format** tool tab, in the **Arrange** group, click the **Align Objects** button, and in the list, click **Distribute Horizontally**.

19   Repeat step 18 to distribute the photos vertically.

20   On the **View** tab, in the **Show** group, clear the **Guides** check box.

      Now let's make a few more adjustments.

21   Click the rectangle shape behind the photos, and drag the rotating handle clockwise until the shape stretches diagonally across the slide. Then drag the shape's middle sizing handles until it is almost as wide as the photos.

22   With the shape still selected, on the **Format** tool tab, in the **Arrange** group, click the **Send Backward** arrow, and then click **Send to Back** so that the shape sits behind the slide title in addition to being behind the photos.

23   Click away from the slide to display the results.

On the finished slide, three equally spaced photos span a diagonal banner.

24   If you want, switch to **Reading** view for a full-screen view of the slide.

❌ CLEAN UP Close the NaturalGardening presentation, saving your changes if you want to.

8

Key points

- A growing trend among presenters is to create graphic-intensive rather than text-intensive presentations.

- If you want to move beyond simple diagrams, you need to know how to manipulate levels of text in shapes and how to format individual shapes and whole diagrams.

- It is important to remember that to be effective, charts need to be simple enough for people to grasp key trends at a glance.

- Knowing how to manipulate graphics on a slide will help you position, align, and stack them to get the effect you want.

Chapter at a glance

Add

Add WordArt text,
page 264

Insert

Insert symbols and equations,
page 267

Seasonal Temperatures				
	Winter❄	Spring☀	Summer☀	Fall✔
Minimum	18	41	73	43
Average	29	57	89	54
Maximum	40	72	105	65

Temperature by Season

To convert to Celsius: $\frac{F-32}{9} x\, 5$

Capture

Capture screen clippings,
page 274

TOOLS WISH LIST

New tablet for travel

Attach

Attach actions to text or objects,
page 281

Top Issues Facing the Company

- External industry pressures
- External customer issues
- High profile internal issues

Add other enhancements

9

IN THIS CHAPTER, YOU WILL LEARN HOW TO

- Add WordArt text.

- Insert symbols and equations.

- Capture screen clippings.

- Create hyperlinks.

- Attach actions to text or objects.

We have looked at some of the more common graphic elements you can add to a slide to reinforce its concepts or make it more attention grabbing or visually appealing. But for some slides, you might need visual elements that are more specialized than pictures, diagrams, and charts. You might also need to add navigation aids or ways to access supporting materials that are external to the presentation.

In this chapter, you'll use WordArt text to create a fancy title. You'll also insert a symbol, build a simple equation, and capture a screen shot from a webpage. Finally, you'll add hyperlinks and action buttons that jump to slides within a presentation, open files and message windows, and display webpages.

PRACTICE FILES To complete the exercises in this chapter, you need the practice files contained in the Chapter09 practice file folder. For more information, see "Download the practice files" in this book's Introduction.

Adding WordArt text

With WordArt, you can create sophisticated text objects that you can move independently, just like text boxes. To insert a WordArt text object, click the WordArt button in the Text group on the Insert tab, and then in the WordArt gallery, click the style you want. Placeholder text in that style appears in a text box in the middle of the slide. After replacing the text, you can edit it, adjust its formatting, and change the WordArt style at any time.

TIP You can select existing text in a placeholder or text box and then click a thumbnail in the WordArt Styles gallery to apply a fancy style to the text.

When a WordArt text object is selected, you can use the commands on the Format tool tab to format it to meet your needs. For example, you can change the fill and outline colors, add effects such as shadows and beveled edges, and change the text direction and alignment.

In this exercise, you'll insert a new WordArt text object and then modify it.

➡ SET UP You need the OrganizationA presentation located in the Chapter09 practice file folder to complete this exercise. Open the presentation, and then follow the steps.

1   With slide **1** displayed, on the **Insert** tab, in the **Text** group, click the **WordArt** button to display the **WordArt** gallery.

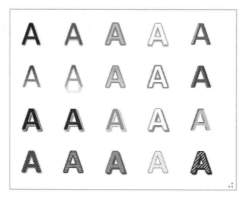

From the WordArt gallery, you can choose from 20 predefined text styles in the presentation's theme colors.

2   In the gallery, click the third thumbnail in the first row (**Fill – Orange, Accent 2, Outline - Accent 2**) to insert a WordArt text object with the selected style into the slide.

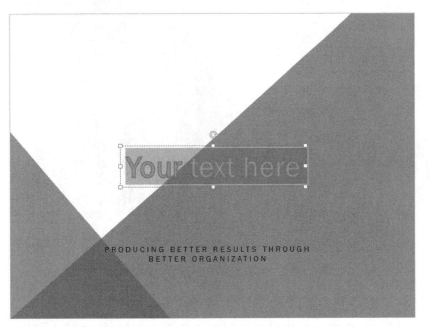

The placeholder WordArt text is formatted according to the style you selected.

3   With the object selected for editing, enter Organization 101.

4   Click the border of the object to select it for manipulation.

TIP A WordArt text object works just like a text box. You click it once to select it for editing and then click its border to select it for manipulation. For information about text boxes, see "Adding text boxes" in Chapter 4, "Work with slide text."

5   Move and resize the object so that its frame spans the middle of the top half of the slide.

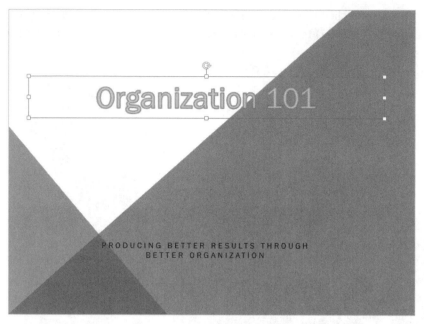

You can move and size a WordArt text object just like any other text box.

Now let's enhance the WordArt text by formatting it in various ways.

6   Select the text, and on the **Format** tool tab, display the **WordArt Styles** gallery, and try a few other styles. When you finish exploring, click the fourth thumbnail in the first row (**Fill – White, Outline – Accent 1, Shadow**).

7   With the text still selected, in the **WordArt Styles** group, click the **Text Fill** arrow. Then in the **Theme Colors** palette, click the fourth swatch in the orange column (**Orange, Accent 2, Lighter 40%**).

8   In the **WordArt Styles** group, click the **Text Outline** arrow, and then in the **Theme Colors** palette, click the fourth swatch in the third column (**Ice Blue, Background 2, Darker 50%**).

9   In the **WordArt Styles** group, click the **Text Effects** button, point to **Transform**, and then in the **Warp** area, click the last thumbnail in the first row (**Triangle Down**).

10   With the text still selected, click the **Text Effects** button again, point to **Reflection**, and then in the **Reflection Variations** area, click the second thumbnail in the second row (**Half Reflection, 4 pt offset**).

TIP The reflection options vary by the amount of reflection and the starting point below the text.

11   Exaggerate the triangle effect by dragging the handle in the middle of the bottom of the frame downward until the reflection sits just above the slide subtitle.

12   Click an edge of the slide to release the selection.

You can use text effects to add drama to presentation titles.

❌ CLEAN UP Close the OrganizationA presentation, saving your changes if you want to.

Inserting symbols and equations

Some slide text requires characters not found on a standard keyboard. These characters might include the copyright (©) or registered trademark (®) symbols, currency symbols (such as € or £), Greek letters, or letters with accent marks. Or you might want to add arrows (such as ⬈ or ⬉) or graphic icons (such as ☎ or ✈). PowerPoint gives you easy access to a huge array of symbols that you can easily insert into any slide. Like graphics, symbols can add visual information or eye-appeal to a slide. However, they are different from graphics in that they are characters associated with a particular font.

TIP You can insert some common symbols by typing a keyboard combination. For example, if you enter two consecutive dashes followed by a word and a space, PowerPoint changes the two dashes to a professional-looking em-dash—like this one. (This symbol gets its name from the fact that it was originally the width of the character *m*.) To use these keyboard shortcuts, display the Backstage view, click Options, and then, on the Proofing page of the PowerPoint Options dialog box, click AutoCorrect Options. On the AutoCorrect page of the AutoCorrect dialog box, ensure that the Replace Text As You Type check box is selected. Then on the AutoFormat As You Type page, select or clear check boxes in the Replace Text As You Type area.

You can insert mathematical symbols, such as π (pi) or ∑ (sigma, or summation), the same way you would insert any other symbol. But you can also create entire mathematical equations on a slide. You can insert some predefined equations, including the Quadratic Formula, the Binomial Theorem, and the Pythagorean Theorem, with a few clicks. If you need something other than these standard equations, you can build your own equations by using a library of mathematical symbols. Equations are accurately rendered mathematical formulas that appear in the slide as fields.

The buttons for inserting symbols and equations are in the Symbols group on the Insert tab.

■ Click the **Symbol** button to display the **Symbol** dialog box.

In the Symbol dialog box you can select from hundreds of symbols and special characters in a variety of fonts.

TIP The Recently Used Symbols area of the Symbol dialog box is dynamic. If you have already explored this dialog box, the symbols you have added to your slides are displayed in this area.

- Click the **Equation** arrow to display the **Equation** gallery, which includes commonly used equations.

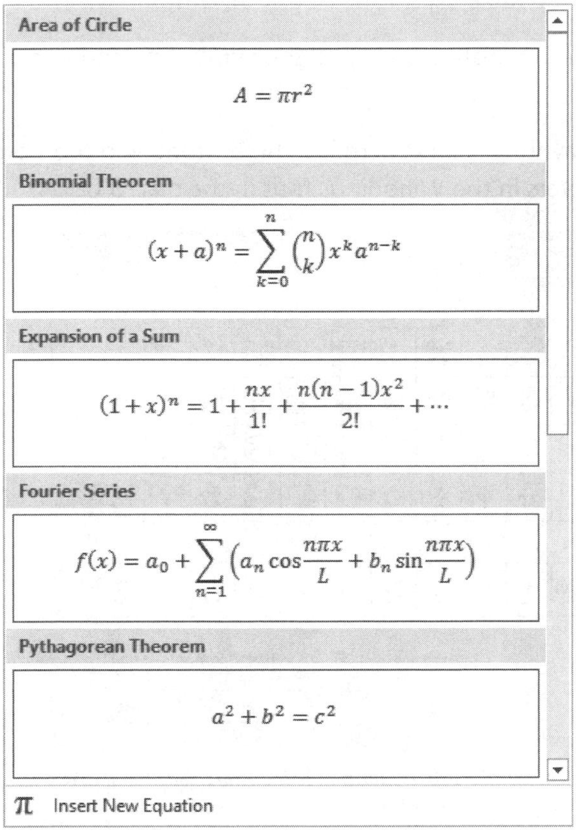

Area of Circle

$$A = \pi r^2$$

Binomial Theorem

$$(x + a)^n = \sum_{k=0}^{n} \binom{n}{k} x^k a^{n-k}$$

Expansion of a Sum

$$(1 + x)^n = 1 + \frac{nx}{1!} + \frac{n(n-1)x^2}{2!} + \cdots$$

Fourier Series

$$f(x) = a_0 + \sum_{n=1}^{\infty} \left(a_n \cos\frac{n\pi x}{L} + b_n \sin\frac{n\pi x}{L} \right)$$

Pythagorean Theorem

$$a^2 + b^2 = c^2$$

π Insert New Equation

Clicking a predefined equation adds it to the slide.

- Click the **Equation** button to insert a box where you can enter an equation. The **Design** tool tab is added to the ribbon, providing access to mathematical symbols, structures such as fractions and radicals, and the **Equation Options** dialog box.

In this exercise, you'll add a symbol to a slide. Then you'll build a simple equation and display it in various ways.

 SET UP You need the NewWaterSaving presentation located in the Chapter09 practice file folder to complete this exercise. Open the presentation, and then follow the steps.

1   Display slide **13**, and in the table, click to the right of **Winter**.

2   On the **Insert** tab, in the **Symbols** group, click the **Symbol** button to open the **Symbol** dialog box.

3   In the dialog box, display the **Font** list, scroll to the bottom, and then click **Wingdings** to display all the characters in the Wingdings font in the dialog box.

Wingdings is one of several symbol fonts available. It includes graphic icons such as scissors, a book, an hourglass, and an airplane.

4   Click an icon that represents winter, such as the snowflake in the fourth row, and click **Insert** to enter the selected symbol at the cursor. Then close the dialog box.

5   Repeat steps 1 through 4 to insert symbols for **Spring**, **Summer**, and **Fall**, switching to different fonts if necessary to find the symbols you want. (We used Webdings for the spring showers and the fall lightning bolt, and Wingdings for the summer sun.)

	Seasonal Temperatures			
	Winter❄	Spring☂	Summer✳	Fall✔
Minimum	18	41	73	43
Average	29	57	89	54
Maximum	40	72	105	65

You can select a symbol and format it by clicking buttons in the Font group of the Home tab.

Next let's insert an equation.

6   Click a blank area of the slide to deselect the table. Then on the **Insert** tab, in the **Symbols** group, click the **Equation** button to insert a box containing an equation placeholder near the middle of the slide. Notice that the **Design** tool tab for equations is active on the ribbon.

7   Select the equation box for manipulation, and drag it to the lower-left corner of the slide, releasing the mouse button when the smart guides indicate that it is aligned with the table above and the footer on the right.

The box in which you build an equation works the same as a text box.

8   Click anywhere in the equation placeholder, and press the **Home** key to position the cursor to the left of the placeholder text. Then enter **To convert to Celsius:** (including the colon and a space).

TROUBLESHOOTING The equation placeholder is a field that is treated as a unit. Clicking the placeholder positions the cursor within the field. You want to enter ordinary text to the left of the placeholder, so be sure to press the Home key rather than simply clicking at the placeholder's left end.

9   Click the equation placeholder, and on the **Design** tool tab, in the **Structures** group, click the **Fraction** button to display the **Fraction** gallery.

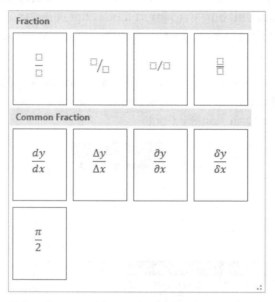

This gallery provides ready-made common fractions, in addition to the structures for creating your own fractions.

10   In the gallery, click the first thumbnail in the first row (**Stacked Fraction**), which inserts the structure for a simple fraction in the field at the cursor.

11   Click the top box in the fraction structure, and enter **F-32**. Then click the bottom box, and enter **9**.

12 Press **End** to move the cursor to the right of the fraction structure. Then press the **Spacebar**, enter x, press the **Spacebar**, and enter 5. Then click a blank area of the slide.

This equation subtracts 32 from the Fahrenheit temperature, divides the result by 9, and then multiplies that result by 5 to yield the Celsius temperature.

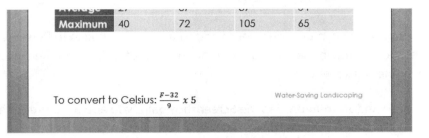

The F variable in the equation is automatically formatted as italic.

PowerPoint has taken care of formatting the fraction so that it looks professional, but let's examine the other available display options.

13 Click the fraction, and then on the **Design** tool tab, in the **Tools** group, click the **Linear** button to change the fraction's format.

The fraction is easier to edit in Linear format.

14 In the **Tools** group, click the **Professional** button to return to the structured format.

15 Right-click the fraction, point to **Math Options**, and then click **Change to Skewed Fraction**.

16 Right-click again, point to **Math Options**, and then click **Change to Stacked Fraction**.

❌ CLEAN UP Close the NewWaterSaving presentation, saving your changes if you want to.

Capturing screen clippings

If you rely on the web as a source of the information you use in your daily life, you might want to include that information in a PowerPoint presentation. PowerPoint 2013 provides a screen clipping tool that you can use to capture an image of anything that is visible on your computer screen.

After you display the content you want to add to a slide, you switch to PowerPoint and click the Screenshot button in the Images group on the Insert tab. You can then insert a screen clipping in one of two ways:

- Click a window thumbnail in the **Screenshot** gallery to add a picture of that window to the slide at the cursor.

- Click **Screen Clipping** at the bottom of the menu, and drag across the part of the screen you want to capture, so only that part is added to the slide as a picture.

In this exercise, you'll capture a screen clipping from a website and then add it to a slide.

SET UP You need the OrganizationB presentation located in the Chapter09 practice file folder to complete this exercise. Be sure that you are connected to the Internet before beginning this exercise. Open the presentation, and then follow the steps.

1   Display slide **4**.

2   Start your web browser, and display a website from which you want to capture a screen clipping. For example, we found a picture of the Microsoft Surface tablet computer on *microsoft.com*.

3   Activate the **OrganizationB** presentation. Then on the **Insert** tab, in the **Images** group, click the **Screenshot** button to display a menu that contains a gallery of the open windows from which you can capture a screen clipping.

Clicking the thumbnail of a window inserts an image of that window in the slide.

4 At the bottom of the gallery, click **Screen Clipping**. Notice that PowerPoint minimizes its program window and covers the entire screen with a translucent white layer.

TIP If you change your mind about capturing the screen clipping, press the Esc key to remove the white layer.

5 On the webpage, point to the upper-left corner of the image you want, and drag down and to the right to select it. For example, we dragged across the picture of the Microsoft Surface tablet.

As you drag, the white translucent layer is removed from the selected area.

When you release the mouse button, PowerPoint inserts the screen clipping into the center of the slide.

The screen clipping is a picture that can be formatted by using the commands on the Format tool tab, just like any other picture.

SEE ALSO For information about formatting pictures, see "Inserting pictures and clip art images" in Chapter 5, "Add simple visual enhancements," and "Editing pictures" in Chapter 8, "Fine-tune visual elements."

❌ CLEAN UP Close the OrganizationB presentation, saving your changes if you want to.

Creating hyperlinks

Presentations that are intended to be viewed electronically often include hyperlinks to provide access to supporting information. That information might be on a hidden slide, in another presentation, in a file on your computer or your organization's network, or on a website. If you use Microsoft Outlook, you can also use a hyperlink to open an email message window so that people viewing the presentation can easily contact you.

You can attach a hyperlink to any selected object, such as text, a graphic, a shape, or a table. Clicking the hyperlinked object then takes you directly to the linked location. Editing the object does not disrupt the hyperlink; however, deleting the object also deletes the hyperlink.

In this exercise, you'll create one hyperlink that opens an email message window and another that opens a document. You'll also create a hyperlink with an informative ScreenTip that starts the default web browser and jumps to a specific webpage.

 SET UP You need the OrganizationC presentation and the Procedures document located in the Chapter09 practice file folder to complete this exercise. Be sure that an email program is configured on your computer and that you are connected to the Internet before beginning this exercise. Open the presentation, and then follow the steps.

1   Display slide **9**, and in the lower-right shape, select the words **Contact Info**.

2   On the **Insert** tab, in the **Links** group, click the **Hyperlink** button to open the **Insert Hyperlink** dialog box.

    KEYBOARD SHORTCUT Press Ctrl+K to open the Insert Hyperlink dialog box. For a complete list of keyboard shortcuts, see "Keyboard shortcuts" at the end of this book.

    Let's set up this hyperlink so that it starts an email message when clicked.

3   In the **Link to** pane, click **E-mail Address** to display the options needed for an email hyperlink in the dialog box.

If you have already created links to email addresses, they appear in the Recently Used E-Mail Addresses box.

4   In the **E-mail address** box, enter david@consolidatedmessenger.com, and then in the **Subject** box, enter Organization presentation. Notice that PowerPoint changes the entry in the **E-mail address** box to **mailto:david@ consolidatedmessenger.com**.

5   Click **OK** to close the dialog box, and then click away from the diagram. Notice that **Contact Info** is now underlined and gray (the color designated by the presentation's theme for hyperlinks).

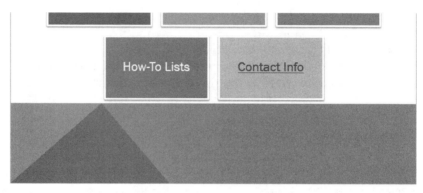

You can attach hyperlinks to the shapes in a diagram as easily as you can to text or a graphic.

6   Switch to **Reading** view, and then in the diagram, click **Contact Info** to start your email program and open a message window with the specified email address entered in the **To** box and the specified subject entered in the **Subject** box.

7   Close the message window without sending the message, and then press **Esc** to return to **Normal** view.

    Now let's attach a hyperlink that opens a file to a graphic.

8   Display slide **5**, and click the graphic.

9   On the **Insert** tab, in the **Links** group, click the **Hyperlink** button. Then in the **Insert Hyperlink** dialog box, in the **Link to** pane, click **Existing File or Web Page** to display the contents of the last folder you accessed.

You can use the Look In box to navigate to a different folder on your computer, or you can click the Browse The Web button to locate a website.

10   With the contents of the **Chapter09** folder displayed, double-click the **Procedures** document.

11   Switch to **Reading** view, and point to the graphic to display a ScreenTip of the hyperlinked file path. Then click the graphic to start Microsoft Word 2013 and open a document about office procedures.

TIP The pointer changes to a pointing hand when you move it over a hyperlinked object. Any time the pointer has this shape, you can click to follow a hyperlink.

12   Exit Word, and then press **Esc** to return to **Normal** view.

Next let's turn a different graphic into a hyperlink that jumps to a webpage.

13   Display slide **6**, and then click the clock to the left of the table.

14   In the **Links** group, click the **Hyperlink** button, and then in the upper-right corner of the **Insert Hyperlink** dialog box, click **ScreenTip** to open the **Set Hyperlink ScreenTip** dialog box.

You can specify the text that will appear when someone points to the clock graphic.

15   In the **ScreenTip text** box, enter Check out this book, and then click **OK**.

16 At the bottom of the **Insert Hyperlink** dialog box, in the **Address** box, enter **http://shop.oreilly.com/product/9780735669093.do**, and click **OK**.

17 Display the slide in **Reading** view, and point to the clock graphic to display the ScreenTip you specified.

18 If you want, click the graphic to start your web browser and jump to the webpage for our book *Microsoft Outlook 2013 Step by Step*.

> **TROUBLESHOOTING** *Microsoft Outlook 2013 Step by Step* will be published by Microsoft Press and will be available from the O'Reilly Media online store in the first quarter of 2013. Before then, clicking the link will display a message that the page you are looking for is not available. If this message appears at a later date, the page address might have changed. If you want, you can search for the book from the message page.

19 Close the browser window, and then press **Esc** to return to **Normal** view.

❌ CLEAN UP **Close the OrganizationC presentation, saving your changes if you want to.**

Adding the same hyperlink to every slide

If you want the same hyperlink to appear on every slide in a presentation, you need to attach the hyperlink to text or an object on the presentation's primary slide master.

To attach a hyperlink to a primary slide master object so that it appears on all the slides in the presentation:

1 On the **View** tab, in the **Master Views** group, click the **Slide Master** button. Then in **Slide Master** view, click the primary master (the top thumbnail).

2 Either create a text box and enter text or insert an object to which you can attach the hyperlink.

> **TIP** You cannot attach a hyperlink to the default placeholders.

3 Select the text or object.

4 On the **Insert** tab, in the **Links** group, click the **Hyperlink** button.

5 In the **Insert Hyperlink** dialog box, set up the hyperlink as usual, and then click **OK**.

6 Switch to **Reading** view, and move through the presentation's slides, checking for the presence of the hyperlink.

Attaching actions to text or objects

In addition to attaching hyperlinks to text or objects by clicking the Hyperlink button, you can attach them by clicking the Action button, which is also in the Links group on the Insert tab. In the dialog box that opens, you can specify whether the action should take place when you point to the linked text or object or when you click it. You can designate a target to which PowerPoint should jump if the link is pointed to or clicked, or designate an action to perform such as starting a program or playing a sound.

If attaching an action to existing text or an object on a slide doesn't suit your needs, you can insert an action button. PowerPoint provides navigation action buttons (Back, Forward, Beginning, End, Home, and Return) and display action buttons (Document, Help, Information, Movie, and Sound), in addition to a generic action button that you can customize.

In this exercise, you'll attach an action that displays a hidden slide when a word is clicked. You'll also attach a sound that plays when you point to a slide title. Finally, you'll create action buttons that you can click to move between presentation slides and an overview slide.

➡ SET UP **You need the JulyMeeting presentation located in the Chapter09 practice file folder to complete this exercise. Open the presentation, and then follow the steps.**

1   Display slide **8**, switch to **Reading** view, and then click the **Next** button to move to the next slide. Press **Esc** to return to **Normal** view.

2   On the **Thumbnails** tab, notice that PowerPoint skipped over slide **9** because it is hidden.

Let's attach an action that jumps to slide 9 when it is clicked.

SEE ALSO For information about hiding slides, see "Adapting presentations for different audiences" in Chapter 13, "Prepare for delivery."

3   On slide **8**, select the words **Equipment replacement**.

4   On the **Insert** tab, in the **Links** group, click the **Action** button to open the **Action Settings** dialog box.

In the Action Settings dialog box, you can specify whether actions should occur when an object is clicked or pointed to.

5   On the **Mouse Click** page, in the **Action on click** area, click **Hyperlink to**, display its list, and then click **Slide** to open the **Hyperlink to Slide** dialog box.

The slide number of the hidden slide is enclosed in parentheses.

6   In the **Slide title** list, click **(9) Equipment Replacement**, and then click **OK**.

7   Click **OK** to close the **Action Settings** dialog box. Then notice that on the slide, the words *Equipment replacement* are now underlined and displayed in the color assigned by the theme to hyperlinks.

On a different slide, let's attach an action that plays a sound when you point to it.

8   Display slide **4**, and select **How Did We Do?**

9   In the **Links** group, click the **Action** button, and then in the **Action Settings** dialog box, click the **Mouse Over** tab. Notice that the options on this page are identical to the **Mouse Click** options.

10   Below the **Action on mouse over** area, select the **Play sound** check box. Then display the list of built-in sounds, click **Applause**, and click **OK**.

11   Switch to **Reading** view, and then point to **How Did We Do?** to play the Applause sound.

12   Right-click the screen, point to **Go to Slide**, and then click **8 Key Spending Areas**.

13   In the bulleted list, click **Equipment replacement** to jump to the hidden slide.

14   Press **Esc** to return to **Normal** view.

Now let's create and format two navigation action buttons that can be used to quickly jump to and from an overview slide.

15   Display slide **6**. Then on the **Insert** tab, in the **Illustrations** group, click the **Shapes** button to display the **Shapes** gallery.

16   In the **Action Buttons** area at the bottom of the gallery, click the **Action Button: Home** icon.

17   In the upper-right corner of the white area of the slide, drag the cross-shaped pointer to create a **Home** action button about half an inch square. When you release the mouse button, the **Action Settings** dialog box opens with the **Hyperlink to** option selected and **First Slide** in the box below. At the bottom of the dialog box, the **Highlight click** check box is selected, but dimmed to indicate that you cannot change this setting.

18   In the dialog box, display the **Hyperlink to** list, and click **Slide** to open the **Hyperlink to Slide** dialog box.

9

19 In the **Slide title** list, click **2. Agenda**, and then click **OK** twice to close the two dialog boxes.

20 With the action button still selected on the slide, on the **Format** tool tab, in the **Shape Styles** group, click the **More** button, and in the gallery, click the third thumbnail in the fourth row (**Subtle Effect – Olive Green, Accent 2**). Then click away from the button to display the results.

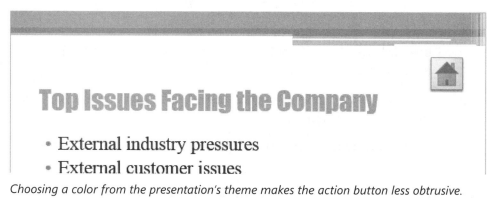

Choosing a color from the presentation's theme makes the action button less obtrusive.

When you click the action button in Reading view or Slide Show view, you'll jump to slide 2, which is an overview of slides 3 through 11. Referring back to this slide after showing half of the listed topics is a good idea, but you might want a quick way of jumping back to slide 6 so that you can resume the discussion.

21 Display slide **2**, and then on the **Insert** tab, in the **Illustrations** group, click the **Shapes** button to display the **Shapes** gallery.

22 In the **Action Buttons** area at the bottom of the gallery, click the **Action Button: Return** icon. Then in the upper-right corner of the white area of the slide, drag the cross pointer to create a **Return** action button about half an inch square. When you release the mouse button, the **Action Settings** dialog box opens with the **Hyperlink to** option set to **Last Slide Viewed**.

23 Click **OK** to accept this setting and close the **Action Settings** dialog box.

24 Change the color of the action button to one that is compatible with the background.

Agenda

- Review of key objectives
- How did we do?

Using the unobtrusive Return button, you can return to the last viewed slide.

25 Display slide **6**, switch to **Reading** view, and then click the **Home** action button to jump to slide **2**.

26 On slide **2**, click the **Return** action button to jump back to slide **6**, and then press **Esc** to return to **Normal** view.

❌ CLEAN UP Close the JulyMeeting presentation, saving your changes if you want to.

Key points

- Fancy titles created with WordArt can have much more impact than regular text.

- The Symbols dialog box provides access not only to the symbols you might need for a slide but also to little icons that can add pizzazz.

- You can construct complex math equations on your slides and have PowerPoint display them in traditional math formats.

- You can capture graphical information from websites or other programs for use on your slides.

- In electronic presentations, you can attach hyperlinks to text or objects to display a slide, presentation, file, or web address.

- Action buttons provide another convenient way to jump to specific locations, play sounds, or run programs.

9

Chapter at a glance

Animate

Animate with ready-made effects,
page 288

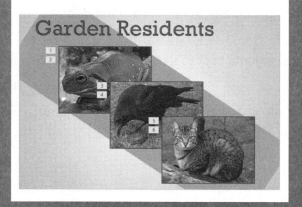

Add

Add audio content,
page 299

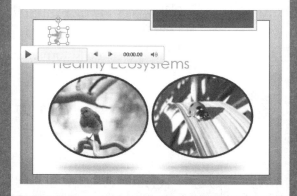

Insert

Insert and play videos,
page 303

Add animations, audio, and videos

10

IN THIS CHAPTER, YOU WILL LEARN HOW TO

- Animate with ready-made effects.
- Customize animation effects.
- Add audio content.
- Insert and play videos.

A Microsoft PowerPoint presentation is usually created to convey a lot of information in a short time. The difference between an adequate presentation and a great presentation often lies in the judicious use of animations, audio content, and videos. By incorporating these dynamic effects, you can grab and keep the attention of your audience. You can emphasize key points, control the focus of the discussion, and entertain in ways that will make your message memorable.

With Microsoft PowerPoint 2013, you have so many opportunities to add pizzazz to your slides that it is easy to end up with a presentation that looks more like an amateur experiment than a professional slide show. When you first start adding animations, audio content, and videos to your slides, it is best to err on the conservative side. As you gain more experience, you'll learn how to mix and match effects to get the results you want for a particular audience.

In this chapter, you'll apply predefined animations to titles, bullet points, and pictures. Then you'll change some of the animation settings to create custom animation schemes. You'll insert an audio clip and an audio file and make various adjustments to their settings. Finally, you'll insert two video files, edit one of them, and format them both.

PRACTICE FILES To complete the exercises in this chapter, you need the practice files contained in the Chapter10 practice file folder. For more information, see "Download the practice files" in this book's Introduction.

Animating with ready-made effects

With all the options available for creating engaging and lively presentations in PowerPoint, you no longer have to settle for static presentations. By applying various types of animations to the text and graphics on your slides, you can keep your audience focused and reinforce the message of your presentation.

You can animate text or an object to make it enter or leave a slide with a particular effect, to emphasize it in a certain way, or to move it across the slide along a particular path. Entrance effects are the most common. To apply one of the 13 ready-made entrance effects, you click the element you want to animate and then select the effect from the Animation gallery. To help you decide which effect to use, you can point to each in turn to display a live preview.

To really emphasize an element, you can animate it with more than one effect. And if you combine animation effects and want to apply the same combination to another object, you can simply copy the set with the Animation Painter, which functions the same way as the Format Painter.

TIP Animations can become tiresome, so it's best to choose one entrance effect for all the objects on your slides, varying only those objects you particularly want to emphasize.

In this exercise, you'll apply predefined animations to a title and subtitle on one slide, to bullet points on another slide, and to pictures on another.

➡ SET UP **You need the NaturalGardenA presentation located in the Chapter10 practice file folder to complete this exercise. Open the presentation, and then follow the steps.**

1   On slide **1**, click the slide title.

2   On the **Animations** tab, in the **Animation** group, click the **More** button to display a menu containing the **Animation** gallery.

   TIP If the menu containing a gallery has a handle in the lower-right corner, you can drag the handle upward until only a couple of rows of thumbnails are visible. This enables you to view the gallery's options while also viewing objects on the slide.

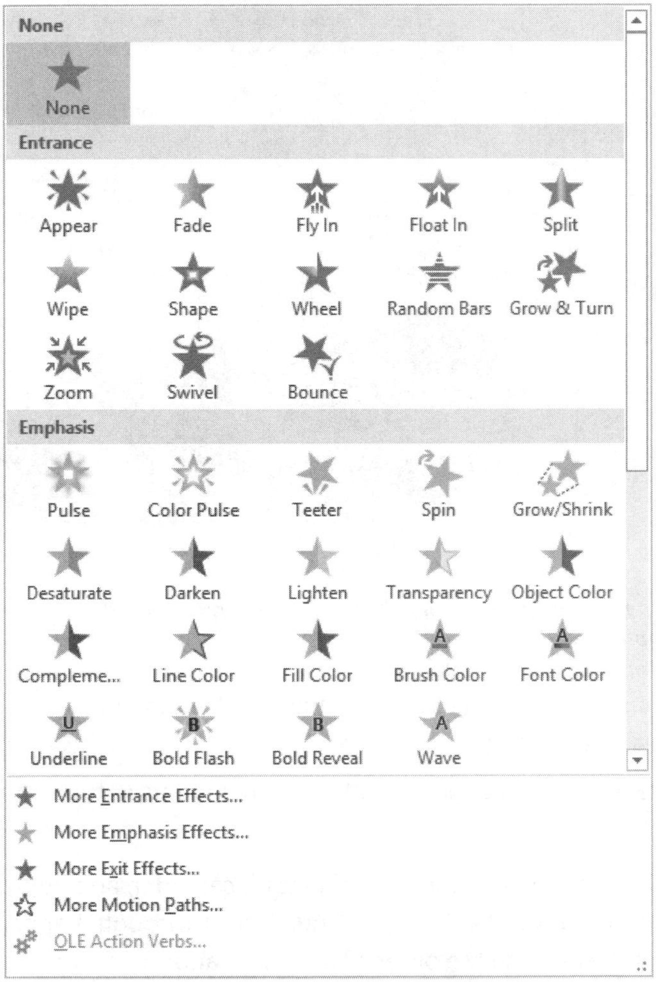

The Animation gallery showing the available Entrance and Emphasis animations. Out of sight are the Exit and Motion Path categories. You can click options at the bottom of the gallery to display more animation effects in each category.

3   In the **Entrance** area, click the **Shape** thumbnail. After PowerPoint displays a live preview of the animation effect, notice that a box containing the number **1** appears to the left of the title, indicating that this element will be the first one animated on this slide.

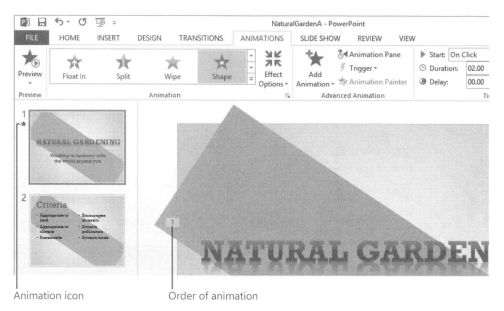

Animation icon   Order of animation

In the Thumbnails pane, the animation icon below the slide number indicates the presence of some form of animation on the slide.

4   Apply the **Shape** animation to the slide's subtitle. Notice that a box containing the number **2** appears to the left of the subtitle.

Now let's animate a list of bullet points so that each appears in turn with the selected animation effect.

5   Display slide **2**, click anywhere in the left content placeholder, and apply the **Shape** animation. Notice that boxes containing the numbers **1** through **3** appear to the left of the bullet points to indicate the order of their animations.

6   Repeat step 5 for the placeholder on the right.

7   In the **Preview** group, click the **Preview** button to display all the animations on slide **2** in the order specified by their animation boxes.

Next let's apply both an Entrance animation effect and an Emphasis animation effect to a couple of photographs.

8   Display slide **3**, click the frog photo, and apply the **Shape** animation.

9   In the **Advanced Animation** group, click the **Add Animation** button, and then in the **Animation** gallery, in the **Emphasis** area, click **Pulse**.

10   Click the **Preview** button to activate both the **Shape** and **Pulse** animations. Notice that boxes containing the numbers **1** and **2** appear to the left of the photo.

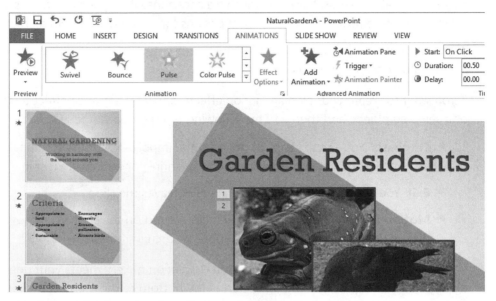

The Shape and Pulse animation effects are applied to the frog photo.

11   Click the frog photo. Then in the **Advanced Animation** group, click the **Animation Painter** button, and click the crow photo.

12   Repeat step 11 to copy the two animations to the cat photo.

13   Preview the animations on this slide.

     Finally, let's preview all the animations.

14   Click slide **1**, switch to **Reading** view, and watch as the title slide is displayed without the title or the subtitle.

15   On the status bar, click the **Next** button repeatedly to display the animation effects on all three slides, and then return to **Normal** view.

CLEAN UP   Close the NaturalGardenA presentation, saving your changes if you want to.

Customizing animation effects

The majority of professional presenter-led presentations don't require much in the way of animation, and you might find that transitions and ready-made animation effects will meet all your animation needs. However, for those occasions when you want a presentation with pizzazz, PowerPoint provides a variety of options for creating your own animation effects.

TIP Animations can be useful for self-running presentations, where there is no presenter to lead the audience from one concept to another.

If you want to create your own animation effects, apply an entrance effect to selected text or a selected object, and then add the following types of ready-made effects:

- **Emphasis** You can increase or decrease the importance of the element by changing its font, size, or style; by making it grow or shrink; or by making it spin.

- **Exit** You can animate the way the element leaves the slide.

- **Motion Path** You can move the element around on the slide in various ways, such as diagonally to the upper-right corner or in a circular motion.

If none of the predefined effects in the Add Animation gallery meets your needs, you can display more effects by clicking an option at the bottom of the menu containing the gallery. These options display dialog boxes with professionally designed animations in four categories: Basic, Subtle, Moderate, and Exciting.

After you apply an animation effect, you can fine-tune its action by using the commands on the Animations tab in the following ways:

- Specify the direction, shape, or sequence of the animation. (The options vary depending on the type of animation you apply.)

- Specify what action will trigger the animation. For example, you can specify that clicking a different object on the slide will animate the selected object.

- As an alternative to clicking the mouse button to build animated slides, have PowerPoint build the slide for you.

- Control the implementation speed (duration) of each animation, or delay an animation effect.

- Change the order of an animation effect.

You can make additional animation adjustments by displaying the Animation pane.

The Animation pane shows all the animations applied to the active slide.

When you click an animation in the Animation pane, an arrow appears to its right. Clicking the arrow displays a menu of actions.

You can perform these actions from the Animation pane to customize an animation.

Clicking Effect Options on the menu provides access to an effect-specific dialog box where you can refine that type of animation in the following ways:

- Specify whether the animation should be accompanied by a sound.

- Dim or hide the element after the animation, or you can have it change to a specific color.

- If the animation is applied to text, animate all the text at once or animate it word by word or letter by letter.

- Repeat an animation and specify what will trigger its action.

- If a slide has more than one level of bullet points, animate different levels separately.

- If an object has text, animate the object and the text together (the default) or separately, or you can animate one but not the other.

All the options for customizing the Diamond animation effect are organized on three pages.

In this exercise, you'll apply effects to an existing animation and change when it starts. Then you'll add sound to a bulleted list, make words appear letter-by-letter, and make them dim to a different color when they have been discussed.

 SET UP You need the NaturalGardenB presentation located in the Chapter10 practice file folder to complete this exercise. Open the presentation, and then follow the steps.

1   With slide **1** displayed, click the slide title, and then on the **Animations** tab, in the **Animation** group, click the **Effect Options** button to display the **Effect Options** gallery.

In the Effect Options gallery, the Shape entrance animation applied to this title has two Direction options, four Shapes options, and one Sequence option.

2   In the **Shapes** area, click **Diamond**. Then display the **Effect Options** gallery again, and in the **Direction** area, click **Out**.

TROUBLESHOOTING Always select the Shape option first. By default, the In direction is applied to whatever Shape option you select.

3   Change the effect options of the subtitle to match those of the title.

4   With the subtitle still selected, in the **Timing** group, display the **Start** list, and click **After Previous**.

5   Switch to **Reading** view, and preview the animation effects on slide **1**.

6   Switch back to **Normal** view, display slide **2**, and then click anywhere in the bulleted list on the left.

7   In the **Advanced Animation** group, click the **Animation Pane** button to open the **Animation** pane.

8   If the **Animation** pane shows only the first animation in each content placeholder, click the chevrons for each placeholder to expand their contents.

   TIP If you have several animations on a slide, being able to expand and collapse sets of animations can help you focus on those you want to work with.

9   In the **Animation** pane, click animation **1**. Then click the arrow on the right, and in the menu, click **Effect Options** to open the **Circle** dialog box.

On the Effect page of the Circle dialog box, you can control direction, attach a sound, specify what happens after the animation, and set the animation grouping.

10　In the **Enhancements** area, display the **Sound** list, and click **Chime**.

11　Display the **After animation** list, and in the palette, click the rightmost red swatch.

12　Display the **Animate text** list, and click **By letter**.

13　Click the **Timing** tab, display the **Duration** list, and click **3 seconds (Slow)**. Then click **OK** to close the dialog box, and watch the effects of your changes to the animation effects.

The Shape animation doesn't work very well with the selected effect options, so let's adjust them.

14　On the slide, click the left content placeholder, and notice that in the **Animation** pane, all the animations for the bullet points in the placeholder are selected.

You can apply animation effects to all the selected bullet points at once.

15   Apply the **Float In** entrance animation to the entire placeholder.

16   In the **Animation** pane, click the arrow to the right of the selected animations, and then click **Effect Options** to open the **Float Up** dialog box.

       TIP By default, the direction of the Float In animation is up.

17   On the **Effect** page, set **Sound** to **Chime**, set **After animation** to the rightmost red swatch in the palette, and set **Animate text** to **By letter**.

18   On the **Timing** page, verify that **Duration** is set to **1 seconds (Fast)**. Then click **OK**.

19   Watch the animation effects, and make any additional adjustments you want to your custom animation effects.

20   When you are satisfied, use the **Animation Painter** to copy the animation effects of the bullet points on the left to those on the right.

21   Switch to **Reading** view, and click the **Next** button repeatedly to display the animated bullet points on slide **2**.

22   When all the bullet points are visible and dimmed to red, press the **Esc** key to return to **Normal** view.

❌ CLEAN UP Close the Animation pane. Then close the NaturalGardenB presentation, saving your changes if you want to.

Adding audio content

In "Adding transitions" in Chapter 5, "Add simple visual enhancements," you added a sound to a slide transition, and in this chapter's previous topic, "Customizing animation effects," you added a sound to an animation effect. You can also enhance your presentations by using the following types of audio content:

- **Audio files** Insert an audio file—for example, a speech or interview—by clicking the **Audio** button in the **Media** group on the **Insert** tab, clicking **Audio On My PC**, and then selecting the file in the **Insert Audio** dialog box.

- **Audio clips** Insert an audio clip by clicking the **Audio** button in the **Media** group, clicking **Online Audio** to display the **Insert Audio** dialog box, where you can search for and select the audio clip you want.

- **Recordings** Record a sound or narration and attach it to a slide, all from within PowerPoint.

  SEE ALSO For information about recording audio content, see the sidebar "Recording presentations" in Chapter 13, "Prepare for delivery."

After you add an audio object, it appears on the slide, represented by an icon. When the audio object is selected, a play bar appears below its icon with controls for playing the audio content, and PowerPoint adds Format and Playback tool tabs to the ribbon. You can customize the icon as follows:

- Drag the object to locate it anywhere on the slide.

- Drag its sizing handles to make it larger or smaller.

- Change the icon's appearance, in much the same way that you would format a picture, by using commands on the Format tool tab.

- Replace the default icon with a picture.

10

You can customize the audio content by using commands on the Playback tab, as follows:

- Edit the audio content so that only part of it plays.
- Make the sound gradually increase and decrease in volume.
- Adjust the volume or mute the sound.
- Specify whether the audio content plays:
  - Automatically when the slide appears.
  - Only if you click its icon.
- Make the audio object invisible while the presentation is displayed in Reading view or Slide Show view.
- Specify that the audio content should play continuously until you stop it.
- Ensure that the audio content starts from the beginning each time it is played.

To play sounds and other audio content, you must have a sound card and speakers installed. In Normal view, you can test the audio content associated with a slide by clicking its icon and then either clicking the Play/Pause button on its play bar or clicking the Play button in the Preview group on the Playback tool tab.

In this exercise, you'll insert an audio clip into a slide, adjust the position of the audio object, change its icon, and make various other adjustments to its settings. Then you'll insert an audio file into another slide and make the file play continuously throughout a presentation.

SET UP You need the HealthyEcosystemsA and AGKCottage presentations, the Bird picture, and the Amanda audio file located in the Chapter10 practice file folder. Open the AGKCottage presentation, and then open the HealthyEcosystemsA presentation. Be sure to turn on your computer's speakers for this exercise. (If you do not have a sound card and speakers, you can still follow the steps, but you won't be able to hear the sound.) Also ensure that your computer is connected to the Internet. Then with HealthyEcosystemsA displayed on your screen, follow the steps.

1   On the **Insert** tab, in the **Media** group, click the **Audio** button, and then click **Online Audio** to open the **Insert Audio** dialog box.

2   In the **Search for** box, enter birds, and then click the **Search** button to display icons of bird call clips available from the Office.com website.

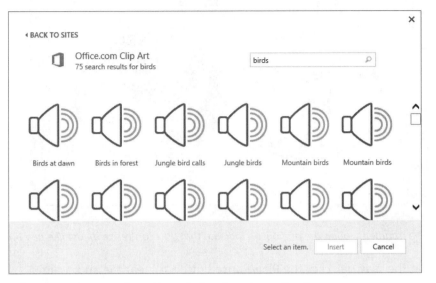

When you point to an icon, PowerPoint plays the audio clip.

TROUBLESHOOTING The audio clips available from Office.com change frequently, so don't worry if the Birds At Dawn clip is not available in your results. Just use a different clip.

3   Preview a few clips. When you are ready, click an audio clip that you think is appropriate for the slide, and then click **Insert**. (We chose Birds Singing.) In the middle of the slide, notice the icon and play bar representing the audio object.

4   Because the icon does not show up against the picture, drag the icon and its play bar to the upper-left corner of the slide to make it more visible.

10

The handles around the audio icon indicate that you can resize it, just like any other object.

5   On the play bar, click the **Play/Pause** button to hear the audio clip.

KEYBOARD SHORTCUT Press Alt+P to play the audio clip. For a complete list of keyboard shortcuts, see "Keyboard shortcuts" at the end of this book.

Now let's customize the audio clip and its icon.

6   With the audio icon selected, on the **Format** tool tab, in the **Adjust** group, click the **Change Picture** button. Then in the **Insert Pictures** dialog box, click **Browse**, navigate to the **Chapter10** practice file folder, and double-click the **Bird** file.

7   On the **Playback** tool tab, in the **Audio Options** group, display the **Start** list, and click **Automatically**. Then select the **Loop until Stopped** check box.

TIP If your presentation might be viewed by people using assistive technologies such as screen readers or text-to-speech tools, you should avoid starting audio clips or files automatically. Instead, allow the user to play the audio content after the tool has finished communicating the slide content.

8   Switch to **Reading** view, and listen as the audio clip plays.

9   Move the pointer over the bird representing the audio object, and when the play bar appears, click the **Play/Pause** button. Then press the **Esc** key to return to **Normal** view.

Next let's attach a "sound track" to a presentation.

10   Display the **AGKCottage** presentation, and view it in **Reading** view, pressing **Esc** after a few slides.

11   With slide **1** displayed, on the **Insert** tab, in the **Media** group, click the **Audio** button, and then click **Audio on My PC** to open the **Insert Audio** dialog box.

TIP Don't be concerned that this Insert Audio dialog box looks very different from the one for finding audio clips. This one is a traditional dialog box for browsing your computer, whereas the one shown earlier is for searching for web content.

12   In the dialog box, navigate to the **Chapter10** practice file folder, and double-click the **Amanda** file.

13   On the **Playback** tab, in the **Audio Options** group, change the **Start** setting to **Automatically**. Then select the **Play Across Slides**, **Loop until Stopped**, and **Hide During Show** check boxes.

14   Switch to **Reading** view, and listen to the audio file as the presentation moves from slide to slide.

15   Press **Esc** to stop the presentation and return to **Normal** view.

❌ CLEAN UP Close the HealthyEcosystemsA and AGKCottage presentations, saving your changes if you want to.

Inserting and playing videos

Sometimes the best way to ensure that your audience understands your message is to show a video. For example, if your company has developed a short advertising video, it makes more sense to include the video in a presentation about marketing plans than to try and describe it with bullet points or even pictures.

In keeping with the trend toward more visual presentations, PowerPoint 2013 has a broad range of video capabilities. You can insert the following types of movies in slides:

- **Video files** You can insert a digital video file in two ways: if a slide has a content placeholder, click the placeholder's **Insert Video** button and then click **From A File** in the **Insert Video** dialog box; if it doesn't have a placeholder, click the **Video** button in the **Media** group on the **Insert** tab, click **Video On My PC**, and then select the file in the traditional browsing Insert **Video** dialog box that appears.

- **Video clips** You can insert a video clip directly from a website in two ways: if the slide has a content placeholder, click the placeholder's **Insert Video** button; if it doesn't, click the **Video** button in the **Media** group and then click **Online Video**. Either method opens the **Insert Video** dialog box, where you can search for and select the clip you want.

  TIP If a video clip is publicly available, you might be able to insert a link to it. You can tell whether a video is publicly available by right-clicking it and looking for a Copy Embed HTML command. If this command is not available, the owner has secured the video, and you cannot play it from anywhere but the site on which it is published. If you are able to copy the embed code, paste it into the From A Video Embed Code box in the Insert Video dialog box, and then click the Insert button. To view the video, switch to Reading view or Slide Show view, and then click the Play/Pause button. PowerPoint then uses the embed code to locate and play the video. Provided the video remains available in its original location, and provided you have an active Internet connection, you will be able to access and play the video from the slide at any time.

Both video files and video clips from websites appear on the slide as video objects that you can size and move to meet your needs. When you select a video object, PowerPoint adds Format and Playback tool tabs to the ribbon.

You can change the way the object appears on the slide as follows:

- Drag the object to locate it anywhere on the slide.

- Drag its sizing handles to make it larger or smaller.

- Use commands on the Format tool tab to change its appearance, in much the same way that you would format a picture.

You can customize the video itself by using commands on the Playback tool tab, as follows:

- Edit the video so that only part of it plays.

  TIP You can find out the total playing time of a video by displaying the Trim Video dialog box.

- Make the video gradually appear and disappear.

- Adjust the volume or mute the sound.

- Specify whether the video plays:

  - Automatically when the slide appears.

  - Only if you click the object.

- Specify that the video should occupy the entire slide space while playing.

- Make the video object invisible while the presentation is displayed in Reading view or Slide Show view.

- Specify that the video should play continuously until you stop it.

- Ensure that the video starts from the beginning each time it is played.

In Normal view, you can test the video associated with a slide by clicking the video object and then either clicking the Play/Pause button on its play bar or clicking the Play button in the Preview group on the Playback tool tab.

In this exercise, you'll insert two videos into a slide, adjust the size of their objects, format the video objects, and make various other adjustments to their settings.

 SET UP You need the HealthyEcosystemsB presentation and the Butterfly and Wildlife video files located in the Chapter10 practice file folder. Open the presentation, and then follow the steps.

10

1   In the left content placeholder, click the **Insert Video** button to open the **Insert Video** dialog box.

You can insert video files, video clips, and video embed codes from this Insert Video dialog box.

2　Adjacent to **From a file**, click the **Browse** button to display a traditional browsing dialog box. Navigate to the **Chapter10** practice file folder, and double-click the **Butterfly** file to insert the video as an object with a play bar below it.

The play bar is similar to the one for an audio object.

3　On the play bar, click the **Play/Pause** button, and watch the video.

4   Repeat steps 1 through 3 to insert the **Wildlife** video in the content placeholder on the right and play the video.

Let's trim this video so that it shows only the animal that looks like a marmot.

5   With the **Wildlife** video selected, on the **Playback** tool tab, in the **Editing** group, click the **Trim Video** button to open the **Trim Video** dialog box.

In the Trim Video dialog box, you can advance through the video frame by frame to identify the start and end times of the segment you want.

6   On the slider below the frame, drag the green start marker to the right until it sits at about the **00:17.020** mark. Then click the **Next Frame** button, pausing after each click, until the first marmot frame comes into view at about the **00:17.292** mark.

7   Drag the red stop marker to the left until it sits at about the **00:20.900** mark. Then click the **Previous Frame** button, pausing after each click, until the last marmot frame comes into view at about the **00:20.790** mark.

   TIP You can also enter specific times in the Start Time and End Time boxes below the slider.

8 Click **OK** to close the dialog box, and then play the trimmed video.

Next let's size the video objects and apply a style to make them look attractive on the slide.

9 Click the **Butterfly** video object, and on the **Format** tool tab, in the **Size** group, click the **Height** arrow until its setting is **3"**.

10 Click the **Wildlife** object, and in the **Size** group, change its **Height** to **3"**.

Because this video object is now too wide, we need to crop it from the left.

11 On the **Format** tool tab, click the **Size** dialog box launcher to display the **Format Video** pane.

12 In the pane, click the **Video** icon, and then click **Crop**.

Format Video	▾ ✕
◇ ◯ ▣ ▤	
▷ **VIDEO**	
◢ **CROP**	
Picture position	
Width	5.33"
Height	3"
Offset X	0"
Offset Y	0"
Crop position	
Width	5.33"
Height	3"
Left	5.08"
Top	3.39"

The crop settings on the Video page of the Format Video pane take the trial-and-error out of any cropping task.

TIP You can use the video settings on this page to adjust the color, brightness, and contrast of the video.

13   In the **Crop position** area, change the **Width** setting to **4"**. Then close the pane.

   TROUBLESHOOTING Be sure to change the Crop Position setting, not the Picture Position setting. Changing Picture Position adjusts the size of the picture within the video frame instead of adjusting the size of the frame.

14   Drag the objects until they are evenly spaced on the slide, using the smart guides to ensure that they are aligned.

15   Select both video objects, and then on the Format tool tab, click the **More** button in the **Video Styles** group to display a menu containing the **Video Styles** gallery.

You can select a frame for the video from the Video Styles gallery, in which 41 frame styles are organized in three categories: Subtle, Moderate, and Intense.

TIP In addition to formatting a video with a ready-made video style, you can choose from the Video Shape, Video Border, and Video Effects galleries to create your own combinations. Just be careful not to overdo it.

16   In the **Intense** area, click the fifth thumbnail in the first row (**Reflected Bevel, Black**). Then click away from the objects to display the results.

The two video objects have rounded frames and reflections.

Finally, let's set up the video for presentation delivery.

17   Click the **Butterfly** object, and on the **Playback** tool tab, in the **Video Options** group, click the **Volume** button, and then click **Mute**.

18   In the **Video Options** group, display the **Start** list, and click **Automatically**. Then select the **Loop until Stopped** check box.

19   Click the **Wildlife** object, set **Volume** to **Mute**, leave **Start** set to **On Click**, and select the **Loop until Stopped** check box.

20   Switch to **Reading** view, and preview and pause the **Butterfly** video. Then preview and pause the **Wildlife** video.

21   Press **Esc** twice to return to **Normal** view.

✖ CLEAN UP Close the HealthyEcosystemsB presentation, saving your changes if you want to.

Key points

- Used judiciously, animated text and graphics add interest to your slides. Combinations of ready-made animations will probably meet almost all of your animation needs.

- You decide how and when the animation occurs, and you can even customize an effect with a sound.

- Audio and video clips can convey information or simply add interest.

- Use audio clips available from Office.com, or supply your own audio files.

- After you insert an audio or video object, you can change the way it looks and the way it plays to suit your needs.

10

Additional techniques

Chapter at a glance

Share

Share presentations in other formats,
page 316

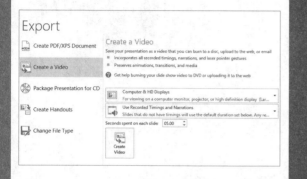

Send

Send presentations directly from PowerPoint,
page 326

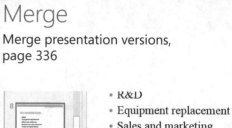

Add

Add and review comments,
page 332

Merge

Merge presentation versions,
page 336

Share and review presentations

11

IN THIS CHAPTER, YOU WILL LEARN HOW TO

- Share presentations in other formats.
- Send presentations directly from PowerPoint.
- Protect presentations by using passwords.
- Add and review comments.
- Merge presentation versions.
- Collaborate with other people.

Many presentations are developed collaboratively by a team of people. You might be the lead developer of some presentations that are reviewed by others, and you might be a reviewer of some presentations that have been developed by colleagues. With Microsoft PowerPoint 2013, you can easily attach a presentation to an email message and send it to someone for review. If you want to send it to someone who doesn't have PowerPoint 2013 installed on his or her computer, you can save the presentation in a different file format. If you want to be sure that only authorized people can review a presentation, you can assign a password.

These days, most presentations are reviewed on the screen. With PowerPoint, it's easy to insert comments, ask questions, and respond to comments made by others. If you send a presentation out for review and receive back a copy with changes, you can merge the reviewed version with your version to simplify the process of reviewing and accepting or rejecting changes. If the presentation is saved in a shared location, several people can make changes that PowerPoint seamlessly incorporates into the same file.

In this chapter, you'll first share presentations in a couple of different formats. You'll send a presentation via email directly from PowerPoint and then password-protect another presentation. You'll review, add, delete, and hide comments, and you'll merge two versions of the same presentation. Finally, we'll briefly discuss the coauthoring capabilities that are available for presentations saved in a shared location.

PRACTICE FILES To complete the exercises in this chapter, you need the practice files contained in the Chapter11 practice file folder. For more information, see "Download the practice files" in this book's Introduction.

Sharing presentations in other formats

When you save a PowerPoint 2013 presentation, the default file format is the .pptx format. To save a presentation in a different file format, display the Save As dialog box from the Backstage view, and then change the Save As Type setting to the format you want to use.

TIP If you are not sure which format will best suit your needs, display the Export page of the Backstage view, and then click Change File Type. In the right pane, PowerPoint displays common file types with descriptions. Double-clicking a file type opens the Save As dialog box with Save As Type already set to that format.

If you want to save the file so that it can be used with an earlier version of PowerPoint, you need to save it in the .ppt format. You do this by changing the Save As Type setting to PowerPoint 97-2003 Presentation.

The format you choose will depend on what you want other people to be able to do with the presentation. If you want people who have PowerPoint installed on their computers to be able to view the presentation with a minimum of fuss, you might want to save it in PowerPoint Show (.ppsx) format. These presentations open automatically in Slide Show view. Another option is to save the presentation in PowerPoint Picture Presentation format, which retains the .pptx format but presents all the elements of each slide as one picture.

You can save presentations in many different formats.

If you want to share a presentation with viewers who might not have PowerPoint 2013 installed on their computers, a simple way to ensure that everyone can view the presentation is to turn it into a video. In PowerPoint 2013, creating presentation videos couldn't be easier. However, video files can be quite large, so before you create a video, you might want to ensure that the presentation is as compact as possible by compressing pictures and media to the smallest size that is suitable for the intended use.

11

When you are ready to turn the presentation into a video, simply click Create A Video on the Export page of the Backstage view, and specify the following:

- The intended viewing device. You can choose a format for computer and high-definition displays, a format for viewing over the Internet and from a DVD, or a format for viewing on portable devices.

- Whether to use recorded timings and narrations. If the presentation has no slide timings or narration, you are given the opportunity to create them before saving the video.

After specifying these options, click Create Video. The Save As dialog box opens with the Save As Type option already set to MPEG-4 Video. (If you want, you can change this setting to Windows Media Video.)Then all you have to do is name the file and specify a location. Depending on the size of the presentation and the amount of media and linked files it contains, the creation process can take quite a while, so be patient!

If you want people who don't have PowerPoint to be able to review the content of a presentation but not change it, save the presentation in one of two formats:

- **PDF (.pdf)** This format is preferred by commercial printing facilities.

- **XPS (.xps)** This format precisely renders all fonts, images, and colors on recipients' computers.

Both the PDF and XPS formats are designed to deliver presentations as electronic representations of the way they look when printed. The text and graphics in .pdf and .xps files are essentially static and content cannot be easily edited. Both types of files can be sent by email to many recipients and can be made available on a webpage for downloading. However, the files are no longer PowerPoint presentations, and they cannot be opened, viewed, or edited in PowerPoint. By default, opening a PDF or XPS file on a computer running Windows 8 displays the file in Windows Reader. (Installing a third-party reader might change this behavior.) You can then scroll through the pages either continuously, one page at a time, or two pages at a time. Opening an XPS file on a computer running Windows 7 displays the file in XPS Viewer.

TIP If you don't want to open a PDF or XPS file in the default program, right-click the file, click Open With, and then click the preferred program. If you want to set a new default for a specific file type, click Choose Default Program, and select from the list or click More Options.

In this exercise, you'll save one presentation as a PowerPoint Show and another as a PowerPoint Picture Presentation. Then you'll save a presentation with slide timings as a video optimized for distribution via the Internet. Finally you'll save one slide of a presentation in XPS format, and you'll view the .xps file.

➡ SET UP You need the CottageShowA, CottageShowB, and WaterUse presentations located in the Chapter11 practice file folder to complete this exercise. Open the three presentations, and then with CottageShowA displayed, follow the steps.

1   With slide **1** of the **CottageShowA** presentation active, display the **Save As** page of the **Backstage** view, and with **Computer** selected, click the **Browse** button in the right pane.

2   In the **Save As** dialog box, display the **Save as type** list, and then click **PowerPoint Show**.

3   Change the file name to CottageShow, and click **Save**. Then close the **CottageShow** presentation.

4   Open **Windows Explorer**, navigate to the **Chapter11** practice file folder, and double-click **CottageShow** to open it in **Slide Show** view. Watch the presentation as it advances automatically from slide to slide while playing the embedded music.

5   Press **Esc** to both end and close the **CottageShow** PowerPoint Show.

11

Next let's save a different presentation as a Picture Presentation.

6　Display the **WaterUse** presentation, open the **Save As** dialog box, change the **Save as type** setting to **PowerPoint Picture Presentation**, change the file name to **WaterUse**, and click **Save**. Then click **OK** to acknowledge the message that the Picture Presentation has been saved in the **Chapter11** practice file folder.

7　Display the **Open** page of the **Backstage** view, open the **Open** dialog box, and in the **Chapter11** practice file folder, double-click **WaterUse**.

8　On slide **1**, click the title, and notice that handles surround the entire slide. Repeat this step on slide **6**.

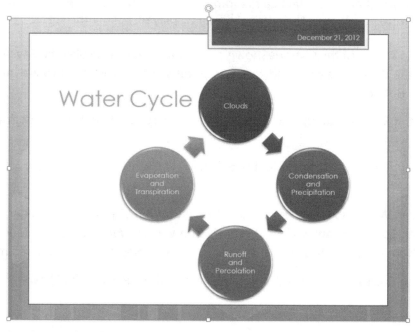

In a PowerPoint Picture Presentation, a slide no longer has discrete elements; they are all combined into one picture.

9   Close the **WaterUse** picture presentation, but leave the **WaterUse** presentation open.

Now let's prepare a presentation so that we can save it as a video.

10   Display the **CottageShowB** presentation, and on slide **1**, click the photo. Then on the **Format** tool tab, in the **Adjust** group, click the **Compress Pictures** button to open the **Compress Pictures** dialog box.

The descriptions after each Target Output type help you select the appropriate setting.

11   Clear the **Apply only to this picture** check box to compress all the pictures in the presentation. Then with **Use document resolution** selected, click **OK**.

TIP For any presentation, you can compact the size of its media files by clicking Compress Media on the Info page of the Backstage view, and then choosing the intended output category.

With that bit of preparation out of the way, let's create the video.

12   Display the **Export** page of the **Backstage** view, and then click **Create a Video** to display the options related to videos.

11

If a presentation does not have slide timings, by default each slide in the video will display for five seconds.

13 In the **Create a Video** pane, click **Computer & HD Displays**, and then in the list of output options, click **Internet & DVD**.

14 Click **Use Recorded Timings and Narrations**, and then click **Preview Timings and Narrations** to display the presentation in **Slide Show** view, where you can check the slide timings and audio.

15 After you have previewed a few slides, press **Esc** to return to the **Export** page.

16 Assume the slide timings are satisfactory, and at the bottom of the right pane, click **Create Video** to open the **Save As** dialog box with the contents of your **Chapter11** practice file folder displayed. Notice that **MPEG-4 Video** is already specified as the file format.

17 In the **Save As** dialog box, change the file name to CottageShow, and click **Save**. Then notice the **Creating Video CottageShow.MP4** indicator on the status bar.

Progress bar

| SLIDE 4 OF 14 | Creating video CottageShow.mp4 | NOTES | COMMENTS |

Cancel button

PowerPoint indicates in the status bar that the video is being created in the background, and provides a Cancel button for aborting the process.

18   The video creation process can take quite a while, so if you want to stop the process, click the **Cancel** button to the right of the progress bar (don't close the presentation). Otherwise, when the progress bar disappears, open **Windows Explorer**, navigate to your **Chapter11** practice file folder, and double-click the **CottageShow** MP4 file to start the video. Click the **Close** button to end it. Then close the **CottageShowB** presentation without saving any changes.

Now let's save one slide in .xps format.

19   Display slide **7** of the **WaterUse** presentation.

20   Open the **Save As** dialog box, and change the **Save as type** setting to **XPS Document**. Notice that the dialog box expands to include options specific to your chosen format.

On the right side of the expanded Save As dialog box, you can select from two video resolutions, depending on the intended distribution method.

21 In the **File name** box, change the name to WaterUseXPS.

22 Click **Minimum size (publishing online)**. Then click **Options** to open the **Options** dialog box.

You can choose options to tailor the .xps file to your needs.

23 In the **Range** area, click **Current slide**.

> **TIP** When you save a presentation in .xps or .pdf format, the Include Non-Printing Information area of the Options dialog box provides a Document Structure Tags For Accessibility check box. Selecting this check box creates files that are tagged in such a way that they are easier for assistive technologies to process them.

24 In the **Include non-printing information** area, clear the **Document properties** check box, select the **Document structure tags for accessibility** check box, and then click **OK**.

25 Back in the **Save As** dialog box, verify that the **Open file after publishing** check box is selected, and then click **Save**.

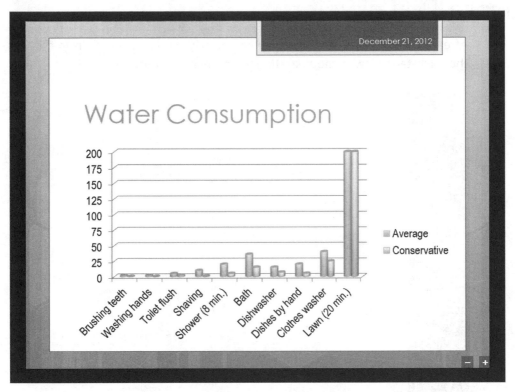

If your computer is running Windows 8, Reader starts and displays slide 7, the only slide in the .xps file. If your computer is running Windows 7, the file opens in XPS Viewer instead.

26 If the file is displayed in **Reader**, close the file by pointing to the top of the screen and dragging down to the bottom. If the file is displayed in **XPS Viewer**, click the **Close** button in the upper-right corner.

❌ CLEAN UP Close the WaterUse presentation.

11

Sending presentations directly from PowerPoint

After you create a presentation, you can quickly send it via email from the Share page of the Backstage view, without starting your email program.

You can send a file as an attachment, a link, a PDF file, or an XPS file. If you subscribe to a fax service, you can also send the file as a fax.

Clicking Send As Attachment opens a message window with the current presentation already attached as a .pptx file. All you have to do is enter the email addresses of anyone you want to receive the message and its attachment. If you want, you can modify the subject line, which contains the name of the presentation you're sending.

TIP If you are working on a presentation that is stored on a Microsoft SkyDrive or Microsoft SharePoint site and you want other people to review the file, you can send an email message with a link to the file by clicking Send A Link in the right pane of the Share page of the Backstage view.

Similarly, you can click Send As PDF or Send As XPS to have PowerPoint save and attach a version of the presentation in the corresponding file format.

In addition to sending a presentation as an email attachment from within PowerPoint, if you have subscribed to an Internet fax service, you can send the presentation as a fax. Although the exact terms vary from one Internet fax service provider to another, these services all enable you to send and receive faxes from your computer without needing a fax machine or dedicated fax line. After establishing an Internet fax service account, you can send the current presentation as a fax by clicking Send As Internet Fax on the Share page. Then all you have to do is follow the procedure specified by your fax service provider.

TIP If you have not subscribed to an Internet fax service before clicking Send As Internet Fax, a message box appears. Clicking OK opens a webpage where you can choose a fax service provider.

In this exercise, you'll attach three presentations to an email message so that you can simulate sending them for review.

➡ SET UP You need the MeetingThemeA, MeetingThemeB, and MeetingThemeC presentations located in the Chapter11 practice file folder to complete this exercise. Be sure to have an email program installed on your computer and an email account set up before beginning this exercise. Microsoft Outlook 2013 is recommended. You can use another email program, but the steps for attaching and sending a message might vary from those given in this exercise. Open the MeetingThemeA presentation, and then follow the steps.

1   Display the **Share** page of the **Backstage** view, and then click **Email**.

2   Click the **Send as Attachment** button in the right pane to start your default email program and open a message window.

> **TROUBLESHOOTING** You might be prompted to supply your user name and password to access your email account.

PowerPoint enters the name of the presentation in the Subject line and attaches the presentation to the message.

3   In the **To** box, enter your own email address.

4   In the message content pane, enter Please review the attached presentations, and let me know which theme you prefer.

5   On the **Message** tab, in the **Include** group, click the **Attach File** button to open the **Insert File** dialog box.

6   Navigate to the **Chapter11** practice file folder.

7   Click **MeetingThemeB**, hold down the **Ctrl** key, click **MeetingThemeC**, and then click **Insert**.

8   On the **Message** tab, in the **Tags** group, click the **High Importance** button.

     If the message recipient is using Outlook, the message header will display a red exclamation mark to indicate that it is important.

9   In the message header, click the **Send** button to send the email message with the attached presentations.

     You'll receive the message the next time you connect to your mail server.

❌ CLEAN UP Close the MeetingThemeA presentation.

Presenting presentations online

Suppose you work with a team whose members are located in various cities in the United States, in addition to places like Denmark and New Zealand. You have developed a presentation to explain the results of your team's work to your managers, and you want to review the presentation with the team. You don't have much time for this review, and you don't want anyone to be able to change the content of the slides.

PowerPoint has the ideal solution for this situation: If you have a Microsoft account, you can use the Microsoft Office Presentation Service to make the presentation available over the Internet so that team members can view the presentation in their web browsers and give feedback via a conference call.

To present the active presentation online:

1   On the **Share** page of the **Backstage** view, click **Present Online**. Then click the **Present Online** button in the right pane to open the **Present Online** dialog box.

    TIP You can also click the Present Online button in the Start Slide Show group on the Slide Show tab. Either way, if this the first time you have used the Office Presentation Service, a message about the service apears. Click Connect in the message box to start the service and display the Present Online dialog box.

2   Click **Send in Email**, and when your email program displays a message containing the link, enter the email addresses of the reviewers, and click **Send**.

3   In the **Present Online** dialog box, click **Start Presentation** to begin the slide show.

    Everyone watching the presentation in their web browser can view all transitions and animations, just as if they were watching the show in the room where you are presenting it.

4   When you reach the last slide, press the **Esc** key to return to **Normal** view.

5   On the **Present Online** tool tab, in the **Present Online** group, click **End Online Presentation**. Then In the message box, confirm that you want to end the presentation.

11

Protecting presentations by using passwords

Sometimes you might want only specified people to be able to view a presentation. Or you might want some people to only be able to view it and others to be able to change it. In both cases, you can control who has access to the presentation and what they can do by assigning one or more passwords to the presentation.

You can assign two types of passwords:

- **Password to open** When you assign a password that must be entered to open the presentation, the presentation is encrypted so that only people with the password can view the presentation.

- **Password to modify** When you assign a password that must be entered to modify the presentation, people who don't have the password can open a read-only version but they cannot make changes or save a copy with a different name.

When you try to open a presentation to which a password has been assigned, the Password dialog box opens. If the password must be entered to open the presentation, you must enter the exact password—including capitalization, numbers, spaces, and symbols. If the password must be entered to modify the presentation, you can either enter the exact password to open it or click Read-Only to open a version that you can view but not modify.

TIP You can also set an encrypting password by displaying the Info page of the Backstage view, clicking the Protect Presentation button, and then clicking Encrypt With Password. Two other options in the Protect Presentation list also help protect presentations. If your organization has implemented Information Rights Management (IRM), you can click Restrict Access to limit who can change, print, or copy a presentation. If you have a digital signature, you can click Add A Digital Signature to attach an electronic stamp of authentication to a presentation to indicate that the file has not been tampered with.

In this exercise, you'll assign a password that people must enter in order to modify a presentation. You'll open a read-only version of the password-protected presentation and then enter the password to open a version that you can edit.

➡ SET UP **You need the Projects presentation located in the Chapter11 practice file folder to complete this exercise. Open the presentation, and then follow the steps.**

1   Open the **Save As** dialog box.

2   At the bottom of the dialog box, click **Tools**, and then in the list, click **General Options** to open the **General Options** dialog box.

You can set encrypted (Password To Open) or unencrypted (Password To Modify) passwords in the General Options dialog box.

3   In the **Password to modify** box, enter Password.

> **TIP** In this exercise, we use a common word that is easy to enter as the password. For maximum protection, use a password of at least eight characters that includes a combination of capital and small letters, digits, and punctuation symbols.

4   Click **OK**, which opens the **Confirm Password** dialog box.

5   In the **Reenter password to modify** box, enter Password, and then click **OK**.

> **TROUBLESHOOTING** If the two passwords you enter do not match exactly, PowerPoint displays a message. Click OK in the message box, click Cancel in the Confirm Password dialog box, and then repeat steps 3 through 5.

6   With the contents of the **Chapter11** practice file folder displayed in the **Save As** dialog box, replace the name in the **File name** box with ProjectsLocked, and then click **Save**.

     Now let's test the password protection. To do this, you need to close the presentation and open it again.

7   In the **Backstage** view, click **Close**.

8   Display the **Backstage** view, and then in the **Recent Presentations** list on the **Open** page, click **ProjectsLocked** to open the **Password** dialog box.

11

If you don't know the password, you can open a read-only copy.

Passwords are case sensitive, so let's test what happens when the wrong combination of capital and small letters is entered.

9   In the **Password** box, enter password, and then click **OK**.

10   When a message box tells you that the password you have entered is incorrect, click **OK**. Then in the **Password** dialog box, click **Read Only** to open a read-only version of the **ProjectsLocked** presentation. Notice in the title bar at the top of the screen that the presentation is designated as **(Read-Only)**.

11   On the slide, double-click in the presentation title, and then press the **Delete** key, which has no effect because you cannot modify the presentation.

12   Close the presentation, and then reopen it.

13   In the **Password** box, enter Password, and then click **OK** to open a version of the presentation that you can modify and save.

> **TIP** To remove the password from a password-protected presentation, open it by using the password, display the Save As dialog box, click Tools, and then click General Options. In the General Options dialog box, remove the password from the password box(es), and click OK. Then click Save to overwrite the password-protected version.

❌ CLEAN UP Close the ProjectsLocked presentation.

Adding and reviewing comments

The development of a presentation, especially one that will be delivered to clients, shareholders, or other important people, is often a collaborative effort, with several people contributing ideas and feedback. Even if you are developing a presentation for your own purposes, you might want to ask other people to review and comment on it before declaring a presentation final.

If you are asked to review a presentation, you can give feedback about a slide without disrupting its text and layout by clicking the Comments button on the status bar and then entering your comment in a box in the Comments pane. If you add a comment without first selecting an object on the slide, a comment icon appears in the upper-left corner of the slide. If you select an object such as the title or a graphic before adding the comment, the comment icon appears in the upper-right corner of the object. When the Comments pane is closed, you can click any comment icon to display the pane and display the comment associated with that icon.

TIP You can also display the Comments pane by clicking the New Comment button in the Comments group on the Review tab.

You can review and manage comments in the following ways:

- **Previous and Next** Click one of these buttons in the **Comments** pane to move backward or forward through the comments, displaying the comment box of each one in turn. If the pane is closed, click one of these buttons in the **Comments** group to display the pane and then perform the same actions.

- **Delete** Click this button in the upper-right corner of a comment box in the **Comments** pane to delete the active comment icon and its comment box. Whether or not the **Comments** pane is displayed, you can delete all the comments on the current slide or all the comments in the entire presentation by clicking the **Delete** arrow in the **Comments** group and then clicking the appropriate option in the list.

  TIP Either option also deletes any slide markup. For information about marking up slides with an electronic pen while reviewing a presentation, see "Delivering presentations" in Chapter 6, "Review and deliver presentations."

- **Show Comments** Click this button in the **Comments** group to open and close the **Comments** pane.

- **Show Markup** Click the **Show Comments** arrow, and then click **Show Markup** to close the **Comments** pane and hide the comment icons so that you can view the slides without extraneous clutter. Click the **Show Comments** button to redisplay both the **Comments** pane and the comment icons.

In this exercise, you'll add and edit comments in a presentation, move among the comments, delete a comment, and hide and display comments. Then you'll remove all comments from the presentation.

11

SET UP You need the HomeHarmony presentation located in the Chapter11 practice file folder to complete this exercise. Open the presentation, and then follow the steps.

1   With nothing selected on slide **1**, on the status bar, click the **Comments** button to display the **Comments** pane.

2   In the **Comments** pane, click the **New** button to open a new comment box with your name at the top. Notice the comment icon in the upper-left corner of the slide.

Comment icon

In the Comments pane, the comment box contains your name and when the comment was created.

3   In the comment box, enter Feng shui not mentioned. Good or bad?

4   Click away from the comment box, and then close the **Comments** pane.

5   Click the comment icon to display the **Comments** pane again, and then display slide **2**.

6   Click anywhere in the bulleted list, and in the **Comments** pane, click the **New** button to attach a comment to the list.

7   In the comment box, enter A graphic would add interest here, and then click away from the comment box.

When you click away from the comment box, a Reply box is added to the initial comment.

Now let's change the comment.

8   In the **Comments** pane, click the comment once to activate it, and then click again to the left of the word *graphic* to position the cursor. Enter tasteful, press the **Spacebar**, and then click away from the comment box.

Let's add one more comment, and then explore ways of reviewing and handling comments.

9   Display slide **1**, double-click the word **Your** in the title, and add a new comment that says Should this be "the Home"?

10 At the top of the slide, click comment icon **1** to activate its comment box, and then in the **Comments** pane, click the **Next** button to move to the next comment.

11 In the **Comments** pane, click the **Previous** button to move back to the first comment.

12 In the upper-right corner of the first comment box, click the **Delete** button.

13 In the **Comments** group, click the **Show Comments** arrow, and then click **Show Markup** to close the **Comments** pane and hide the comment icon attached to the slide title.

14   Display slide **2**, and verify that the comment icon is hidden there also.

15   In the **Comments** group, click the **Show Comments** button to display the **Comment** pane and redisplay the comment icons.

16   In the **Comments** group, click the **Delete** arrow, and then in the list, click **Delete All Comments and Ink in this Presentation**.

17   When asked to confirm that you want to delete all the comments, click **Yes**.

✖ CLEAN UP   **Close the HomeHarmony presentation without saving it.**

Merging presentation versions

Sometimes you might want to compare two versions of the same presentation. For example, if you have sent a presentation out for review by a colleague, you might want to compare his or her edited version with the original presentation so that you can incorporate the changes you like and reject those you don't.

Instead of comparing two open presentations visually, you can tell PowerPoint to compare the presentations and merge the differences into one presentation. The differences are recorded in the merged presentation as revisions. From within that one presentation, you can view the suggested changes and accept or reject them.

TIP Although differences between presentations are marked as revisions, you cannot track changes in a PowerPoint presentation the way you can in a Microsoft Word document.

In this exercise, you'll merge two versions of the same presentation. You'll then review the changes and accept those you like.

➔ SET UP   **You need the MeetingSH and MeetingTA presentations located in the Chapter11 practice file folder to complete this exercise. (MeetingSH was last edited by Sidney Higa, and MeetingTA was last edited by Terry Adams.) Open the MeetingTA presentation, and then follow the steps.**

1   On the **Review** tab, in the **Compare** group, click the **Compare** button to open the **Choose File to Merge with Current Presentation** dialog box.

2   Navigate to the **Chapter11** practice file folder, and double-click **MeetingSH** to compare the two presentations and flag the differences in **MeetingTA**.

Slide 9 is displayed because Sidney Higa suggested deleting this slide—a change to the presentation. But first let's address any changes to slide content.

3   Display slide **1**, and notice that the **Details** page of the **Revisions** pane flags both the slide differences (changes to slide content) and the presentation differences (adding or deleting slides).

4   At the top of the pane, click **Slides** to display that page.

The Revisions pane has two pages that help you decide which version of each slide to keep.

5   Notice that the **Slides** page displays slide **1** from Sidney Higa's presentation and that she has changed **Company Meeting** to **Annual Meeting**. On the right side of the slide, click the revision icon attached to the slide title placeholder, which is identified as **Rectangle 7**.

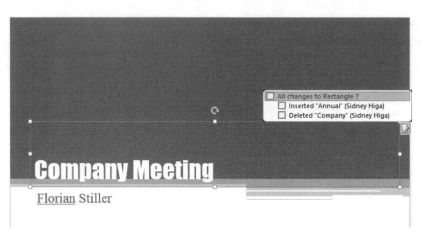

You can choose individual changes or accept or reject all of them.

6   In the **Revisions** pane, click **Details**. Then in the **Slide Changes** area, click **Rectangle 7: Company meeting**, which also expands the revision icon attached to the slide title to show this revision's change options.

7   In the revision box, select the **All changes to Rectangle 7** check box to accept the change from **Company Meeting** to **Annual Meeting**.

8   On the **Review** tab, in the **Compare** group, click the **Next** button to display slide **2**, where there are changes to the bullet points.

9   In the revision box, select the **Deleted "our"** check box to delete the word *our* from the fifth bullet point. Then reverse this step by clearing the check box.

   TIP You can select and clear any check box to determine whether or not you like each change.

10   Accept all the changes, and then click the **Next** button.

11   Repeat step 10 to accept all the changes for slide **5** and slide **7**, clicking **Next** after slide **7**.

12   When PowerPoint displays a message that it has reached the end of all the slide changes, click **Continue**.

   PowerPoint indicates that Sidney Higa has deleted slide 9 from the presentation. Let's evaluate this presentation change, which is flagged with an orange revision box at the bottom of the screen.

13   In the orange revision box at the bottom of the screen, select the check box to accept the slide deletion. Notice that although the slide disappears, on the **Thumbnails** tab, an icon between slide **8** and slide **9** indicates the change.

14   Point to the icon on the **Thumbnails** tab to display a ScreenTip that explains how you can click the icon to view the deleted slide details.

15   Click the icon to display the revision box.

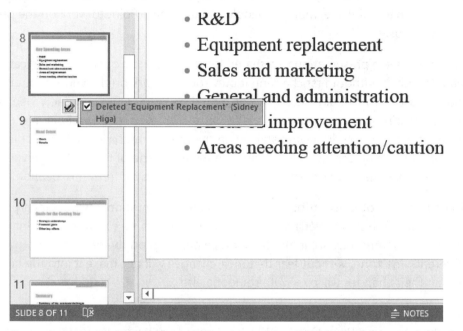

If you change your mind, you can easily reinsert deleted slides by clearing the check box.

Now let's check the revisions we've made.

16   On the **Review** tab, in the **Compare** group, click the **Next** button to return to the title change on slide **1**.

17   In the **Compare** group, click the **Reject** button to restore the original slide title. Then click **Next**.

18   To apply all the remaining revision decisions, in the **Compare** group, click the **End Review** button.

19   When a message box appears asking you to confirm that you want to end the review, click **Yes**, which accepts all the changes and closes the **Revisions** pane.

❌ CLEAN UP   Close the MeetingTA presentation, saving your changes if you want to.

Collaborating with other people

Whether you work for a large organization or a small business, you might need to collaborate with other people on the development of a presentation. Or perhaps you are working with a team of students or volunteers on a presentation that requires input from everyone. No matter what the circumstances, it can be difficult to keep track of different versions of a presentation produced by different people. If you store a presentation in a shared location such as a SharePoint site, multiple people can use PowerPoint to work on the presentation simultaneously.

After you save a presentation to a shared location, you can open it and indicate that you want to edit it, without first checking it out. You can work on the version that is stored on the site just as you would a presentation stored on your own computer. When another contributor begins making changes to the file stored on the site, PowerPoint alerts you to that person's presence by displaying an icon on the taskbar, and a list of the people currently working on the presentation is available on the Info page of the Backstage view. You can send an email message or instant message to these people from this location.

As you and the other contributors work with the presentation, saving it incorporates any changes into the shared version. In this way, several people can work efficiently on a presentation, whether they are in the same office building, on the other side of town, or in a different time zone, without fear that their changes will not make it into the final version or that their changes will overwrite someone else's.

Team members who travel frequently can review presentations stored on SkyDrive while traveling, by using PowerPoint 2013 Web App. If they have a Windows smartphone, they can also use PowerPoint 2013 Mobile to view and edit presentations. PowerPoint Web App and PowerPoint Mobile allow collaboration among team members no matter where they are and whether or not PowerPoint 2013 is available. Although a more in-depth discussion of these programs is beyond the scope of this book, if you are a "road warrior," you will certainly want to research them further.

Key points

- For distribution purposes, you can save a presentation in several different file formats, including PowerPoint Show, PowerPoint Picture Presentation, PDF, and XPS.

- You can send a presentation in a variety of formats via email.

- Assigning a password ensures that only people who know the password can review and work on the presentation.

- When you review a presentation created by someone else, you can add comments to give feedback. You can also use comments in your own presentations to remind yourself of outstanding issues and tasks.

- When you receive reviewed versions of a presentation, you can merge them so that all the changes are recorded in one presentation.

- If your organization is running SharePoint, you can collaborate on a presentation stored on a SharePoint site. By using PowerPoint Web App, you and your colleagues can also collaborate on a presentation stored on a SkyDrive site.

11

Chapter at a glance

View

View and change slide masters, page 344

Create

Create themes, theme colors, and theme fonts, page 353

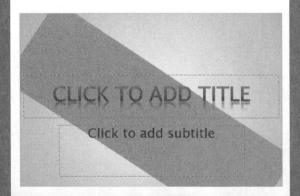

Design

Design slide layouts, page 362

Save

Save custom design templates, page 369

Create custom presentation elements

IN THIS CHAPTER, YOU WILL LEARN HOW TO

- View and change slide masters.

- Create themes, theme colors, and theme fonts.

- Design slide layouts.

- Save custom design templates.

  In addition to using the built-in design elements of Microsoft PowerPoint 2013, you can create your own designs, themes, theme color schemes, theme font sets, layouts, and templates. Why would you want to create your own elements rather than use those that come with PowerPoint? If your organization has established a corporate or brand image through the use of a logo, a color scheme, or other visual cues, you might be required to incorporate that branding into presentations that will be presented outside the organization. Even if branding is not an issue, you might want to establish a unique look for all your presentations to identify your work.

  In this chapter, you'll view and edit the slide masters for a presentation, changing the layout, text formatting, and bullet formatting, and adding a picture to the background. You'll create sets of theme colors and theme fonts and save the color/font combination as a new theme. You'll then create a master layout, save a presentation as a design template, and create a presentation based on the template.

  PRACTICE FILES To complete the exercises in this chapter, you need the practice files contained in the Chapter12 practice file folder. For more information, see "Download the practice files" in this book's Introduction.

Viewing and changing slide masters

When you create a presentation, the slides take on the characteristics of the template on which the presentation is based. PowerPoint templates use masters to determine their basic design. By default, each PowerPoint presentation has three masters:

- **Slide master** This set of masters controls the look of all the slides in a presentation, including the theme, text placement, background graphics, and other slide elements. The set contains a master design for most of the layouts you are likely to need when using that particular template.

- **Handout master** This master controls the look of any handouts you prepare for distribution to your audience.

- **Notes master** This master controls the look of speaker notes (if you choose to print them).

  SEE ALSO For information about handouts and speaker notes, see "Preparing speaker notes and handouts" in Chapter 6, "Review and deliver presentations."

When you create a presentation, its slides assume the design of their slide masters. The slide masters contain placeholders for a title, bullet points, or other content, depending on the particular layout. Most slide masters also contain placeholders for the date and time, footer information, and slide number. The placeholders control the position of the elements on the slide. Text placeholders also control the formatting of their text.

On an individual slide, you can make changes to the design elements provided by the master, but you can change the basic design only on the master itself. When you change a design element on the master, all the slides reflect the change.

TIP To override the master design for a particular slide, you use commands on the Home and Design tabs. For example, you can remove a background graphic from a slide by clicking the Hide Background Graphics button in the Background group on the Design tab.

To make changes to a presentation's masters, you need to switch to Slide Master view by clicking the Slide Master button in the Master Views group on the View tab. In this view, the Thumbnails pane displays the primary master, which controls the base layout, followed by all the available layout variations. The layout selected in the Thumbnail pane is displayed in the Slide pane. PowerPoint adds a Slide Master tab to the ribbon and hides the tabs that aren't needed in this view.

The first thumbnail shows the primary master, and the remaining thumbnails show the masters for the slide layouts.

By using commands on the Slide Master tab, you can make the following adjustments:

- Make another set of masters available to the presentation and preserve that set so that it remains available even if it is not currently used in the presentation.

- Add a new layout with the same background, title, and footer style to which you can add your own placeholders.

- Delete or rename a selected layout.

- Specify which placeholders will be included on the selected layout.

- Select and fine-tune the theme applied to the master set.

- Control the background color, texture, and graphics.

- Set the default slide size for the presentation.

Clicking the Close Master View button in the Close group returns you to the view from which you switched to Slide Master view. You can also click any view button on the View Shortcuts toolbar at the right end of the status bar to close Slide Master view.

While you are working in Slide Master view, you can use the commands on the other tabs in the following ways:

- **Home** Format a text placeholder on a master by selecting it and then clicking buttons in the Font and Paragraph groups.

- **Insert** Add objects such as graphics and WordArt text to a master by clicking buttons.

- **Transitions** Apply transitions by clicking buttons.

- **Animations** Animate parts of a slide by clicking buttons.

- **Review** Use the proofing and language tools.

For slides designed to contain bullet points, you can format bulleted lists by specifying the bullet's size, shape, and color. You can also control the indenting of bullet levels and the distance from the bullet to its text, by displaying the rulers and moving markers, as follows:

- **First Line Indent** The upper triangle controls the first line of the paragraph.

- **Hanging Indent** The lower triangle controls the left edge of the remaining lines of the paragraph.

- **Left Indent** The small square controls how far the entire paragraph sits from the edge of the text object.

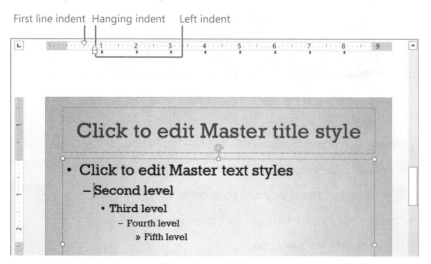

You can click any bullet point to display its indent markers on the horizontal ruler.

To adjust the relationship between the first and remaining lines of a bullet point, drag the First Line Indent and Hanging Indent markers to the left or right on the ruler. To adjust the distance of the bullet point from the left edge of the text object, drag the Left Indent marker.

In this exercise, you'll view a presentation's masters in Slide Master view. You'll add a graphic to the background and change character formatting. Then you'll change bullet characters and adjust bullet spacing. Finally, you'll remove the footer placeholders from the Title Slide layout.

SET UP You need the NaturalA presentation located in the Chapter12 practice file folder to complete this exercise. Open the presentation, and then follow the steps.

1   With slide **1** displayed in **Normal** view, switch to **Slide Master** view.

    Other than the gradient background, the masters don't reflect the formatting of the presentation's slides, which has been applied manually on a slide-by-slide basis. Let's implement the formatting in the masters so that we don't have to do it manually on each slide.

2   Switch to **Normal** view, and on slide **1**, click the diagonal shape to select it. Then copy it.

    KEYBOARD SHORTCUT Press Ctrl+C to copy a selected item. For a complete list of keyboard shortcuts, see "Keyboard shortcuts" at the end of this book.

3   Switch back to **Slide Master** view. Then scroll to the top of the **Thumbnail** pane, click the primary master (the top thumbnail), and paste the diagonal shape into that master.

    KEYBOARD SHORTCUT Press Ctrl+V to paste a cut or copied item.

4   Notice that because the primary master controls the basic characteristics of all the layouts, the graphic fills their backgrounds as well. The shape is selected, so PowerPoint adds the **Format** tool tab to the ribbon.

5   On the **Format** tool tab, in the **Arrange** group, click the **Send Backward** arrow, and then click **Send to Back** to move the shape behind the other elements on the primary master.

12

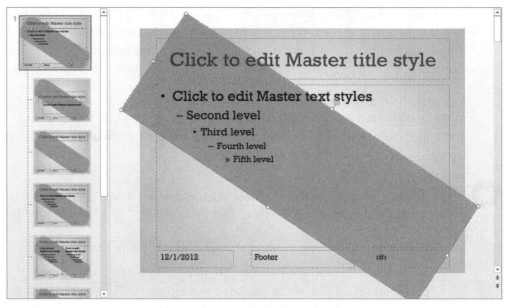

In the Thumbnail pane, the change is reflected in all of the layouts.

6   Switch to **Normal** view, and on slide **1**, select and delete the shape that was drawn manually on the slide. Notice that the appearance of the slide remains the same, because the shape is now supplied by the slide master.

7   Click anywhere in the title placeholder, and select all the text. Then on the **Home** tab, in the **Clipboard** group, click the **Format Painter** button.

    KEYBOARD SHORTCUT   Press Ctrl+A to select all the text in a placeholder.

8   Switch back to **Slide Master** view, where the **Title Slide** layout is selected by default, and drag the **Format Painter** pointer across the text in the placeholder for the presentation's title.

9   Enlarge the title placeholder by dragging its handles upward and toward the edges of the slide. Then click away from the placeholder to display the result.

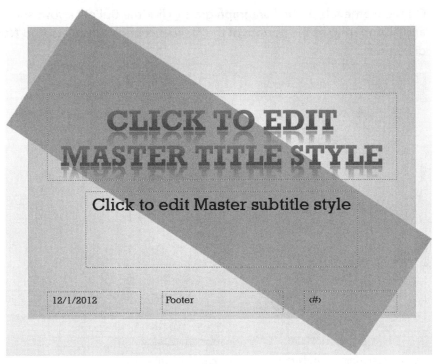

On any slide you create with the Title Slide layout, the title will now be formatted as shown on this master.

10   Repeat steps 7 and 8 to copy the formatting of the subtitle on the presentation's title slide to the master **Title Slide** layout.

11   Repeat steps 7 and 8 again to copy the formatting of the title of slide **2** in the presentation to the title of the primary master, which copies it to all the layouts with slide titles.

TIP At its bigger size, the title placeholder text breaks to two lines and overflows its placeholder. However, if you want slide titles in the presentation to be only one line long, you shouldn't adjust the size of this placeholder.

Now let's change the formatting of the bulleted lists on the slide masters.

12   Display the rulers.

13   With the primary master displayed, click anywhere in the phrase **Click to edit Master text styles** in the bulleted list placeholder.

12

14　On the **Home** tab, in the **Paragraph** group, click the **Bullets** arrow, and click **Bullets and Numbering** at the bottom of the menu to open the **Bullets And Numbering** dialog box.

You can change the bullet's symbol, color, and relative size.

15　Click **Picture** to open the **Insert Pictures** dialog box.

Choosing a picture bullet in place of a standard bullet can add a unique touch to your presentation.

16   In the **Office.com Clip Art** search box, enter bullet, and then click the **Search** button. Scroll through the gallery of images, click any red image (we chose the first image in the last row), and then click **Insert**.

17   Click anywhere in the phrase **Second level**, display the **Bullets and Numbering** dialog box, and click **Customize** to open the **Symbol** dialog box.

> **SEE ALSO** For more information about inserting symbols, see "Inserting symbols and equations" in Chapter 9, "Add other enhancements."

18   Change the **Font** to **Wingdings**, and double-click a symbol that is compatible with the picture you selected for the first-level bullet. Then click **OK**.

19   Back in the **Bullets and Numbering** dialog box, set the **Color** of the new bullet to **Dark Red** and its **Size** to **90**, and then click **OK** to implement your changes in all the layouts with bulleted lists.

20   Click the first-level bullet point, and on the horizontal ruler, drag the **Hanging Indent** marker (the lower triangle) to the right to the **0.5** inch mark. Then click the second-level bullet point, and drag its **Hanging Indent** marker to the **1** inch mark.

You've changed the bullet characters and spacing in the first-level and second-level bullet points.

TROUBLESHOOTING Dragging the Hanging Indent marker also drags the Left Indent marker, so increasing the distance between the bullet and the text in the first line also increases the indentation of the second and subsequent lines. If you drag the Left Indent marker instead, all three markers move on the ruler, changing the indentation of the paragraph while maintaining the relationship of the bullet and the text.

21 Switch to **Normal** view, and display slide **2**, noticing the effects of the changes you made to the primary master.

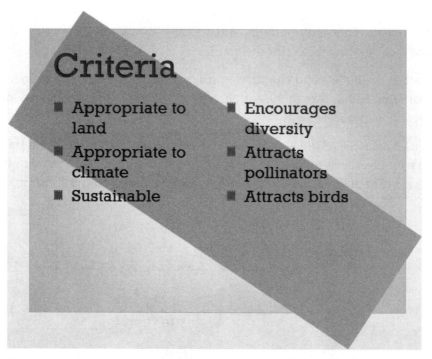

The changes to the primary master are reflected on all layouts with content placeholders.

We don't need date, footer information, and slide number placeholders on the Title Slide layout. Let's remove them.

22 Display the **Title Slide** layout in **Slide Master** view, and on the **Slide Master** tab, in the **Master Layout** group, clear the **Footers** check box.

TIP You cannot remove the footer placeholders from the primary master. You must remove them from the individual layouts.

❌ CLEAN UP Turn off the rulers. Then close the NaturalA presentation, saving your changes if you want to.

Creating themes, theme colors, and theme fonts

As you learned in Chapter 3, "Work with slides," a simple way to dress up a presentation is to apply a theme to make its colors, fonts, formatting, graphics, and other elements consistent from slide to slide. Understanding theme colors and theme fonts can help you create professional-looking presentations that use an appealing balance of color and text. You're not limited to using a presentation's theme colors and theme fonts, but because they have been selected by professional designers and are based on good design principles, using them ensures that your slides will be pleasing to the eye.

Every theme is assigned 12 complementary colors designed to be used for the following elements of a slide:

- **Text/Background** These four colors are for dark text on a light background or light text on a dark background.

- **Accent 1 through Accent 6** These six colors are for objects other than text.

- **Hyperlink** This color is to draw attention to hyperlinks.

- **Followed Hyperlink** This color is to indicate visited hyperlinks.

When you click a color arrow, such as the Font Color arrow in the Font group on the Home tab, the Theme Colors palette displays 10 of the 12 theme colors, each with an additional five light to dark shades. (The two background colors are not represented in this palette.)

SEE ALSO For information about using non-theme colors, see the sidebar "Non-theme colors" in Chapter 3, "Work with slides."

If you like all the elements of a theme except its color scheme, you can choose a different predefined set of theme colors without otherwise affecting the overall look of the theme. To view the theme colors you can apply to a presentation while in Normal view, display the Colors gallery from the Variants group on the Design tab. In Slide Master view, display this gallery from the Background group on the Slide Master tab. In either view, when you find a set of theme colors you like, simply click it to change the colors of all the slides in the presentation.

In addition to changing the set of theme colors, you can change the set of theme fonts. Displaying the Fonts gallery from either the Variants group on the Design tab or the Background group on the Slide Master tab shows a list of all the predefined combinations. In

12

each combination, the first font (called the *heading font*) is used for slide titles, and the second font (called the *body font*) is used for other slide text.

TIP Also associated with each theme is a set of theme effects. Using theme effects ensures that the shapes in the presentation have a consistent look. Clicking the Effects button in either the Variants group on the Design tab or the Background group on the Slide Master tab displays a gallery of effect combinations to choose from.

If none of the sets of theme colors is exactly what you're looking for, you can create your own by clicking Customize Colors at the bottom of the menu containing the Colors gallery and assembling colors in the Create New Theme Colors dialog box. You can also create a custom set of theme fonts by clicking Customize Fonts at the bottom of the menu containing the Fonts gallery and then specifying the font combination you want in the Create New Theme Fonts dialog box. After you save either type of custom combination, it is applied to all the slides or slide masters in the presentation.

TIP The simplest way to create a new theme color or theme font set is by altering an existing one.

When you apply a different theme color or theme font set to a presentation, your changes are stored with the presentation and do not affect the underlying theme. If you want to be able to use your custom theme color and theme font combination with other presentations, you can save the combination as a new theme that you can then apply to another presentation with a few clicks.

TIP You can set a custom theme, or any theme, as the default for all new presentations by right-clicking the theme's thumbnail in the Themes gallery on the Design tab in Normal view, and then clicking Set As Default Theme.

In this exercise, you'll apply a different theme color set and a different set of theme fonts to a presentation in Slide Master view. Next you'll create theme colors and theme fonts for a photo album and make them available for reuse. Then you'll save the color/font combination as a new theme that you can apply to any presentation.

SET UP You need the AnnualMeeting and PhotoAlbum presentations located in the Chapter12 practice file folder to complete this exercise. Open both presentations, and then with AnnualMeeting displayed, follow the steps.

1   Switch to **Slide Master** view, and then display the primary master.

2   On the **Slide Master** tab, in the **Background** group, click the **Colors** button to display a menu containing the **Colors** gallery.

Each set of theme colors is represented in the Colors gallery by 8 of its 12 available colors.

3   In the gallery, point to a few color sets to display live previews of their effects on the active slide.

4   Click **Yellow** to apply that theme color set to the presentation.

> **TIP** The theme retains all of its other characteristics, such as the fonts and back-ground graphic; only the colors change.

Next let's apply a different set of theme fonts.

5   In the **Background** group, click the **Fonts** button to display a menu containing the **Fonts** gallery.

Each set of theme fonts includes two fonts or two variations of the same font.

6   In the **Fonts** gallery, point to a few font sets to display live previews of their effects on the active slide.

7   In the gallery, click **Arial Black-Arial** to apply that theme font set to the presentation.

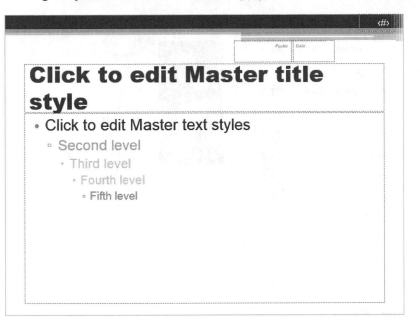

The theme colors and theme fonts applied to the primary master are also applied to all the other masters in the presentation.

8   Save the **AnnualMeeting** presentation, but don't close it.

Now let's create custom theme colors and custom theme font sets for a different presentation.

9   Display the **PhotoAlbum** presentation in **Slide Master** view. Then display the **Colors** gallery, and click **Blue**.

The Blue theme color set has some interesting colors, but the presentation title is too sedate. Let's change the color assigned to text.

10 Display the **Colors** gallery, and then at the bottom of the gallery, click **Customize Colors** to open the **Create New Theme Colors** dialog box.

12

Each color scheme consists of 12 colors assigned to the 12 possible design elements of a presentation.

11   Click the **Text/Background - Light 2** button to display a menu containing the **Theme Colors** and **Standard Colors** palettes.

12   In the **Theme Colors** palette, click the second swatch from the right in the top row (**Orange, Hyperlink**). Notice that the **Sample** pane changes to show the new color combination.

13   Click the **Accent 1** button, and in the **Theme Colors** palette, click the fourth swatch in the top row (**Light Blue, Text 2**).

14   Click the **Text/Background - Light 1** button, and at the bottom of the menu, click **More Colors** to open the **Colors** dialog box.

15   If the **Standard** tab is not displayed, click it to display its color wheel.

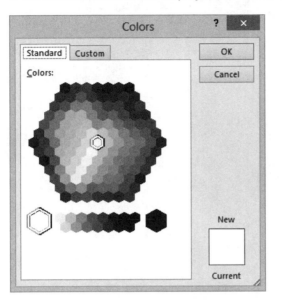

The color wheel has light and dark shades of three primary colors (blue, red, and yellow), three secondary colors (violet, orange, and green), and tertiary colors created by mixing a primary color with a secondary color.

16   In the color wheel, click a lime green color, and then click **OK**.

17   In the **Name** box at the bottom of the **Create New Theme Colors** dialog box, change the name of the new theme to My Custom Colors, and then click **Save** to apply the change to the slides.

18   Display the **AnnualMeeting** presentation in **Slide Master** view, and then display the **Colors** gallery. Notice that the custom set of theme colors is now available for use with other presentations.

12

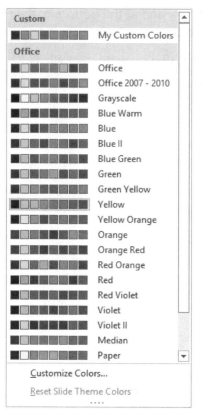

The new set of theme colors is available in the Custom area at the top of the Colors gallery so that it is easy to apply to any presentation.

Now let's create a custom set of theme fonts.

19 Switch back to the **PhotoAlbum** presentation. Then in the **Background** group, click the **Fonts** button, and in the **Fonts** gallery, click **Consolas-Verdana** as a starting point for a new font set.

20 Click the **Fonts** button again, and then at the bottom of the menu, click **Customize Fonts** to open the **Create New Theme Fonts** dialog box.

When choosing fonts, try to find a combination that reflects the tone of your presentation.

21   Click the **Heading font** arrow, and then in the list, click **Arial Rounded MT Bold**.

22   In the **Name** box at the bottom of the dialog box, change the name of the new font set to **My Custom Fonts**, and then click **Save**.

23   In the **Background** group, click the **Fonts** button, and verify that your combination is listed in the **Custom** area of the **Fonts** gallery.

24   Switch to **Normal** view, and view the slides of the presentation with the new colors and fonts in place.

> **TROUBLESHOOTING** If you create a set of theme fonts and PowerPoint doesn't update the slides to reflect the change, click each text placeholder, press Ctrl+A to select all its text, and then press Ctrl+Spacebar. This removes any local formatting and reapplies the formatting defined by the attached theme.

Let's save the theme colors and theme fonts as a new theme.

25   Switch to **Slide Master** view. In the **Edit Theme** group, click the **Themes** button, and then at the bottom of the menu, click **Save Current Theme** to open the **Save Current Theme** dialog box.

> **TIP** By default, the dialog box displays the contents of the Document Themes folder, which is located at C:\Users\<username>\AppData\Roaming\Microsoft\Templates\Document Themes. Custom theme colors and theme fonts are saved in subfolders of this folder so that they are available in their galleries for use in other presentations.

12

26   In the **File name** box at the bottom of the dialog box, change the name of the new theme to **My Theme**, and then click **Save**.

27   Close the **PhotoAlbum** presentation, saving your changes if you want to.

28   Display the **AnnualMeeting** presentation in **Normal** view. Then on the **Design** tab, in the **Themes** group, point to the second thumbnail in the gallery to display the ScreenTip **My Theme**.

29   Click the **My Theme** thumbnail to apply the custom theme to the presentation.

30   On slide **1**, select the presentation title, and on the **Home** tab, in the **Font** group, click the **Font Color** arrow. Notice that the **Theme Colors** palette reflects the custom theme colors stored as part of the custom theme. Then click the lime green theme color to make the title stand out.

> **TIP** To delete a custom theme, theme color set, or theme font set, display its gallery, right-click its thumbnail, and click Delete. Then click Yes to confirm the deletion.

❌ CLEAN UP If you want, delete the custom theme, theme colors, and theme fonts. Then close the AnnualMeeting presentation, saving your changes if you want to.

Designing slide layouts

PowerPoint 2013 comes with many standard layouts—enough to suit most presentations. However, one of the slides in a presentation might require a completely different layout. If the same custom layout is likely to be used more than once in a presentation, you can save time by adding the layout to the slide master set so that you can use it anytime you need it. Clicking the Insert Layout button in the Edit Master group on the Slide Master tab adds a new layout to the master set, with a title but no other content. You can then insert place-holders and arrange and format them the way you want them.

In this exercise, you'll create a slide master layout with placeholders for a title and a paragraph of text. Then you'll create another layout with placeholders for a title and pictures.

SET UP You need the NaturalB presentation located in the Chapter12 practice file folder and three photographs to complete this exercise. Open the presentation, display the rulers, and then follow the steps.

1   Switch to **Slide Master** view. Then with the **Title Slide** layout displayed, on the **Slide Master** tab, in the **Edit Master** group, click the **Insert Layout** button.

2   With the new slide layout selected, in the **Master Layout** group, click the **Insert Placeholder** arrow to display the **Placeholder** gallery.

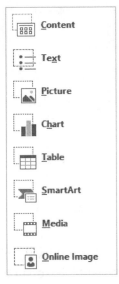

You can draw placeholders for any of these types of content.

3   In the gallery, click **Text**. Then move the cross pointer over the slide, and drag to create a text placeholder the width of the title placeholder and about **3** inches high. (Drag from about the **-1.5** inch mark to the **1.5** inch mark on the vertical ruler.)

12

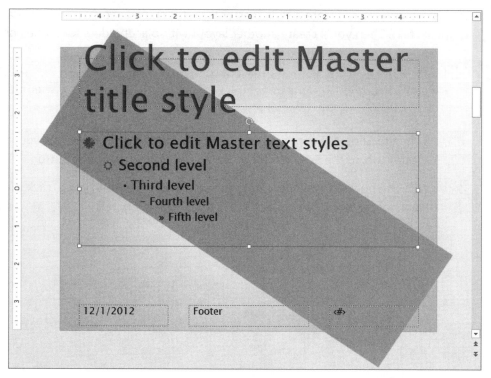

When you finish dragging, PowerPoint adds the five default bullet levels defined on the primary master to the text placeholder of the new slide layout.

Let's format the text placeholder to display an italic paragraph, instead of a bulleted list.

4 In the text placeholder, point to the bullet to the left of **Second level**, and when the cursor changes to a four-headed arrow, click to select that bullet-point level and all the levels below it. Then press the **Delete** key.

5 With the cursor at the end of the first-level bullet point, on the **Home** tab, in the **Paragraph** group, click the **Bullets** arrow, and in the **Bullets** gallery, click **None**.

6 With the cursor at the end of the paragraph, press **Ctrl+A** to select all the text in the placeholder, and then in the **Font** group, click the **Italic** button.

KEYBOARD SHORTCUT Press Ctrl+I to italicize the selected text.

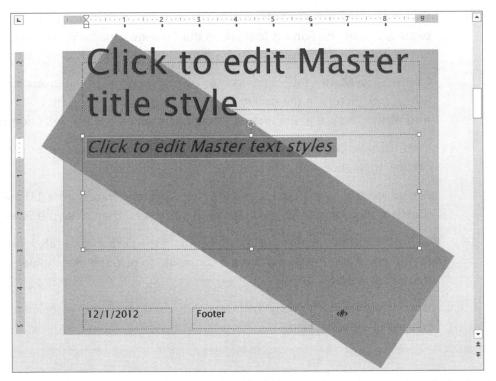

Because you removed the bullet formatting, the indent markers have moved on the horizontal ruler.

Next let's create a picture layout.

7   On the **Slide Master** tab, in the **Edit Master** group, click the **Insert Layout** button to add another slide layout to the master set.

8   Switch to **Normal** view, and display slide **3**. Then select the cat, crow, and frog pictures, and copy them.

9   Switch to **Slide Master** view, display the new master layout (the third one below the primary master), and paste in the pictures.

TIP If you want the pictures to appear on all slides, paste them into the primary master instead.

To make it easier to add pictures to slides with this layout, let's replace the pictures with placeholders.

10 Click a blank area of the slide layout to release the selection. Then click the frog picture, and on the **Format** tool tab, in the **Arrange** group, click the **Selection Pane** button to open the **Selection** pane, where the frog picture is designated as **Picture 5**.

11 On the **Slide Master** tab, in the **Master Layout** group, click the **Insert Placeholder** arrow, click **Picture** in the gallery, and then drag a picture placeholder on top of the frog picture. Notice that a **Picture Placeholder** appears in the **Selection** pane.

12 In the pane, click **Picture 5**, and then press **Delete**, leaving the picture placeholder occupying its spot in the slide.

13 Repeat steps 11 and 12 to replace the crow (**Content Placeholder 11**) and cat (**Content Placeholder 10**) with picture placeholders. Then close the **Selection** pane.

14 Select the bottom picture placeholder, and on the **Format** tool tab, in the **Shape Styles** group, use the **Shape Outline** command to give the placeholder a **Dark Red** frame that is **3 pt** wide.

15 Use **Format Painter** to copy the frame of the bottom picture placeholder to the other two picture placeholders.

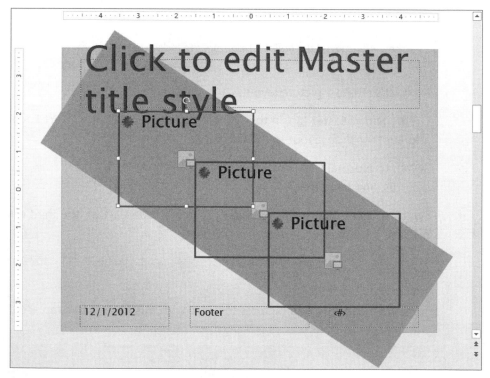

Each picture placeholder contains a Pictures button.

Now let's give the new layouts meaningful names and then test them.

16 With the picture layout still selected, on the **Slide Master** tab, in the **Edit Master** group, click the **Rename** button to open the **Rename Layout** dialog box.

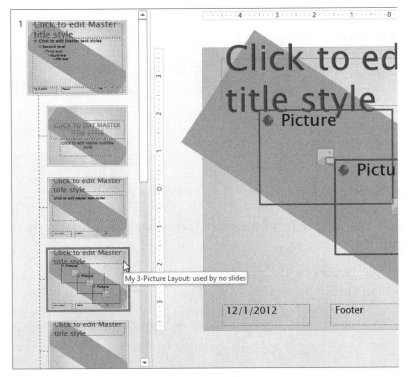

Providing a name for your custom layout will identify the layout in the New Slide gallery.

17 In the **Layout name** box, enter **My 3-Picture**, and then click **Rename**.

18 On the **Thumbnail** tab, point to the layout to display its name in a ScreenTip.

The ScreenTip also tells you how many slides are using this layout.

19 Repeat steps 16 and 17 to rename the first layout master you created as **My Text Paragraph**.

20 Switch to **Normal** view. Then with slide **3** selected, click the **New Slide** arrow to display a menu containing the **New Slide** gallery.

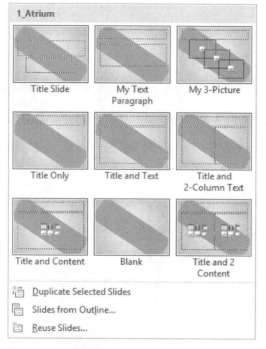

The gallery now includes thumbnails of your custom layouts.

21 In the gallery, click **My Text Paragraph**. Then add another slide by clicking **My 3-Picture** in the gallery.

22 Test the new layouts by adding a title and a paragraph to slide **4** and a title and pictures to slide **5**. (We used the **NativePlant1**, **NativePlant2**, and **NativePlant3** photos in the **Chapter12** practice file folder.)

This slide uses the NativePlant1, NativePlant2, and NativePlant3 picture files in the My 3-Picture layout.

❌ CLEAN UP **Turn off the rulers, and then close the NaturalB presentation, saving your changes if you want to.**

Saving custom design templates

Suppose you have spent a lot of time customizing the slide masters of a particular presentation and you think you might want to use the new design for future presentations. Or suppose your company requires that all official presentations use a customized set of masters that include a logo, contact information, a specific background, and bullets and text in colors that reflect the company's branding. In cases like these, you can save a customized presentation as a design template. You can then use it as the basis for new presentations.

12

In earlier versions of PowerPoint, templates were saved by default in a hidden folder stored at C:\Users\< *user name*>\AppData\Roaming\Microsoft\Templates. By default, PowerPoint 2013 saves templates in the My Documents\Custom Office Templates folder, which the program creates the first time you save either a custom theme or theme component, or a template. However, PowerPoint doesn't make the templates you save available from the New page of the Backstage view until you designate the Custom Office Templates folder as the default personal templates location on the Save page of the PowerPoint Options dialog box.

TIP You can designate any folder as the default personal templates folder. (The folder you designate must already exist.) If you created templates with an earlier version of Power-Point, you might want to designate the C:\Users\<user *name*>\AppData\Roaming\Microsoft\ Templates folder so that those templates will be available on the New page.

If you store a template in a folder that is not the default personal templates location, you can browse to that folder in File Explorer and double-click the template file to start PowerPoint and open a new presentation based on the template.

In this exercise, you'll save a presentation as a template, set the default personal templates location, and then create a presentation based on the template.

➡ SET UP **You need the NaturalC presentation located in the Chapter12 practice file folder to complete this exercise. Open the presentation, and then follow the steps.**

TIP This exercise assumes that you haven't previously designated a default personal templates folder.

1   Display the **Save As** page of the **Backstage** view, and with **Computer** selected, click **Browse**.

2   In the **Save As** dialog box, change the **Save as type** option to **PowerPoint Template**. In the **Address** box at the top of the dialog box. Then notice that the default folder is **Custom Office Templates**.

3   In the **File name** box, enter Natural, and then click **Save**.

    With the Natural template saved in the specified folder, we can edit it and save it just like any other presentation. Let's edit the template to make it more generic.

4   With the title slide displayed, select all the text in the title placeholder, and press the **Delete** key. Then click away from the placeholder to display the instruction **CLICK TO ADD TITLE**.

5   Repeat step 7 for the subtitle.

6   In the **Thumbnails** pane, click slide **2**. Then hold down the **Shift** key, and click slide **5**.

7   With slides **2** through **5** selected, press **Delete**.

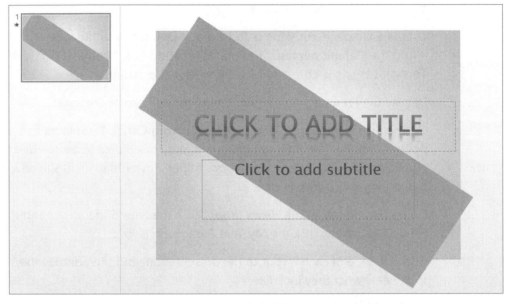

The template now contains only the title slide, which has two placeholders that are empty except for placeholder instructions.

8   On the **Quick Access Toolbar**, click the **Save** button. Then from the **Backstage** view, close the template.

KEYBOARD SHORTCUT Press Ctrl+S to save the presentation.

Now let's start a new presentation based on the template.

9   Display the **New** page of the **Backstage** view, and to the right of **Featured**, click **Custom** or **Personal**. Notice that the new template does not appear on this page.

12

TIP If you save a theme or theme component first, PowerPoint adds a Custom page to the New page in Backstage view. If you save a template first, PowerPoint adds a Personal page instead. After you have created multiple items, the themes and theme components are gathered together in a folder on this page, and the templates are gathered together in another folder. As a result, your New page might behave slightly differently than described in this exercise.

10   Open the **PowerPoint Options** dialog box by clicking **Options** in the **Backstage** view, and in the left pane, click **Save**.

11   On the **Save** page, copy the path from the **Default local file location** box, and paste it into the **Default personal templates location** box. Then add Custom Office Templates to the end, and click **OK** to save the setting.

12   Display the **New** page again, and then click **Custom** or **Personal**.

13   On the **displayed** page, either click the **Custom Office Templates** folder, and then double-click the **Natural** thumbnail, or simply double-click the **Natural** thumbnail if you have no Custom Office Templates folder. PowerPoint creates a new presentation based on your custom template.

14   On the **Home** tab, in the **Slides** group, click the **New Slide** arrow, and then in the **New Slide** gallery, click the **My Text Paragraph** layout.

15   Add one slide of each layout to the presentation, and then display the slides in turn to preview what they look like.

❌ CLEAN UP Close the presentation without saving your changes. If you want, delete the Natural template from your My Documents\Custom Office Templates folder.

Key points

- The slide master set controls the basic design of all slides in a presentation. You can make global changes by editing text and objects on the primary master and on the layout variations in the set.

- If the themes, theme colors, and theme fonts that come with PowerPoint don't meet your needs, you can create your own and then make any combination available to all your presentations as a custom theme.

- To create your own layouts, you can manipulate existing objects on the masters. Or you can add an entirely new layout and build it from scratch.

- After setting up a presentation to look the way you want, you can save it as a design template for use as the basis for other presentations.

12

Chapter at a glance

Adapt

Adapt presentations for different audiences,
page 376

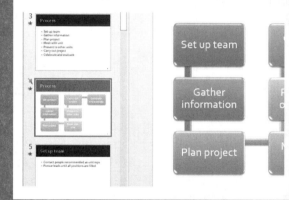

Rehearse

Rehearse presentations,
page 380

Prepare

Prepare presentations for travel,
page 386

Prepare for delivery 13

IN THIS CHAPTER, YOU WILL LEARN HOW TO

- Adapt presentations for different audiences.

- Rehearse presentations.

- Prepare presentations for travel.

The goal of all the effort involved in creating a presentation is to be able to effectively deliver it to a specific audience. With Microsoft PowerPoint 2013, you can deliver presentations in several ways, and you need to prepare the presentation accordingly to ensure its success.

If your presentation will be delivered in person, you might want to hide individual slides that are not appropriate to show to all audiences. If you know that you'll be giving variations of the same presentation to different audiences, you can prepare a master set of slides and then save subsets as separate presentations that you'll show to each audience. To appropriately fit your presentation to its allotted time, you can tailor the speed at which slides appear. If you are delivering the presentation in a remote location, you'll want to use the Package For CD feature to ensure that you take all the necessary files with you.

In this chapter, you'll adapt a presentation for two audiences, first by creating a custom slide show, and then by hiding a slide. You'll rehearse a presentation so that you can have PowerPoint set the appropriate slide timing for each slide. You'll also save a presentation package on a CD.

PRACTICE FILES To complete the exercises in this chapter, you need the practice files contained in the Chapter13 practice file folder. For more information, see "Download the practice files" in this book's Introduction.

Adapting presentations for different audiences

If you plan to deliver variations of the same presentation to different audiences, you should prepare one presentation containing all the slides you are likely to need for all the audiences. Then you can select slides from the presentation that are appropriate for a particular audience and group them as a custom slide show. When you need to deliver the presentation for that audience, you open the main presentation and show the subset of slides by choosing the custom slide show from a list.

For example, suppose you need to pitch an idea for a new product or service to both a team of project managers and a company's executive team. Many of the slides would be the same for both groups, but the presentation to the executive team might include more in-depth competitive and financial analysis. You would develop the executive team's presentation first and then create a custom slide show for the project managers by using a subset of the slides in the executive presentation.

During a presentation, you might sometimes want to be able to make an on-the-spot decision about whether to display a particular slide. You can give yourself this flexibility by hiding the slide so that you can skip over it if its information doesn't seem useful to a particular audience. If you decide to include the slide's information in the presentation, display it by pressing the letter *H* or by using the Go To Slide command.

In this exercise, you'll select slides from an existing presentation to create a custom slide show for a different audience. You'll also hide a slide and then redisplay it.

SET UP You need the CommunityProjects presentation located in the Chapter13 practice file folder to complete this exercise. Open the presentation, and then follow the steps.

1   On the **Slide Show** tab, in the **Start Slide Show** group, click the **Custom Slide Show** button, and then click **Custom Shows** to open the **Custom Shows** dialog box.

2   Click **New** to open the **Define Custom Show** dialog box.

The slides in the active presentation are listed in the box on the left.

3 Replace the name in the **Slide show name** box with Managers.

4 In the **Slides in presentation** list, select the slide **1** check box, and then click **Add** to transfer slide **1** to the **Slides in custom show** box on the right.

5 Repeat step 4 to add slides **2** through **6**, **9**, **10**, and **14** through **16**.

You can change the order of the slides by clicking the Up or Down button or remove a slide by clicking the Remove button.

6 Click **OK** to define 11 of the 16 available slides as the custom show for managers.

7 In the **Custom Shows** dialog box, click **Show** to start the **Managers** custom slide show.

8 Advance through all the slides, including the blank one at the end of the show. As you move from slide to slide, notice the slide numbers in the lower-right corner of the screen.

13

Let's remove one of the slides from the custom show.

9   In **Normal** view, on the **Slide Show** tab, in the **Start Slide Show** group, click the **Custom Slide Show** button, and then in the list, click **Custom Shows**.

10   In the **Custom Shows** dialog box, verify that **Managers** is selected, and then click **Edit** to open the **Define Custom Show** dialog box.

11   In the **Slides in custom show** list, click slide **3**, and then click the **Remove** button.

     TIP The slide is removed from the custom slide show, not from the presentation.

12   Click **OK,** and then close the **Custom Shows** dialog box.

     As we previously demonstrated, you can start the custom show from the Custom Shows dialog box, but for a smoother delivery, let's set up the presentation to display only the subset of slides in the Managers custom show.

13   With slide **1** displayed in **Normal** view, on the **Slide Show** tab, in the **Set Up** group, click the **Set Up Slide Show** button to open the **Set Up Show** dialog box.

14   In the **Show slides** area, click **Custom show**, which activates the box below it.

If the presentation contains more than one custom show, you can select the one you want from the Custom Show list.

15   Click **OK** to close the dialog box, switch to **Slide Show** view, and then advance
      through the 10 slides of the **Managers** custom show and the ending black slide.

      Let's hide slide 4 in the main presentation.

16   In the **Thumbnails** pane, click slide **4**, and then on the **Slide Show** tab, in the **Set Up**
      group, click the **Hide Slide** button.

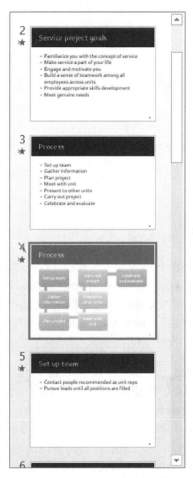

*In the Thumbnails pane, there is now a diagonal line through
the number 4 and the slide contents are dimmed
to indicate that slide 4 is hidden.*

TIP You can also right-click the slide thumbnail and then click Hide Slide.

13

17   Display slide **1**, switch to **Reading** view, and click the **Next** button to display slide **2**. Then click **Next** again. Notice that PowerPoint skips slide **3** because it is not included in the custom show and skips slide **4** because it is hidden.

18   Click the **Previous** button to move back to slide **2**.

19   Right-click anywhere on the screen, point to **Go to Slide**, and then click **(3) Process** to display the hidden slide.

> **TIP** Because you removed slide 3 from the Managers custom show, slide 4 in the main presentation is slide 3 in Managers. The number is in parentheses because the slide is hidden.

20   Press **Esc** to return to **Normal** view.

❌ CLEAN UP **Close the CommunityProjects presentation, saving your changes if you want to.**

Rehearsing presentations

As we've demonstrated, when delivering a presentation, you can move from slide to slide manually by clicking the mouse button, pressing keys, or clicking commands. By adding transitions, you can have PowerPoint display each slide for a predefined length of time before displaying the next slide. In automatically advancing presentations, the length of time a slide appears on the screen is controlled by its slide timing.

To apply a timing to one slide, to a group of slides, or to an entire presentation, first select the slides, and then in the Advance Slide area of the Timing group on the Transitions tab, select the After check box and enter the number of minutes and seconds you want each slide to remain on the screen. By default, each slide timing is divided equally among the animated items on a particular slide. So if a slide has a title and four bullet points that are all animated and you assign a timing of one minute to the slide, the five elements will appear at 12-second intervals.

TIP If you are delivering the presentation in Slide Show view and you want to prevent PowerPoint from advancing to the next slide according to a slide timing, press the letter *S* on your keyboard, or right-click the current slide and click Pause. To continue the presentation, press the letter *S* again, or right-click the slide and click Resume.

If you don't know how much time to allocate for the slide timings of a presentation, you can rehearse the presentation. PowerPoint automatically tracks and sets the timings for you, reflecting the amount of time you spend on each slide during the rehearsal. Then during presentation delivery, PowerPoint displays each slide for the length of time you indicated during the rehearsal. In this way, you can synchronize an automatic slide show with a live narration or demonstration.

TIP If your presentation will be delivered as a slide show, you should consider omitting slide timings so that people viewing the slides can advance at their own speed. Otherwise, people with visual impairments or who use accessibility tools might not finish reading the content before the slide advances.

In this exercise, you'll set the timing for one slide and apply it to an entire presentation. Then you'll rehearse the presentation and have PowerPoint set slide timings according to the amount of time you display each slide during the rehearsal.

➡ SET UP **You need the Journal presentation located in the Chapter13 practice file folder to complete this exercise. Open the presentation, and then follow the steps.**

1   On the **Transitions** tab, in the **Timing** group, in the **Advance Slide** area, select the **After** check box, and then at the right end of the adjacent box, click the up arrow three times to change the setting to **00:03.00**.

   TIP Because both check boxes in the Advance Slide area are selected, the slide will advance either after three seconds or when you click the mouse button. The ability to click in addition to setting slide timings is useful when you're running short on time during a presentation and need to speed things up.

2   Switch to **Reading** view, and watch as slide **1** is displayed for three seconds and then slide **2** appears. Then return to **Normal** view.

3   Switch to **Slide Sorter** view.

13

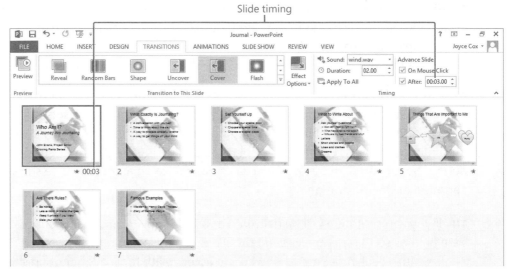

Slide timing

The slide timing appears below the lower-left corner of slide 1, which is the only slide with a slide timing.

4   With slide **1** selected, in the **Timing** group, click the **Apply To All** button.

TIP When you click Apply To All, all the transition effects of the current slide are copied to the other slides. If you have applied different transitions to different slides, those individually specified transitions are overwritten. So it's a good idea to apply all the effects you want the slides to have in common first. Then you can select individual slides and customize their effects. For information about transitions, see "Adding transitions" in Chapter 5, "Add simple visual enhancements."

5   Switch to **Reading** view, watch as the slides advance, and then when the black screen is displayed, click it to return to **Slide Sorter** view.

Now let's rehearse the presentation and have PowerPoint apply slide timings based on the amount of time each slide remains on the screen. First we have to delete the automatic slide timings.

6   Select slide **1**. In the **Advance Slide** area of the **Timing** group, clear the **After** check box, and then click **Apply To All**.

7   With slide **1** selected, on the **Slide Show** tab, in the **Set Up** group, click the **Rehearse Timings** button. When PowerPoint switches to **Slide Show** view and starts the presentation, notice the **Recording** toolbar in the upper-left corner of the screen.

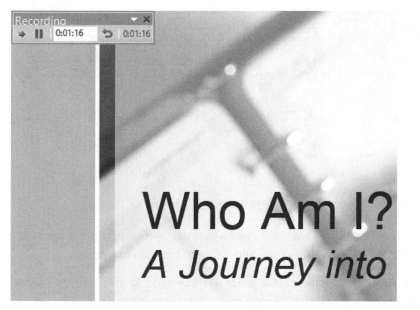

The Slide Time counter tracks the time slide 1 remains on the screen, and the Presentation Time counter accumulates the display time of all the slides.

8   Wait several seconds, and then on the **Recording** toolbar, click the **Next** button to display the next slide and start the **Slide Time** counter over at **0:00:00**.

9   Work your way slowly through the presentation, clicking **Next** until you reach slide **6**. Then allow the **Slide Time** counter to record for a few seconds.

Let's repeat the rehearsal for this slide.

10   On the **Recording** toolbar, click the **Repeat** button to reset the **Slide Time** counter for slide **6** to **0:00:00**.

11   When a message tells you that the recording has been paused, click **Resume Recording** and rehearse the delivery for slide **6** again.

TIP If you want to start the entire rehearsal over again, click the Close button on the Recording toolbar, and when a message asks whether you want to keep the existing timings, click No.

12   Click **Next** to move to the last slide, wait a few seconds, and then click **Next** again.

13   When a message tells you the total delivery time and asks whether you want to save the recorded slide timings, click **Yes** to end the rehearsal and redisplay the presentation in **Slide Sorter** view with slide **1** active.

13

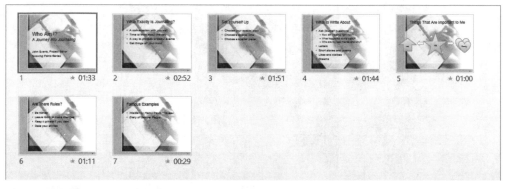

The recorded timings are displayed below each slide.

14 Click the **Transitions** tab, and notice that the rehearsed timing for slide **1** appears in the **After** box in the **Advance Slide** area of the **Timing** group.

15 If the **After** setting for slide **1** is not a whole second, click the **Up** button to the right of the box to adjust the time up to the next whole second.

> **TIP** You can manually adjust the timing of any slide by selecting it and changing the setting in this box.

16 Switch to **Reading** view, and watch as the slides advance according to the recorded timings.

17 Press **Esc** at any time to stop the presentation.

✖ CLEAN UP Close the Journal presentation, saving your changes if you want to.

Recording presentations

For a really smooth delivery, you might want to record your presentation so that you can hear yourself in action and correct any flaws before you have to perform before a live audience. You might also want to record a presentation that people will view on their own computers rather than at a speaker-led meeting. When you record a presentation, you can specify whether you want to record only slide and animation timings or only narrations and laser pointer movements, and you can record an entire presentation or only a specific slide.

To record a presentation:

1. Ensure that your computer has a sound card, microphone, and speakers. Test the microphone before beginning the recording.

2. Open the presentation you want to record.

3. With slide **1** displayed, on the **Slide Show** tab, in the **Set Up** group, click the **Record Slide Show** button to open the **Record Slide Show** dialog box.

   TIP If you don't want to record the entire presentation, click the Record Slide Show arrow, and then click Start Recording From Current Slide.

4. If you don't want to record timings or narrations and laser pointer movements, clear the corresponding check box. Then click **Start Recording**.

   PowerPoint switches to Slide Show view, starts the presentation, and displays the Recording toolbar in the upper-left corner of the screen. The Slide Time counter tracks the length of time the slide remains on the screen.

5. Discuss the points associated with the current slide, just as if you were delivering the presentation to a live audience, and then move to the next slide.

   TIP You can pause the recording by clicking the Pause button on the Recording toolbar, and you can repeat the recording for the current slide by clicking the Repeat button.

6. When you have finished, press the **Esc** key to stop recording. Display the presentation in **Slide Sorter** view, where the narration appears on each slide as a sound object and the slide timings appear below the lower-right corner of each slide.

7. Test the recording by running the presentation in **Reading** view, where each slide is accompanied by its recorded narration.

If you are not satisfied with the narration for a particular slide, you can delete its sound icon just like any other object, and then record that slide again.

If you are archiving a presentation and want to add comments to a specific slide, you don't have to record the entire presentation. Display the slide in Normal view, and on the Insert tab, in the Media group, click the Audio button, and then click Record Audio. After recording your comments, name the sound file for that slide, and click OK. The narration is then attached to a sound icon on the slide.

TIP If you anticipate that your presentation will be viewed by people with hearing disabilities, be sure to add alt text to the sound object to describe the content of the narration.

13

Preparing presentations for travel

When you develop a presentation on the computer from which you will be delivering it, all the fonts, linked objects, and other components of the presentation will be available when the lights go down and you launch your first slide. However, if you will deliver your presentation from a different computer, you need to ensure that the fonts, linked objects, and any other necessary items will all be available when you need them.

You can use the Package For CD feature to help you gather all the presentation components and save them to a CD or other type of removable media so that they can be transported to a different computer. Linked and embedded items, such as fonts, sounds, videos, and any other files used by the presentation, are included in the presentation package by default. You also have the option of assigning a password to open or modify the presentation, and of using the Document Inspector to remove any personal or confidential information from the packaged file.

TIP PowerPoint 2013 does not support the direct burning of content to a DVD. If you prefer to burn to a DVD rather than a CD, first use the Package For CD feature to create a presentation package in a folder on your computer, and then use DVD-burning software to copy the package to the DVD.

You can add more than one presentation to the same presentation package, and you can include files not specifically related to the presentation. If you add more than one presentation, you can specify the order in which the presentations should run. PowerPoint assembles all the files, adds an autorun file, and creates a folder of supporting files.

To run a packaged presentation from CD on a computer that does not have PowerPoint 2013 installed, you need the Microsoft PowerPoint Viewer. With some earlier versions of PowerPoint, the PowerPoint Viewer was automatically included with the packaged presentation. However, it's not included with PowerPoint 2013; it must be downloaded from the Microsoft Download Center website and installed on the computer in order to use it.

TIP When you insert the presentation CD into your CD/DVD drive, the AutoPlay dialog box opens so that you can indicate whether you want to display an HTML introductory screen (called a *splash screen*) for the presentation. This screen provides a link for downloading the Viewer. After the Viewer is installed, clicking the name of the presentation on the HTML splash screen runs the presentation.

In this exercise, you'll use Package For CD to create a presentation package on a CD.

SET UP You need the GettingOrganized presentation and the Procedures document located in the Chapter13 practice file folder to complete this exercise. Be sure to have a blank CD available. If your computer does not have a CD/DVD burner, you can follow along with the exercise by creating a presentation package in a folder. Open the presentation, and then follow the steps.

1   Display the **Export** page of the **Backstage** view, click **Package Presentation for CD**, and then click the **Package for CD** button in the right pane to open the **Package for CD** dialog box.

You can add files to or remove files from the Files To Be Copied list.

2   Replace the name in the **Name the CD** box with **Organization**.

3   Click **Options** to open the **Options** dialog box.

By default, the presentation's linked files and embedded TrueType fonts will be included in the presentation package.

13

TIP If the presentation includes fonts that don't come with the version of Windows running on the presentation computer or with the Microsoft Office 2013 programs, be sure to leave the Embedded TrueType Fonts check box selected. Then the presentation will look the same on a computer on which the fonts aren't installed as it does on your computer. You can embed fonts when you package a presentation, or you can do it when you first save the presentation. (Only TrueType and OpenType fonts can be embedded.) In the Save As dialog box, click Tools, click Save Options, and on the Save page of the PowerPoint Options dialog box, select the Embed Fonts In The File check box. Then click Embed Only The Characters Used In The Presentation to embed only the characters in the font set that are actually used, or click Embed All Characters to embed the entire font set.

4   Select the **Inspect presentations for inappropriate or private information** check box, and then click **OK**.

5   Insert a blank CD in your CD/DVD burner, and if the **AutoPlay** dialog box opens, close it.

6   In the **Package for CD** dialog box, click **Copy to CD**.

   TROUBLESHOOTING If your computer does not have a CD/DVD burner, click Copy To Folder instead. Then in the Copy To Folder dialog box, specify the folder in which you want to store the package, clear the Open Folder When Complete check box, and click OK.

7   When a message asks you to verify that you want to include linked content, click **Yes**.

8   When the **Document Inspector** dialog box opens so that you can inspect the presentation file for personal or confidential information, click **Inspect**.

9   When the inspection results are displayed, click **Remove All** to the right of **Document Properties and Personal information** (ignore any other results). Then close the **Document Inspector** dialog box.

   SEE ALSO For more information about the Document Inspector, see "Finalizing presentations" in Chapter 6, "Review and deliver presentations."

10   When the files required for the **GettingOrganized** presentation have been copied and the CD is ejected, click **No** in the message box that appears, indicating that you don't want to copy the same package to another CD.

11   Close the **Package for CD** dialog box.

If you have access to a different computer, you should now test whether you can run the presentation from the CD. If the other computer does not have PowerPoint 2013 installed on it, you will need to download and install the PowerPoint Viewer as described in the Tip preceding the Set Up instructions for this exercise.

❌ CLEAN UP Close the GettingOrganized presentation.

Key points

- An efficient way to create versions of the same presentation for different audiences is to gather subsets of the presentation's slides in custom slide shows. You can also hide slides and then display them only if appropriate.

- You can manually assign slide timings, or you can rehearse the presentation and have PowerPoint track the amount of time each slide is displayed during the rehearsal.

- To be sure you have all the required files when delivering a presentation from a computer other than the one on which it was developed, create a presentation package.

- You can deliver a presentation on a computer on which PowerPoint is not installed by downloading the PowerPoint Viewer.

13

Chapter at a glance

Change

Change default program options,
page 391

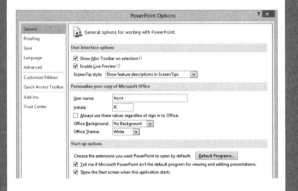

Customize

Customize the ribbon,
page 403

Manipulate

Manipulate the Quick Access Toolbar,
page 410

Work in PowerPoint more efficiently

14

IN THIS CHAPTER, YOU WILL LEARN HOW TO

- Change default program options.

- Customize the ribbon.

- Manipulate the Quick Access Toolbar.

If you use Microsoft PowerPoint 2013 only occasionally, you might be perfectly happy creating presentations with the wide range of tools we have already discussed in this book. And you might be comfortable with the default working environment options and behind-the-scenes settings. However, if you create many presentations of various types, you might want to streamline the development process or change aspects of the program to make it more suitable for the kinds of presentations you create.

In this chapter, you'll take a tour of the pages of the PowerPoint Options dialog box to understand the ways in which you can customize the program. Then you'll manipulate the ribbon and the Quick Access Toolbar to put the tools you need for your daily work at your fingertips.

PRACTICE FILES To complete the exercises in this chapter, you need the practice files contained in the Chapter14 practice file folder. For more information, see "Download the practice files" in this book's Introduction.

Changing default program options

In earlier chapters, we mentioned that you can change settings in the PowerPoint Options dialog box to customize the PowerPoint environment in various ways. After you work with PowerPoint for a while, you might want to refine more settings to tailor the program to the way you work. Knowing which settings are where in the PowerPoint Options dialog box makes the customizing process more efficient.

In this exercise, you'll open the PowerPoint Options dialog box and explore several of the available pages.

➜ SET UP **You don't need any practice files to complete this exercise. Start a new, blank presentation, and then follow the steps.**

TIP As you work your way through this exercise, don't worry if the settings in your PowerPoint Options dialog box are different from ours. Settings can vary depending on changes you might have made while working through the exercises and depending on which programs you have installed. Also don't worry about the height of the dialog box; for screen shot purposes, we sized the dialog box to best fit its contents.

1 Display the **Backstage** view, and then click **Options** to open the **PowerPoint Options** dialog box with the **General** page displayed.

The General page includes three categories of options that affect program features and the user interface.

2 If having the **Mini Toolbar** appear when you select text is more of a hindrance than a help, disable that feature by clearing the **Show Mini Toolbar on selection** check box. Similarly, if you don't use Live Preview, clear the **Enable Live Preview** check box.

Now let's adjust the display of ScreenTips, verify the user name and initials, and change the background of the user interface.

3 Display the **ScreenTip style** list, and click **Don't show feature descriptions in ScreenTips**.

4 In the **Personalize your copy of Microsoft Office** area, verify that the information in the **User name** and **Initials** boxes are correct, or change them to the way you want them to appear.

5 Display the **Office Theme** list, and click **Dark Gray**.

6 Change any other options you think would help you work more efficiently, and then click **OK** to close the **PowerPoint Options** dialog box. Notice the gray background of the program window.

7 In the **Font** group, point to the **Bold** button to display its ScreenTip, which now includes only the button name and its keyboard shortcut.

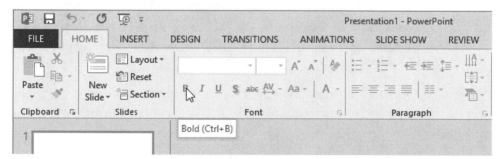

The ScreenTip no longer includes a description and is much less intrusive.

Now let's take a tour of the other pages in the PowerPoint Options dialog box.

14

8   Open the **PowerPoint Options** dialog box, and in the left pane, click **Proofing**.

The Proofing page provides options for adjusting the AutoCorrect settings and for refining the spell-checking process.

SEE ALSO For information about AutoCorrect and checking spelling, see "Checking spelling and choosing the best wording" in Chapter 4, "Work with slide text."

9   Display the **Save** page.

The Save page provides options for changing the default file format, AutoRecover file save rate, save locations, shared-document merge behavior, and whether fonts are embedded in the file.

10   Display the **Language** page.

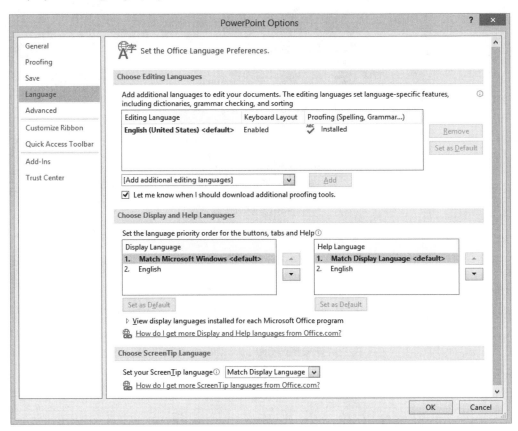

On the Language page, you can make additional editing languages available and specify the Display, Help, and ScreenTip languages.

11   Display the **Advanced** page.

The Advanced page includes options related to editing content; displaying presentations on the screen; printing, saving, and sharing presentations; and a variety of other options.

12 Scroll the **Advanced** page to explore all the options on this page.

Although these options are labeled Advanced, *they are the ones you're most likely to want to adjust to suit the way you work.*

13   Skipping over **Customize Ribbon** and **Quick Access Toolbar**, which we discuss in later topics in this chapter, display the **Add-Ins** page.

The Add-Ins page displays all the active and inactive add-ins installed on your computer. You can add new ones and remove any you no longer need.

SEE ALSO For information about add-ins, see the sidebar "Using add-ins" at the end of this topic.

14

14   Display the **Trust Center** page.

The Trust Center page provides information about privacy, security, and the Trust Center.

15   In the **Microsoft PowerPoint Trust Center** area, click **Trust Center Settings**.

On the pages of the Trust Center, you can control actions PowerPoint takes in response to presentations from people, companies, or locations or containing ActiveX controls or macros.

16   In the left pane of the **Trust Center** dialog box, click **File Block Settings**.

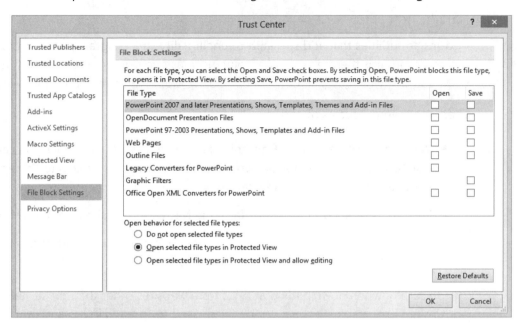

On the File Block Settings page, you can control actions PowerPoint takes in response to presentations of various file formats, filters, and converters.

17   Explore the other pages of the **Trust Center** dialog box, and then close it to return to the **PowerPoint Options** dialog box.

❌ CLEAN UP Reverse any changes you don't want to keep before moving on. Then close the PowerPoint Options dialog box.

Using add-ins

Add-ins are utilities that add specialized functionality to a program but aren't full-fledged programs themselves. PowerPoint includes two primary types of add-ins: COM add-ins (which use the Component Object Model) and PowerPoint add-ins.

There are several sources of add-ins:

- You can purchase add-ins from third-party vendors—for example, you can purchase an add-in that allows you to assign keyboard shortcuts to PowerPoint commands that don't already have them.

- You can download free add-ins from the Microsoft website or other websites.

- When installing a third-party program, you might install an add-in to allow it to interface with Microsoft Office 2013 programs.

TIP Be careful when downloading add-ins from websites other than those you trust. Add-ins are executable files that can easily be used to spread viruses and otherwise wreak havoc on your computer. For this reason, default settings in the Trust Center intervene when you attempt to download or run add-ins.

To use some add-ins, you must first install them on your computer and then load them into your computer's memory, as follows:

1   At the bottom of the **Add-Ins** page of the **PowerPoint Options** dialog box, display the **Manage** list, click either **COM Add-ins** or **PowerPoint Add-ins**, and then click **Go** to open an **Add-Ins** dialog box corresponding to the type of add-in you chose.

2   In the dialog box, click **Add** or **Add New**.

3   In the **Add Add-In** dialog box, navigate to the folder where the add-in you want to install is stored, and double-click its name.

4   In the list of available add-ins in the **Add-In** dialog box, select the check box of the new add-in, and then click **OK** or **Load** to make the add-in available for use in PowerPoint.

Customizing the ribbon

The ribbon is designed to make all the commonly used commands visible, so that everyone can more easily discover the full potential of the program. But many people use PowerPoint to perform the same set of tasks all the time, and for them, the visibility of buttons (or even entire groups of buttons) that they never use is just another form of clutter.

SEE ALSO For information about hiding and displaying the ribbon, see "Working in the PowerPoint 2013 user interface" in Chapter 1, "Explore Microsoft PowerPoint 2013."

Would you prefer to have fewer commands available, not more? Or would you prefer to have more specialized groups of commands? Clicking Customize Ribbon in the left pane of the PowerPoint Options dialog box displays the Customize Ribbon page, where you can make these kinds of changes.

You can add commands from the left list box to groups and tabs in the right list box.

You can customize the ribbon in the following ways:

- If you rarely use a tab, you can turn it off.

- If you use the commands in only a few groups on each tab, you can remove the groups you don't use. (The group is not removed from the program, just from its tab.)

- You can move a predefined group by removing it from one tab and then adding it to another.

- You can duplicate a predefined group by adding it to another tab.

- You can create a custom group on any tab and then add commands to it. (You cannot add commands to a predefined group.)

- For the ultimate in customization, you can create a custom tab. For example, you might want to do this if you use only a few commands from each tab and you find it inefficient to flip between them.

Don't be afraid to experiment with the ribbon to come up with the configuration that best suits the way you work. If at any point you find that your new ribbon is harder to work with instead of easier, you can always reset everything back to the default configuration.

TIP If you have upgraded from PowerPoint 2003 or an earlier version, you might identify a few commands that no longer seem to be available. A few old features have been abandoned, but others that people used only rarely have simply been pushed off to one side. If you miss one of these sidelined features, you can make it a part of your PowerPoint environment by adding it to the ribbon. You can find a list of all the commands that do not appear on the ribbon but are still available in PowerPoint by displaying the Customize Ribbon page of the PowerPoint Options dialog box and then clicking Commands Not In The Ribbon in the Choose Commands From list.

In this exercise, you'll turn off tabs, remove groups, create a custom group, and add a command to the new group. Then you'll create a tab and move predefined groups of buttons to it. Finally, you'll reset the ribbon to its default state.

 SET UP **You need the ColorDesign presentation located in the Chapter14 practice file folder to complete this exercise. Open the presentation, and then follow the steps.**

1   Open the **PowerPoint Options** dialog box, and then click **Customize Ribbon**.

2 In the **Main Tabs** list box on the right of the **Customize Ribbon** page, clear the check boxes of the **Insert**, **Design**, **Transitions**, **Animations**, and **Slide Show** tabs. Then click **OK** to display only four tabs on the ribbon.

   TIP You cannot turn off the File tab.

   Let's redisplay the Design tab and then remove one of its groups.

3 Display the **Customize Ribbon** page of the **PowerPoint Options** dialog box, and in the list box on the right, select the **Design** check box. Then click the adjacent plus sign to display the groups on this tab.

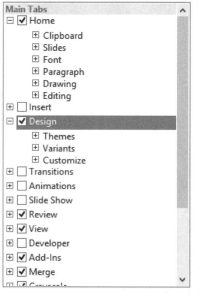

The Design tab has three groups: Themes, Variants, and Customize.

4 Above the left list box, display the **Choose commands from** list, and click **Main Tabs**. Then in the list box, click the plus sign adjacent to **Design** to display the groups that are predefined for this tab.

5 In the right list box, click the **Variants** group, and then click **Remove**.

   TIP The group is removed from the list box on the right and will no longer appear on the Design tab on the ribbon. But it is still available in the list box on the left. You can add it back to the Design tab, or add it to a different tab, at any time.

14

Now let's customize the Home tab.

6   If the **Home** tab is not expanded in the right list box, click the plus sign adjacent to **Home** to displays its groups, and then click the word **Home**.

7   Below the right list box, click **New Group**. When the **New Group (Custom)** group is added to the bottom of the **Home** group list, click **Rename**, enter Final in the **Display name** box, and click **OK**. Then click the **Move Up** button until the **Final (Custom)** group is at the top of the **Home** group list, which will place it at the left end of the **Home** tab.

You have created a Final (Custom) group on the Home tab.

8   Above the left list box, display the **Choose commands from** list, and click **File Tab** to list only the commands that are available in the **Backstage** view.

9   In the commands list, click **Inspect Document**, and click **Add**. Then repeat this step to add **Mark as Final** to the **Final (Custom)** group.

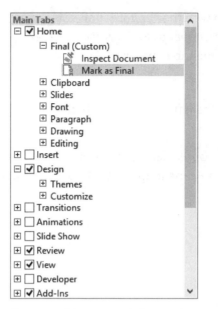

You can add commands to a custom group, but not to a predefined group.

10   In the right list box, remove the **Font**, **Paragraph**, and **Drawing** groups from the **Home** tab.

Next let's create a custom tab.

11   In the right list box, click the word **Home**, and then below the list box, click **New Tab**. Notice that the new tab is selected for display on the ribbon and has been given one custom group.

12   Remove the custom group from the **New Tab (Custom)** tab.

13   Click **New Tab (Custom)**, and then click **Rename**. In the **Rename** dialog box, enter **Formatting** in the **Display name** box, and click **OK**.

> **TIP** The name appears on the ribbon with the capitalization you use in the Rename dialog box. If you want *Formatting* to appear as *FORMATTING*, enter it that way. However, bear in mind that entering the tab name with an initial capital letter visually identifies it as a custom tab.

14   Display the **Main Tabs** commands in the left list box, and then expand the **Home** and **Design** tabs.

15   With the new **Formatting (Custom)** tab selected in the right list box, add the **Font**, **Paragraph**, and **Drawing** groups from **Home** in the left list box, and then add **Variants** from **Design**.

You have moved groups from the Home and Design tabs to a new Formatting (Custom) tab.

16 In the **PowerPoint Options** dialog box, click **OK**.

This customized ribbon includes modified Home and Design tabs and a new Formatting tab.

17 Click the title of slide **1** to select it, and then click the **Formatting** tab.

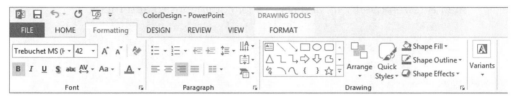

The new Formatting tab, which includes groups formerly found on the Home and Design tabs.

Let's finish this exercise by restoring the default ribbon configuration.

18 Display the **Customize Ribbon** page of the **PowerPoint Options** dialog box. In the lower-right corner, click **Reset**, and then click **Reset all customizations**.

19 When you are asked to confirm that you want to delete all ribbon and Quick Access Toolbar customizations, click **Yes**.

20 Click **OK** to close the **PowerPoint Options** dialog box.

❌ CLEAN UP Close the ColorDesign presentation.

14

Manipulating the Quick Access Toolbar

By default, the Save, Undo, Repeat/Redo, and Start From Beginning buttons appear on the Quick Access Toolbar. If you regularly use a few buttons that are scattered on various tabs of the ribbon and you don't want to create a custom tab, you might want to add these frequently used buttons to the Quick Access Toolbar. They are then always visible in the upper-left corner of the program window.

Clicking the Customize Quick Access Toolbar button at the right end of the Quick Access Toolbar displays a menu that lists commonly used commands. Check marks appear to the left of commands currently available on the Quick Access Toolbar. You can click these commands to remove them, and click other commands to add them.

Customize Quick Access Toolbar
New
Open
✓ Save
Email
Quick Print
Print Preview and Print
Spelling
✓ Undo
✓ Redo
✓ Start From Beginning
Touch/Mouse Mode
More Commands...
Show Below the Ribbon

You can customize the Quick Access Toolbar by selecting or clearing buttons on the Customize Quick Access Toolbar menu.

As you add buttons to the Quick Access Toolbar, it expands to accommodate them. If you add many buttons, some of them might not be visible, defeating the purpose of adding them. To resolve this problem, you can move the Quick Access Toolbar below the ribbon by clicking the Customize Quick Access Toolbar button, and then clicking Show Below The Ribbon.

Clicking More Commands on the Customize Quick Access Toolbar menu opens the PowerPoint Options dialog box with the Quick Access Toolbar page displayed. This page gives you more options for displaying commands on the toolbar.

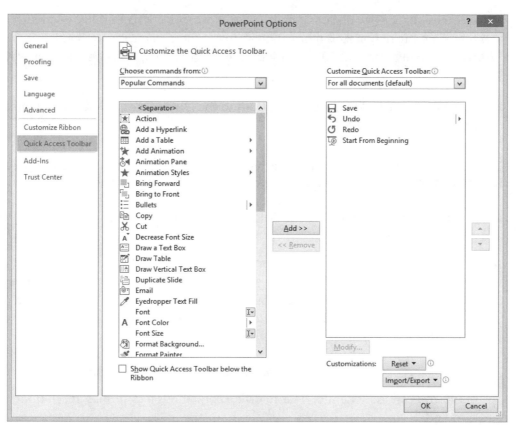

You can customize the Quick Access Toolbar by moving commands from the left list box to the right list box.

From this PowerPoint Options dialog box page, you can customize the Quick Access Toolbar in the following ways:

- Define a custom Quick Access Toolbar for all presentations, or you can define a custom Quick Access Toolbar for a specific presentation.

- Add any command from any group of any tab, including tool tabs, to the toolbar.

- Display a separator between different types of buttons.

- Move buttons around on the toolbar until they are in the order you want.

- Reset everything back to the default Quick Access Toolbar configuration.

14

TIP If you use only a few buttons, you can add those buttons to the Quick Access Toolbar and then hide the ribbon. For information about hiding and displaying the ribbon, see "Working in the PowerPoint 2013 user interface" in Chapter 1, "Explore Microsoft Power-Point 2013."

In this exercise, you'll add a couple of buttons to the Quick Access Toolbar for all presentations, and then you'll test the buttons.

SET UP You need the BuyersSeminar presentation located in the Chapter14 practice file folder to complete this exercise. Open the presentation, and then follow the steps.

1   Open the **PowerPoint Options** dialog box, and then in the left pane, click **Quick Access Toolbar**.

   TIP If you want to create a Quick Access Toolbar that is specific to the active presentation, on the right side of the Quick Access Toolbar page, display the Customize Quick Access Toolbar list, and click For <name of presentation>. Then any command you select will be added to the toolbar for that specific presentation instead of the toolbar for all presentations.

2   At the top of the **Popular Commands** list on the left, double-click **Separator**.

   TIP You can use separator lines to divide commands into groups, making them easier to find.

3   Scroll down the **Popular Commands** list, click the **Quick Print** command, and then click **Add**.

   TIP You can also add the Quick Print button to the Quick Access Toolbar by clicking the Customize Quick Access Toolbar button.

4   Display the **Choose commands from** list, and click **Insert Tab**.

5   Repeat step 3 to add the **Screen Clipping** command to the right list box.

	Save
↶	Undo
↻	Redo
	Start From Beginning
	<Separator>
	Quick Print
	Screen Clipping

You have moved one command from the Backstage view and another from the Insert tab to the Quick Access Toolbar.

6   In the right list box, click **Start From Beginning**, and click the **Remove** button. Then click **OK** to close the **PowerPoint Options** dialog box.

The Quick Access Toolbar now includes three default buttons and two custom buttons, separated by a line.

To print a presentation with the default settings, you no longer have to go to the Print page of the Backstage view, and to capture a picture of the screen, you no longer need to switch to the Insert tab.

Let's restore the default Quick Access Toolbar.

7   Display the **Quick Access Toolbar** page of the **PowerPoint Options** dialog box, click **Reset**, and then click **Reset only Quick Access Toolbar**.

8   In the **Reset Customizations** message box, click **Yes** to return the **Quick Access Toolbar** to its default contents. Then click **OK** to close the **PowerPoint Options** dialog box.

❌ CLEAN UP Close the BuyersSeminar presentation without saving it.

14

Customizing the status bar

You can easily add or remove controls from the status bar by right-clicking any blank area of the status bar and then, on the Customize Status Bar menu, clicking the control you want to add or remove.

Customize Status Bar	
✓ View Indicator	Slide 1 of 9
Theme	"Oriel"
✓ Number of Authors Editing	
✓ Spell Check	
✓ Language	
✓ Signatures	Off
✓ Information Management Policy	Off
✓ Permissions	Off
✓ Upload Status	
✓ Document Updates Available	No
✓ Notes	
✓ Comments	
✓ View Shortcuts	
✓ Zoom Slider	
✓ Zoom	70%
✓ Zoom to Fit	

On the Customize Status Bar menu, a check mark indicates a control that is currently shown or will be shown when information of that type is available.

Key points

- The PowerPoint environment is flexible and can be customized to meet your needs.

- Most of the settings that control the working environment are gathered on the pages of the PowerPoint Options dialog box.

- You can customize the ribbon to put precisely the presentation development tools you need at your fingertips.

- You can provide one-click access to any command by adding its button to the Quick Access Toolbar, either for all presentations or for the active presentation.

Glossary

accessible content Content that is optimized for consumers with disabilities and for assistive devices such as electronic readers.

action button A ready-made button that you can insert into a presentation and use to define hyperlinks.

add-in A utility that adds specialized functionality to a program but that does not operate as an independent program.

adjustment handle A diamond-shaped handle used to adjust the appearance but not the size of most shapes. For example, you can adjust a rounded rectangle to be more or less rounded.

animation In PowerPoint, an effect that you can apply to text or an object to produce an illusion of movement.

attribute Individual items of character formatting, such as style or color, that determine how text looks.

AutoCorrect A feature that automatically detects and corrects misspelled words and incorrect capitalization. You can add your own AutoCorrect entries.

background The colors, shading, texture, and graphics, that appear behind the text and objects on a slide.

body font The second font listed in a set of theme fonts, which is by default applied to all text except headings.

bullet point An item in a list in which each list entry is preceded by a symbol.

caption Descriptive text associated with a figure, photo, illustration, or screen shot.

case The capitalization (uppercase or lowercase) of a word or phrase. In title case, the first letter of all important words is capitalized. In sentence case, only the first letter of the first word is capitalized.

category axis The axis used for plotting categories of data in a chart. Also called the *x-axis*.

cell A box formed by the intersection of a row and column in a worksheet or a table, in which you enter information.

cell address The location of a cell, expressed as its column letter and row number, as in A1.

character formatting Formatting you can apply to selected typographical characters.

chart A diagram that plots a series of values in a table or worksheet.

chart area A region in a chart that is used to position chart elements, render axes, and plot data.

clip art image A piece of free, ready-made art that is distributed without copyright. Usually a cartoon, sketch, illustration, or photograph.

Clipboard A storage area shared by all Office programs where cut or copied items are stored.

color gradient A gradual progression from one color to another color, or from one shade to another shade of the same color.

color scheme See *theme colors*.

column Either the vertical arrangement of text into one or more side-by-side sections, or the vertical arrangement of cells in a table or worksheet.

comment An annotation that is associated with text or an object to provide context-specific information or reviewer feedback.

connection point A point on a shape to which another shape can be connected.

connector A line that connect two shapes and that moves if the shapes are moved.

content placeholder See *placeholder*.

contextual tab See *tool tab*.

cursor A representation on the screen of the input device pointer location.

custom slide show A set of slides extracted from a presentation to create a slide show for an audience that doesn't need to view the entire presentation.

cycle diagram A diagram that shows a continuous process.

data marker A customizable symbol or shape that identifies a data point on a chart. Data markers can be bars, columns, pie or doughnut slices, dots, and various other shapes and can be various sizes and colors.

data point An individual value plotted in a chart.

data series Related data points that are plotted in a chart.

design template A file that contains masters that control the formatting of a presentation, including placeholder sizes and positions; background design, graphics, and color schemes; fonts; and the type and size of bullets.

destination file The file into which a linked or embedded object is inserted. When you change information in a destination file, the information is not updated in the source file. See also *source file*.

diagram A drawing that is used to present relationships between abstract ideas and data. For example, an organizational chart or a Venn diagram.

dialog box launcher On the ribbon, a button at the bottom of some groups that opens a dialog box with features related to the group.

Document Inspector A tool that automates the process of detecting and removing all extraneous and confidential information from a presentation.

dragging A way of moving objects by selecting them and then, while the selection device is active (for example, while you are holding down the mouse button), moving the selection to the new location.

embedded object An object that is wholly inserted into a file. Embedding the object, rather than simply inserting or pasting its contents, ensures that the object retains its original format. If you open the embedded object, you can edit it with the toolbars and menus from the program used to create it.

encrypting To programmatically disguise content to hide its substance.

file format The structure or organization of data in a file. The file format is usually indicated by the file name extension.

file name extension A set of characters added to the end of a file name that identifies the file type or format.

First Line Indent marker The triangle-shaped control, on the top of the horizontal ruler, that indicates the position of the first line of the paragraph.

font A graphic design applied to a collection of numbers, symbols, and characters. A font describes a certain typeface, which can have qualities such as size, spacing, and pitch.

font effect An attribute, such as superscript, small capital letters, or shadow, that can be applied to a font.

font size The height (in points) of a collection of characters, where one point is equal to approximately 1/72 of an inch.

font style The emphasis given to a font by using formatting such as bold, italic, underline, or color.

footer One or more items of information, typically at the bottom of a slide and typically containing elements such as the page number and the date.

gallery Rich, customizable list boxes that can be used to organize items by category, display them in flexible column-based and row-based layouts, and represent them with images and text. Depending on the type of gallery, live preview is also supported.

graphic Any image, such as a picture, photograph, drawing, illustration, or shape, that can be placed as an object on a slide.

grayscale The spectrum (range) of shades of black in an image.

group (ribbon) A set of buttons on a tab that all relate to the same type of object or task.

grouping To assemble several objects, such as shapes, into a single unit so that they act as one object. Grouped objects can easily be moved, sized, and formatted.

handle A small circle, square, or set of dots that appears at the corner or on the side of a selected object and facilitates moving, sizing, reshaping, or other functions pertaining to the object.

handout master A template that defines the layout for the printed handout pages distributed to a presentation's audience.

Handout Master view The view from which you can change the overall look of audience handouts.

Hanging Indent marker The triangle-shaped control, on the bottom of the horizontal ruler, that indicates the left edge of the second and subsequent lines of the paragraph.

heading font The first font listed in a set of theme fonts, which is by default applied to all slide titles..

hierarchy diagram A diagram that illustrates the structure of an organization or entity.

hyperlink A connection from a hyperlink anchor, such as text or a graphic, that you can follow to display a link target such as a file, a location in a file, or a website. Text hyperlinks are usually formatted as colored or underlined text, but sometimes the only indication is that when you point to them, the pointer changes to a hand..

Hypertext Markup Language (HTML) A formatting language that uses tags to mark elements in a document to indicate how web browsers should display them to the user and should respond to user actions.

icon A small picture or symbol representing a command, file type, function, program, or tool.

Indent marker One of four controls located on the horizontal ruler that indicate how far text is indented from the left or right margin.

keyboard shortcut Any combination of keystrokes that can be used to perform a task that would otherwise require a mouse or other pointing device.

kiosk mode A display mode in which a single window takes over the whole screen and the desktop is inaccessible.

Left Indent marker The square-shaped control, on the bottom of the horizontal ruler, that indicates how far text is indented from the left margin.

legend A key that identifies the data series plotted in the chart.

line break A manual break that forces the text that follows it to the next line.

link See *hyperlink*; *linked object*.

linked object An object that is inserted into a slide but that still exists in its source file. When information is linked, the slide is updated automatically if the information in the original document changes.

Live Preview A feature that temporarily displays the effect of applying a specific format to the selected element.

master A slide or page on which you define formatting for all slides or pages in a presentation. Each presentation has a set of masters for slides, as well as masters for speaker notes and audience handouts.

Microsoft Office Clipboard See *Clipboard*.

Microsoft PowerPoint Viewer A viewer with which you can display presentations on a computer that does not have PowerPoint installed.

Mini Toolbar A toolbar that is typically displayed after you select text on a slide so that you can quickly format the text.

Normal view A view that displays three panes: Thumbnails, Slide, and Notes.

notes master A template that defines the formatting and content used by speaker notes pages.

Notes Master view The view from which you can change the overall look of speaker notes pages.

Notes Page view The view in which you can add speaker notes that contain objects such as tables, charts, and graphics.

Notes pane The pane in Normal view in which you enter notes that you want to accompany a slide. You print these notes as speaker notes pages.

object An item, such as a graphic, video clip, sound file, or worksheet, that can be inserted into a PowerPoint slide and then selected and modified.

Outline pane The pane that appears in Outline view on the left side of the program window and that displays all the text of the presentation in outline form.

Outline view A view that displays three panes: Outline, Slide, and Notes.

Package for CD A feature to help you gather all the components of a presentation and store them to a CD or another type of removable media so that they can be transported to a different computer.

palette A collection of color swatches that you can click to apply a color to selected text or an object. PowerPoint has three palettes: Theme Colors, Standard, and Recently Used.

paragraph formatting Formatting that controls the appearance of a paragraph. Examples include indentation, alignment, line spacing, and pagination.

password The string of characters that must be entered to open a password-protected presentation for editing.

path A sequence of folders that leads to a specific file or folder. A backslash is used to separate each folder in a Windows path, and a forward slash is used to separate each directory in an Internet path.

photo album A specific kind of presentation into which you can insert and arrange collections of digital images.

picture A photograph, clip art image, illustration, or another type of image created with a program other than PowerPoint.

picture diagram A diagram that uses pictures to convey information, rather than or in addition to text.

pixel The smallest element used to form the composition of an image on a computer monitor. Computer monitors display images by drawing thousands of pixels arranged in columns and rows.

placeholder A area on a slide designed to contain a specific type of content that you supply.

plot area In a two-dimensional chart, the area bounded by the axes, including all data series. In a three-dimensional chart, the area bounded by the axes, including the data series, category names, tick-mark labels, and axis titles.

point The unit of measure for expressing the size of characters in a font, where 72 points equals 1 inch.

Portable Document Format (PDF) A fixed-layout file format in which the formatting of the document appears the same regardless of the computer on which it is displayed.

PowerPoint Web App An app that you can use to review and edit a presentation in your web browser when you're working with a presentation that is stored on a Microsoft SharePoint site or on a Microsoft SkyDrive. The web app runs directly in your web browser instead of on your computer. Web apps are installed in the online environment in which you're working and are not part of the desktop program that you install directly on your computer.

Presenter view A tool with which you can control a presentation on one monitor while the audience views the presentation's slides in Slide Show view on a delivery monitor or projector screen.

process diagram A diagram that visually represents the ordered set of steps required to complete a task.

property Settings of a file that you can change, such as the file's name and read-only status, as well as attributes that you can't directly change, such as the file's size and creation date.

Quick Access Toolbar A small, customizable toolbar that displays frequently used commands.

read-only A setting that allows a file to be read or copied, but not changed or saved. If you change a read-only file, you can save your changes only if you give the file a new name.

Reading view The view in which each slide fills the screen. You can click buttons on the navigation bar to move through or jump to specific slides.

relationship diagram A diagram that shows convergent, divergent, overlapping, merging, or containment elements.

ribbon A user interface design that organizes commands into logical groups, which appear on separate tabs.

Rich Text Format (RTF) A format for text and graphics interchange that can be used with different output devices, operating environments, and operating systems.

rotating handle A small green handle that you can use to adjust the angle of rotation of a shape.

screen clipping An image of all or part of the content displayed on a computer screen. Screen clippings can be captured by using a graphics capture tool such as the Screen Clipping tool included with Office 2013 programs.

ScreenTip A note that appears on the screen to provide information about the program interface or certain types of document content, such as proofing marks and hyperlinks within a document.

selecting To specify, or highlight, an object or block of text so that you can manipulate or edit it in some way.

series axis The optical axis that is perpendicular to the x-axis and y-axis, usually the "floor." Also called the *z-axis*.

shape An object created by using drawing tools or commands.

sizing handle A small circle, square, or set of dots that appears at the corner or on the side of a selected object. You drag these handles to change the size of the object horizontally, vertically, or proportionally.

slide library A type of SharePoint document library that is optimized for storing and reusing PowerPoint slides.

slide master The set of slides that stores information about a presentation's design template, including font styles, placeholder sizes and positions, background design, and color schemes.

Slide Master view The view from which you make changes to the slide masters.

Slide pane The area in Normal view that shows the currently selected slide as it will appear in the presentation.

Slide Show view The view in which you deliver an electronic presentation to an audience.

Slide Sorter view The view in which the slides of the presentation are displayed as thumbnails so that you can easily reorganize them.

slide timing The time a slide will be displayed on the screen before PowerPoint moves to the next slide.

smart guide A vertical or horizontal dotted line that appears on a slide to help align slide elements.

SmartArt graphic A predefined set of shapes and text used as a basis for creating a diagram.

source file A file that contains information that is linked, embedded, or merged into a destination file. Updates to source file content are reflected in the destination file when the data connection is refreshed. See also *destination file*.

source program The program used to create a linked or embedded object. To edit the object, you must have the source program installed on your computer.

splitting To separate a single cell into two or more cells.

stack A set of graphics that overlap each other.

status bar A program window element, located at the bottom of the program window, that displays indicators and controls.

subpoint A subordinate item below a bullet point in a list.

tab (ribbon) An organizational element of the ribbon that displays related groups of buttons.

table One or more rows of cells commonly used to display numbers and other items for quick reference and analysis. Items in a table are organized in rows and columns.

template A file that can contain predefined formatting, layout, text, or graphics, and that serves as the basis for new presentations with a similar design or purpose.

text box A movable, resizable container used to insert text on a slide with a different position or orientation than the text in placeholders.

theme A set of unified design elements that combine color, fonts, and effects to provide a professional look for a presentation.

theme colors A set of twelve balanced colors that you can apply to slides, notes pages, or audience handouts. A color scheme consists of light and dark background colors, light and dark text colors, six accent colors, and two colors for hyperlinks.

theme fonts A set of two fonts: one applied to slide titles (heading font) and one applied to all other text on a slide (body font).

Thesaurus A feature that looks up alternative words, or *synonyms*, for a word.

thumbnail A small representation of an item, such as a slide or theme. Thumbnails are typically used to provide visual identifiers for related items.

Thumbnails pane The pane in Normal view that displays thumbnails of the slides in a presentation and allows you to display a specific slide by clicking its thumbnail.

tick-mark A small line of measurement, similar to a division line on a ruler, that intersects an axis in a chart.

title bar The horizontal bar at the top of a window that contains the name of the window. Most title bars also contain boxes or buttons for closing and resizing the window.

title slide The introductory slide in a presentation.

tool tab A tab containing commands that are relevant only when you have selected a particular object type. See also *tab*.

transition An effect that specifies how the display changes as you move from one slide to another.

value axis The axis used for plotting values in a chart. Also called the *y-axis*.

View Shortcuts toolbar The toolbar at the right end of the status bar that contains tools for switching between views of slide content and changing the view of the open presentation.

watermark A faint text or graphic image that appears on the page behind the main content of a slide.

Web App See *PowerPoint Web App*.

web browser Software that interprets HTML files, formats them into webpages, and displays them. A web browser, such as Internet Explorer, can follow hyperlinks, respond to requests to download files, and play sound or video files that are embedded in webpages.

webpage A World Wide Web document. A webpage typically consists of an HTML file, with associated files for graphics and sets of instructions called *scripts*. It is identified by a Uniform Resource Locator (URL).

WordArt object A text object you create with ready-made effects and to which you can apply additional formatting options.

x-axis The axis used for plotting categories of data in a chart. Also called the *category axis*.

y-axis The axis used for plotting values in a chart. Also called the *value axis*.

z-axis The optical axis that is perpendicular to the x-axis and y-axis, usually the "floor." Also called the *series axis*.

Keyboard shortcuts

Throughout this book we provide information about how to perform tasks quickly and efficiently by using keyboard shortcuts. This section presents information about keyboard shortcuts that are built in to Microsoft PowerPoint 2013 and Microsoft Office 2013, and about custom keyboard shortcuts.

TIP In the following lists, keys you press at the same time are separated by a plus sign (+), and keys you press sequentially are separated by a comma (,).

PowerPoint 2013 keyboard shortcuts

This section provides a comprehensive list of keyboard shortcuts built into PowerPoint 2013. The list has been excerpted from PowerPoint Help and formatted in tables for convenient look up.

Move between panes

Action	Keyboard shortcut
Move clockwise among panes in Normal view	F6
Move counterclockwise among panes in Normal view	Shift+F6
Switch between Slides and Outline tabs in the Outline and Slides pane in Normal view	Ctrl+Shift+Tab

Work in an outline

Action	Keyboard shortcut
Promote a paragraph	Alt+Shift+Left Arrow
Demote a paragraph	Alt+Shift+Right Arrow
Move selected paragraphs up	Alt+Shift+Up Arrow
Move selected paragraphs down	Alt+Shift+Down Arrow
Show heading level 1	Alt+Shift+1
Expand text below a heading	Alt+Shift+Plus Sign
Collapse text below a heading	Alt+Shift+Minus Sign

Work with shapes, objects, and WordArt

Select a shape

Action	Keyboard shortcut
Select a single shape	Tab or Shift+Tab
Group selected shapes	Ctrl+G
Ungroup a group of shapes	Ctrl+Shift+G
Copy object attributes	Ctrl+Shift+C
Paste object attributes	Ctrl+Shift+V

Show or hide a grid or guides

Action	Keyboard shortcut
Show or hide the grid	Shift+F9
Show or hide guides	Alt+F9

Select text and objects

Action	Keyboard shortcut
Select one character to the right	Shift+Right Arrow
Select one character to the left	Shift+Left Arrow
Select to the end of a word	Ctrl+Shift+Right Arrow
Select to the beginning of a word	Ctrl+Shift+Left Arrow
Select one line up (with the cursor at the beginning of a line)	Shift+Up Arrow
Select one line down (with the cursor at the beginning of a line)	Shift+Down Arrow
Select an object (when the text inside the object is selected)	Esc
Select another object (when one object is selected)	Tab or Shift+Tab until the object you want is selected
Select text within an object (with an object selected)	Enter
Select all objects	Ctrl+A (on the Slides tab)
Select all slides	Ctrl+A (in Slide Sorter view)
Select all text	Ctrl+A (on the Outline tab)

Delete and copy text and objects

Action	Keyboard shortcut
Delete one character to the left	Backspace
Delete one word to the left	Ctrl+Backspace
Delete one character to the right	Delete
Delete one word to the right (The cursor must be between words to do this)	Ctrl+Delete
Cut selected object or text	Ctrl+X
Copy selected object or text	Ctrl+C
Paste cut or copied object or text	Ctrl+V
Undo the last action	Ctrl+Z
Redo the last action	Ctrl+Y
Copy formatting only	Ctrl+Shift+C
Paste formatting only	Ctrl+Shift+V
Open the Paste Special dialog box	Ctrl+Alt+V

Move around in text

Action	Keyboard shortcut
Move one character to the left	Left Arrow
Move one character to the right	Right Arrow
Move one line up	Up Arrow
Move one line down	Down Arrow
Move one word to the left	Ctrl+Left Arrow
Move one word to the right	Ctrl+Right Arrow
Move to the end of a line	End
Move to the beginning of a line	Home
Move up one paragraph	Ctrl+Up Arrow
Move down one paragraph	Ctrl+Down Arrow
Move to the end of a text box	Ctrl+End
Move to the beginning of a text box	Ctrl+Home
Move to the next title or body text placeholder If it is the last placeholder on a slide, this will insert a new slide with the same slide layout as the original slide	Ctrl+Enter
Move to repeat the last Find action	Shift+F4

Move around in and work on tables

Action	Keyboard shortcut
Move to the next cell	Tab
Move to the preceding cell	Shift+Tab
Move to the next row	Down Arrow
Move to the preceding row	Up Arrow
Insert a tab in a cell	Ctrl+Tab
Start a new paragraph	Enter
Add a new row at the bottom of the table	Tab at the end of the last row

Edit a linked or embedded object

1 Press **Tab** or **Shift+Tab** to select the object you want.

2 Press **Shift+F10** to display the shortcut menu.

3 Press the **Down Arrow** key until the **Object** command is selected, press the **Right Arrow** key to select **Edit**, and then press **Enter**.

TIP The name of the command in the shortcut menu depends on the type of embedded or linked object. For example, an embedded Microsoft Excel worksheet has the command *Worksheet Object*, whereas an embedded Microsoft Visio Drawing has the command *Visio Object*.

Format and align characters and paragraphs

Change or resize the font

Action	Keyboard shortcut
Open the Font dialog box to change the font	Ctrl+Shift+F
Increase the font size	Ctrl+Shift+>
Decrease the font size	Ctrl+Shift+<

Apply character formats

Action	Keyboard shortcut
Open the Font dialog box to change the formatting of characters	Ctrl+T
Change the case of letters between sentence, lowercase, or uppercase	Shift+F3
Apply bold formatting	Ctrl+B
Apply an underline	Ctrl+U
Apply italic formatting	Ctrl+I
Apply subscript formatting (automatic spacing)	Ctrl+Equal Sign
Apply superscript formatting (automatic spacing)	Ctrl+Shift+Plus Sign
Remove manual character formatting, such as subscript and superscript	Ctrl+Spacebar
Insert a hyperlink	Ctrl+K

Copy text formats

Action	Keyboard shortcut
Copy formats	Ctrl+Shift+C
Paste formats	Ctrl+Shift+V

Align paragraphs

Action	Keyboard shortcut
Center a paragraph	Ctrl+E
Justify a paragraph	Ctrl+J
Left-align a paragraph	Ctrl+L
Right-align a paragraph	Ctrl+R

Manage a presentation

Use the following keyboard shortcuts while running a presentation in Slide Show view.

Run a slide show

Action	Keyboard shortcut
Start a presentation from the beginning	F5
Perform the next animation or advance to the next slide	N, Enter, Page Down, Right Arrow, Down Arrow, or Spacebar
Perform the previous animation or return to the previous slide	P, Page Up, Left Arrow, Up Arrow, or Backspace
Go to a specific slide number	Number+Enter
Display a blank black slide, or return to the presentation from a blank black slide	B or Period
Display a blank white slide, or return to the presentation from a blank white slide	W or Comma
Stop or restart an automatic presentation	S
End a presentation	Esc or Hyphen
Erase on-screen annotations	E
Go to the next slide, if the next slide is hidden	H
Set new timings while rehearsing	T
Use original timings while rehearsing	O
Use mouse-click to advance while rehearsing	M
Re-record slide narration and timing	R
Return to the first slide	Press and hold right and left mouse buttons for 2 seconds
Show or hide the arrow pointer	A or =
Change the pointer to a pen	Ctrl+P
Change the pointer to an arrow	Ctrl+A
Change the pointer to an eraser	Ctrl+E
Show or hide ink markup	Ctrl+M
Hide the pointer and navigation button immediately	Ctrl+H
Hide the pointer and navigation button in 15 seconds	Ctrl+U
View the All Slides dialog box	Ctrl+S
View the computer task bar	Ctrl+T

Action	Keyboard shortcut
Display the shortcut menu	Shift+F10
Go to the first or next hyperlink on a slide	Tab
Go to the last or previous hyperlink on a slide	Shift+Tab
Perform the "mouse click" behavior of the selected hyperlink	Enter while a hyperlink is selected
Broadcast the open presentation to a remote audience by using PowerPoint Web App	Ctrl+F5

Use media shortcuts during a presentation

Action	Keyboard shortcut
Stop media playback	Alt+Q
Toggle between play and pause	Alt+P
Go to the next bookmark	Alt+End
Go to the previous bookmark	Alt+Home
Increase the sound volume	Alt+Up
Decrease the sound volume	Alt+Down
Seek forward	Alt+Shift+Page Down
Seek backward	Alt+Shift+Page Up
Mute the sound	Alt+U

TIP Press F1 during a presentation to display a list of controls.

Browse web presentations

Use the following keyboard shortcuts while displaying a web presentation in Windows Internet Explorer.

Action	Keyboard shortcut
Move forward through the hyperlinks in a web presentation, the Address bar, and the Links bar	Tab
Move back through the hyperlinks in a web presentation, the Address bar, and the Links bar	Shift+Tab
Perform the "mouse click" behavior of the selected hyperlink	Enter
Go to the next slide	Spacebar

Use the Selection pane feature

Use the following keyboard shortcuts in the Selection pane. To display the Selection pane, press Alt, then H, then S, then L, and then P.

Action	Keyboard shortcut
Cycle the focus through the different panes	F6
Display the context menu	Shift+F10
Move the focus to a single item or group	Up Arrow or Down Arrow
Move the focus from an item in a group to its parent group	Left Arrow
Move the focus from a group to the first item in that group	Right Arrow
Expand a focused group and all its child groups	* (on numeric keypad only)
Expand a focused group	+ (on numeric keypad only)
Collapse a focused group	- (on numeric keypad only)
Move the focus to an item and select it	Shift+Up Arrow or Shift+Down Arrow
Select a focused item	Spacebar or Enter
Cancel selection of a focused item	Shift+Spacebar or Shift+Enter
Move a selected item forward	Ctrl+Shift+F
Move a selected item backward	Ctrl+Shift+B
Show or hide a focused item	Ctrl+Shift+S
Rename a focused item	F2
Switch the keyboard focus within the Selection pane between tree view and the Show All and Hide All buttons	Tab or Shift+Tab
Collapse all groups (The focus must be in the tree view of the Selection pane to use this shortcut)	Alt+Shift+1
Expand all groups	Alt+Shift+9

Office 2013 keyboard shortcuts

This section provides a comprehensive list of keyboard shortcuts available in all Office 2013 programs, including PowerPoint.

Display and use windows

Action	Keyboard shortcut
Switch to the next window	Alt+Tab
Switch to the previous window	Alt+Shift+Tab
Close the active window	Ctrl+W or Ctrl+F4
Restore the size of the active window after you maximize it	Alt+F5
Move to a pane from another pane in the program window (clockwise direction). If pressing F6 does not display the pane that you want, press Alt to put the focus on the ribbon, and then press Ctrl+Tab to move to the pane	F6 or Shift+F6
Switch to the next open window	Ctrl+F6
Switch to the previous window	Ctrl+Shift+F6
Maximize or restore a selected window	Ctrl+F10
Copy a picture of the screen to the Clipboard	Print Screen
Copy a picture of the selected window to the Clipboard	Alt+Print Screen

Use dialog boxes

Action	Keyboard shortcut
Move to the next option or option group	Tab
Move to the previous option or option group	Shift+Tab
Switch to the next tab in a dialog box	Ctrl+Tab
Switch to the previous tab in a dialog box	Ctrl+Shift+Tab
Move between options in an open drop-down list, or between options in a group of options	Arrow keys
Perform the action assigned to the selected button; select or clear the selected check box	Spacebar
Select an option; select or clear a check box	Alt+ *the underlined letter*
Open a selected drop-down list	Alt+Down Arrow

Action	Keyboard shortcut
Select an option from a drop-down list	*First letter of the list option*
Close a selected drop-down list; cancel a command and close a dialog box	Esc
Run the selected command	Enter

Use edit boxes within dialog boxes

An edit box is a blank box in which you enter or paste an entry.

Action	Keyboard shortcut
Move to the beginning of the entry	Home
Move to the end of the entry	End
Move one character to the left or right	Left Arrow or Right Arrow
Move one word to the left	Ctrl+Left Arrow
Move one word to the right	Ctrl+Right Arrow
Select or unselect one character to the left	Shift+Left Arrow
Select or unselect one character to the right	Shift+Right Arrow
Select or unselect one word to the left	Ctrl+Shift+Left Arrow
Select or unselect one word to the right	Ctrl+Shift+Right Arrow
Select from the insertion point to the beginning of the entry	Shift+Home
Select from the insertion point to the end of the entry	Shift+End

Use the Open and Save As dialog boxes

Action	Keyboard shortcut
Open the Open dialog box	Ctrl+F12 or Ctrl+O
Open the Save As dialog box	F12
Open the selected folder or file	Enter
Open the folder one level above the selected folder	Backspace
Delete the selected folder or file	Delete
Display a shortcut menu for a selected item such as a folder or file	Shift+F10
Move forward through options	Tab
Move back through options	Shift+Tab
Open the Look In list	F4 or Alt+I
Refresh the file list	F5

Use the Backstage view

Action	Keyboard shortcut
Display the Open page of the Backstage view	Ctrl+O
Display the Save As page of the Backstage view (when saving a file for the first time)	Ctrl+S
Continue saving an Office file (after giving the file a name and location)	Ctrl+S
Display the Save As page of the Backstage view (after initially saving a file)	Alt+F+S
Close the Backstage view	Esc

TIP You can use dialog boxes instead of Backstage view pages by selecting the Don't Show The Backstage When Opening Or Saving Files check box on the Save page of the PowerPoint Options dialog box. Set this option in any Office program to enable it in all Office programs.

Navigate the ribbon

1   Press **Alt** to display the KeyTips over each feature in the current view.

2   Press the letter shown in the KeyTip over the feature that you want to use.

TIP To cancel the action and hide the KeyTips, press Alt.

Change the keyboard focus without using the mouse

Action	Keyboard shortcut
Select the active tab of the ribbon and activate the access keys	Alt or F10. Press either of these keys again to move back to the document and cancel the access keys
Move to another tab of the ribbon	F10 to select the active tab, and then Left Arrow or Right Arrow
Expand or collapse the ribbon	Ctrl+F1
Display the shortcut menu for the selected item	Shift+F10

Action	Keyboard shortcut
Move the focus to select each of the following areas of the window:	F6
■ Active tab of the ribbon	
■ Any open panes	
■ Status bar at the bottom of the window	
■ Your document	
Move the focus to each command on the ribbon, forward or backward, respectively	Tab or Shift+Tab
Move among the items on the ribbon	arrow keys
Activate the selected command or control on the ribbon	Spacebar or Enter
Display the selected menu or gallery on the ribbon	Spacebar or Enter
Activate a command or control on the ribbon so that you can modify a value	Enter
Finish modifying a value in a control on the ribbon, and move focus back to the document	Enter
Get help on the selected command or control on the ribbon	F1

Undo and redo actions

Action	Keyboard shortcut
Cancel an action	Esc
Undo an action	Ctrl+Z
Redo or repeat an action	Ctrl+Y

Change or resize the font

TIP The cursor must be inside a text box when you use these shortcuts.

Action	Keyboard shortcut
Change the font	Ctrl+Shift+F
Change the font size	Ctrl+Shift+P
Increase the font size of the selected text	Ctrl+Shift+>
Decrease the font size of the selected text	Ctrl+Shift+<
Change the font	Ctrl+Shift+F

Move around in text or cells

Action	Keyboard shortcut
Move one character to the left	Left Arrow
Move one character to the right	Right Arrow
Move one line up	Up Arrow
Move one line down	Down Arrow
Move one word to the left	Ctrl+Left Arrow
Move one word to the right	Ctrl+Right Arrow
Move to the end of a line	End
Move to the beginning of a line	Home
Move up one paragraph	Ctrl+Up Arrow
Move down one paragraph	Ctrl+Down Arrow
Move to the end of a text box	Ctrl+End
Move to the beginning of a text box	Ctrl+Home
Repeat the last Find action	Shift+F4

Move around in and work in tables

Action	Keyboard shortcut
Move to the next cell	Tab
Move to the preceding cell	Shift+Tab
Move to the next row	Down Arrow
Move to the preceding row	Up Arrow
Insert a tab in a cell	Ctrl+Tab
Start a new paragraph	Enter
Add a new row at the bottom of the table	Tab at the end of the last row

Access and use panes and galleries

Action	Keyboard shortcut
Move to a pane from another pane in the program window	F6
When a menu is active, move to a pane	Ctrl+Tab
When a pane is active, select the next or previous option in the pane	Tab or Shift+Tab

Action	Keyboard shortcut
Display the full set of commands on the pane menu	Ctrl+Spacebar
Perform the action assigned to the selected button	Spacebar or Enter
Open a drop-down menu for the selected gallery item	Shift+F10
Select the first or last item in a gallery	Home or End
Scroll up or down in the selected gallery list	Page Up or Page Down
Close a pane	Ctrl+Spacebar, C
Open the Clipboard	Alt+H, F, O

Access and use available actions

Action	Keyboard shortcut
Display the shortcut menu for the selected item	Shift+F10
Display the menu or message for an available action or for the AutoCorrect Options button or the Paste options button	Alt+Shift+F10
Move between options in a menu of available actions	Arrow keys
Perform the action for the selected item on a menu of available actions	Enter
Close the available actions menu or message	Esc

Find and replace content

Action	Keyboard shortcut
Open the Find dialog box	Ctrl+F
Open the Replace dialog box	Ctrl+H
Repeat the last Find action	Shift+F4

Use the Help window

Action	Keyboard shortcut
Open the Help window	F1
Close the Help window	Alt+F4
Switch between the Help window and the active program	Alt+Tab
Return to the Help table of contents	Alt+Home

Action	Keyboard shortcut
Select the next item in the Help window	Tab
Select the previous item in the Help window	Shift+Tab
Perform the action for the selected item	Enter
Select the next hidden text or hyperlink, including Show All or Hide All at the top of a Help topic	Tab
Select the previous hidden text or hyperlink	Shift+Tab
Perform the action for the selected Show All, Hide All, hidden text, or hyperlink	Enter
Move back to the previous Help topic (Back button)	Alt+Left Arrow or Backspace
Move forward to the next Help topic (Forward button)	Alt+Right Arrow
Scroll small amounts up or down, respectively, within the currently displayed Help topic	Up Arrow, Down Arrow
Scroll larger amounts up or down, respectively, within the currently displayed Help topic	Page Up, Page Down
Display a menu of commands for the Help window. This requires that the Help window have the active focus (click in the Help window)	Shift+F10
Stop the last action (Stop button)	Esc
Print the current Help topic
If the cursor is not in the current Help topic, press F6 and then press Ctrl+P	Ctrl+P
In a Table of Contents in tree view, select the next or previous item, respectively	Up Arrow, Down Arrow
In a Table of Contents in tree view, expand or collapse the selected item, respectively	Left Arrow, Right Arrow

TIP To assign custom keyboard shortcuts to menu items, recorded macros, and Visual Basic for Applications (VBA) code in PowerPoint, you must use a third-party add-in. For links to current add-ins, refer to PowerPoint Help.

Index

Symbols and Numbers

A

aligning *(continued)*
    slide elements, 35
    text in placeholders, 104, 109
    text in table cells, 217
    text in text boxes, 131
alternative words, using Thesaurus to find, 119, 123
alt text, attaching
    to diagrams, 148
    to graphics, 238
    to pictures, 144
    to text boxes, 131
animating
    bullet points, 290, 294
    pictures, 290
    slide titles, 288
animation, *defined*, 415
animation effects, 288
    adding sounds, 294, 297
    copying, 288, 291
    customizing, 292, 295
    previewing, 290
    refining, 292
    turning off, 184
Animation gallery, 288
Animation Painter, 288, 291, 298
Animation pane, 293
Animations tab, 24
annotations, adding to graphics, 129, 143
appearance of ribbon, 16
arranging
    graphics, 255
    windows, 35, 38
artistic effects for pictures, 230, 236
Artistic Effects gallery, 236
assigning passwords, 330
attaching
    actions, 281
    hyperlinks, 277
attributes
    defined, 415
    applying, 105, 107
audience-specific presentations, 376
audio clips, 299, 301
audio content. *See also* sounds
    adding to slides, 299
    customizing, 300, 302

    looping, 300, 302
    pausing, 303
    playing, 299, 302
    playing across slides, 303
    testing, 300
    trimming, 300
    volume, 300
audio files, 299
audio icons, 299
    hiding, 300
    moving, 301
AutoCorrect
    defined, 415
    customizing, 111, 113
    options, setting, 394
AutoCorrect dialog box, 112, 113
AutoFit, 112, 116
    default settings, 112
automatic updating of pictures, 141
autosave time interval, 49, 395

B

background theme colors, 353
backgrounds, 87, 89
    defined, 415
    hiding, 91
    of pictures, removing, 230, 234
    of user interface, 393
Backstage view, 12, 26
    Account page, 26
    Export page, 196
    Info page, 198, 199
    New page, 26
    Open page, 28
    Print page, 184, 187
    Save As page, 47
    Share page, 326
banded rows in tables, 218
banners, 179, 181
bar charts, 244
Basic animation effects, 292
bitmaps, 146
black and white slides, 35, 185, 187
black last slide, eliminating, 37, 207
black pause screen, 206

slides, 81
tables, 217
text, 60, 63
text boxes, 130, 133
to first slide, 121
to last slide, 141
multi-line text boxes, 129, 135
muting video sound, 310

N

narration, turning off, 184
navigating
  among slides, 30, 31
  with action buttons, 283
  with actions, 281
Navigation pane (Save As dialog box), 51
new folders, saving presentations in, 48, 54
New page (Backstage), 26
New Slide gallery, 67, 368
non-English words/phrases, marking, 119, 121
Normal view, 15, 33, 37
  defined, 418
  hiding panes, 35, 37
  sizing panes, 35, 37, 190
notes
  adding headers/footers, 193
  adding to slides, 189, 190
  layout, 190
  printing, 186, 194
  taking in OneNote, 197
notes masters, 190, 344
  defined, 418
Notes Master view, 35
  defined, 418
Notes Page view, 34, 189, 190
  defined, 418
Notes pane, 16
  defined, 418
number styles, formatting , 104
numeric data, displaying visually, 154. *See also* charts

O

objects
  defined, 418
  attaching hyperlinks, 277
  changing order, 256
  embedded vs. linked, 221
  embedded worksheets, 221
  formatting, 226
  hiding on slides, 256
  sizing/moving/aligning, 224
  updating, 225
Office 365, 4
Office 2013 RT, 4
off-slide content, 199
OneNote notes, 197
Open dialog box, 31
Open page (Backstage), 28
opening
  files with hyperlinks, 276, 278
  outlines as presentations, 70
  presentations, 28, 30
  presentations from File Explorer, 21
  Text pane (diagrams), 149
Options dialog box, 324
order
  of graphics, 256, 257, 347
  of objects, 256
  of slides, 80
orientation
  of slides, 181
  of text boxes, 130, 131
Outline pane, 57
  defined, 418
Outline view, 15, 33, 36
  defined, 418
outlines. *See also* borders
  expanding/collapsing, 62
  exporting presentations as, 68
  importing, 69
  opening as presentations, 70
  printing, 186
  viewing, 36
overhead projectors, 178, 179

P

About the authors

Joyce Cox

Joyce has more than 30 years' experience in the development of training materials about technical subjects for non-technical audiences, and is the author of dozens of books about Microsoft Office and Windows technologies. She is the Vice President of Online Training Solutions, Inc. (OTSI).

As President of and principal author for Online Press, she developed the Quick Course series of computer training books for beginning and intermediate adult learners. She was also the first managing editor of Microsoft Press, an editor for Sybex, and an editor for the University of California.

Joan Lambert

Joan has worked in the training and certification industry for 16 years. As President of OTSI, Joan is responsible for guiding the translation of technical information and requirements into useful, relevant, and measurable training and certification tools.

Joan is a Microsoft Office Certified Master, a Microsoft Certified Application Specialist Instructor, a Microsoft Certified Technology Specialist, a Microsoft Certified Trainer, and the author of more than two dozen books about Windows and Office (for Windows and Mac). Joan enthusiastically shares her love of technology through her participation in the creation of books, learning materials, and certification exams. She greatly enjoys communicating the benefits of new technologies by delivering training and facilitating Microsoft Experience Center events.

Joan currently lives in a nearly perfect small town in Texas with her daughter, Trinity Preppernau.

The team

This book would not exist without the support of these hard-working members of the OTSI publishing team:

- Jan Bednarczuk
- Rob Carr
- Susie Carr
- Jeanne Craver
- Kathy Krause
- Marlene Lambert
- Jaime Odell
- Jean Trenary

We are especially thankful to the support staff at home who make it possible for our team members to devote their time and attention to these projects.

Rosemary Caperton provided invaluable support on behalf of Microsoft Learning.

Online Training Solutions, Inc. (OTSI)

OTSI specializes in the design, creation, and production of Office and Windows training products for information workers and home computer users. For more information about OTSI, visit:

www.otsi.com

Microsoft

How to download your ebook

Thank you for purchasing this Microsoft Press® title. Your companion PDF ebook is ready to download from O'Reilly Media, official distributor of Microsoft Press titles.

To download your ebook, go to
http://aka.ms/PowerPoint2013sbs/files
and follow the instructions.

Please note: You will be asked to create a free online account and enter the access code below.

Your access code:

> ## DNNXPNM

Microsoft® PowerPoint® 2013 Step by Step

Your PDF ebook allows you to:

- Search the full text
- Print
- Copy and paste

Best yet, you will be notified about free updates to your ebook.

If you ever lose your ebook file, you can download it again just by logging in to your account.

Need help? Please contact:
mspbooksupport@oreilly.com
or call 800-889-8969.

What do you think of this book?

We want to hear from you!
To participate in a brief online survey, please visit:

microsoft.com/learning/booksurvey

Tell us how well this book meets your needs—what works effectively, and what we can do better. Your feedback will help us continually improve our books and learning resources for you.

Thank you in advance for your input!